Ditch Witch of South Carolina
3405 Main Street
Columbia, South Carolina 29203
Phone 803 - 779-4143

To Tom
From Papa Jack
Walt Lowe 8-09

The Human Side

of Sales Management

BURTON BIGELOW

Consultant to Management

Englewood Cliffs, N. J., PRENTICE-HALL, INC.

Fifth printing ....January, 1967

TO MY WIFE, SALLY JANE

*Whose dedicated toil and tears gave
the manuscript for this book
its final perfection.*

What You Can Expect From This Book

This book was put together as a *practical working manual* for the top executive who must *motivate* and *manage* people. People are the most important element in business; they make up at once the manager's chief problem and his greatest opportunity.

The manager must UNDERSTAND people. That is the first necessity. If he is surprised, shocked, puzzled, frustrated, or made angry or impatient when he encounters that crazy-quilt response-mechanism which is the human being, then he is ill-prepared to *manage* them. For surprise, shock, puzzlement, frustration, anger and impatience are not among the ingredients in the tested prescription for successful management.

The manager must be prepared to recognize and successfully deal with the inevitable weaknesses of people. That is the second necessity. If his workers are not dominated and debilitated by the swarm of faults, foibles and fears which beset them daily, it will be due in the main to his vigilance, insight and skill, for the average group is not able to deal with their own negatives without the help of a leader.

The manager must have a deep and profound faith in the intrinsic, but unseen, gifts and capacities of people, those talents which lie hidden deep beneath the surface, waiting to be discovered, developed and utilized. This is the third necessity. He needs to possess not only faith that the indwelling aptitudes are *there,* but he must also have the insight to *discover* them, plus the brooding patience to nurture them to full flower. Finally, he must command the skill to put the developed abilities to work in the common cause.

To equip the manager to understand the *whole* man; to help him recognize and counterbalance men's inevitable *weaknesses;* to implant faith in the *dormant capacities* of his fellow men, and to point up his skill in developing these hidden talents—these necessities are likewise the major objectives of this book.

It is slanted at the management of salesmen and their field managers. Most of its examples are taken from the field of selling and sales management.

Yet, not a single one of its principles need be altered if the reader wishes to manage men in other pursuits. Salesmen come from all walks of life; they exhibit almost every conceivable pattern of life-trends; they test every managerial capacity.

The contradictions they exhibit, other men present; the weaknesses they are heir to, other men inherit; the potentialities for success which they possess and so deftly conceal, men in other lines also own, and likewise bury deep within themselves far from the glimpse of the casual managerial eye.

The intuitive insight which salesmen respect in their managers, other men honor; the arts and skills of leadership to which they respond, lift other men out of their daily doldrums and send them singing on their way to success, regardless of their line of endeavor.

But no matter how artful his leadership, the mature manager is not likely to exclaim: "I have fully fathomed man!" Indeed, he is more likely to agree with the shrewd and canny comment of Robert Burns, who regarded the human enigma as an enigma still:

> *Good Lord, what is man! for as simple he looks,*
> *Do but try to develop his hooks and his crooks,*
> *With his depths and his shallows, his good and his evil,*
> *All in all, he's a problem must puzzle the devil.*

BURTON BIGELOW
Santa Barbara, California

Table of Contents

CHAPTER I

Salesmen Are People

A recently-appointed member of Lincoln's cabinet received, from an aged mother out in Ohio, a letter asking a slight favor for her young son. The new official, unduly puffed up with his own importance, replied saying—"Dear Madam: I am now so busy with the affairs of the *nation* that I have no time for the problems of the *individual.*"

The old lady, unimpressed by his high station, took her quill in hand, and in a cramped and aged script, she responded:

"*So fur, the Almighty ain't been that busy!*"

Consider the INDIVIDUALITY of Each Man

The sales manager who hopes to lead his men to success must not forget that *salesmen are people!* He must go even one step further; he must not forget that each one thinks of himself first as an *individual* and only rarely as a member of the team. If the sales manager would come close to him, he must come close to him as the one, the only, the unique, the never-before-born, and the never-again-to-live—John Q. Salesman. This separative sense of personal individuality is a necessity to John Q. Salesman. It is a deep-seated, instinctive defense-mechanism, a desperate device which he hopes will prevent one of those vague and indefinable catastrophes which all men fear—that of being swallowed up by the great crowd of men and women who people the earth and thus losing that most precious of all possessions, that one asset which distinguishes him from all other human beings—his individuality. His name is the tag, the label which defines,

1

confines, delimits, and separates that single individuality from the mass; and so the sound of his name, the repetition of it, reassures him, perhaps not consciously, but subconsciously. (And since his fear is subconscious, too, it is quite correct to apply the remedy in the same area!)

If you and I could step back in time and go out to visit the lady in Ohio, we would find her, as we already know, familiar with the Bible. And it would be a safe wager that we would find her, too, one who loves the Twenty-Third Psalm, because that is the *personal* psalm, the psalm of personal *promise* and *reassurance*. It quiets those inner personal fears which are the inevitable counterpart of ego-centered individuality. The Twenty-Third Psalm doesn't speak to the world, nor to a nation. It speaks to one man; it talks straight to *me*, about *me*. Even as I read it, it compels me to confess my confidence:

> The Lord is *my* Shepherd;
> *I* shall not want.
> He maketh *me* to lie down in green pastures;
> He leadeth *me* beside the still waters.
> He restoreth *my* soul:
> He leadeth *me* in the paths of righteousness for his name's sake.
> Yea, though *I* walk through the valley of the shadow of death,
> *I* will fear no evil:
> For Thou art with *me*;
> Thy rod and Thy staff, they comfort *me*.
> Thou preparest a table before *me*
> In the presence of *mine* enemies:
> Thou annointest *my* head with oil:
> *My* cup runneth over.
> Surely goodness and mercy shall follow *me*
> All the days of *my* life:
> And *I* will dwell in the house of the Lord forever.

In those seventeen lines of blank verse, there are seventeen personal pronouns—I's, or me's, or my's, or mine's. That explains why it is the most popular psalm in the Good Book. And, it is another bit of age-old evidence showing that we who manage men must deal with them not as *things*, but as *people*; not as *groups*, but as *individuals*.

It will be said, perhaps, that every sales manager knows this, and, moreover, that most of them practice it. But for the benefit of those hard-boiled managers who prefer to check themselves rigorously, let us examine a few areas in which the individualistic-human concept is likely to be overlooked.

MEETINGS: As a tool of sales management, meetings have an important place; but it is well to check whether you are trying to do in meetings what can be better done with the *individual* approach. In some companies, "meeting-itis" becomes a disease. Starting with the executives, it soon infects the sales force, particularly if they are physically concentrated in one office. To give product talks, to announce the details of a new campaign or promotion, to make a quick (but not too penetrating) survey of opinions or attitudes—for such purposes, meetings are often adequate. But plans are seldom evolved in a meeting; neither are meetings noted for getting action, unless the plans are already made, the tasks already assigned and scheduled, and the meetings used merely as a dispatching or kickoff device.

Recognize HIS Special Needs

Consequently, either before or immediately after a meeting, it is wise for the sales manager to ask himself: In what respect does this meeting fail to meet the needs of individual salesmen? Are there individual exceptions to be discussed? For example: Are there territories in which the deal will receive extraordinarily good (or poor) reception? Are there special travel allowances for the mountainous areas of the Great Divide country? If the generalizations made in the meeting are not capable of immediate application in all territories, then some further work with individual salesmen is indicated.

In such cases, it is too often the habit of the sales manager to shrug off the specialized situations and say: "Joe can figure out how to change the deal for his territory." Probably Joe does know WHAT needs changing, but he is afraid to take the initiative. Perhaps Joe does have ideas; but doesn't know how far he can go in changing policy, or prices, or allowances, or terms. Even if Joe is aggressive and full of initiative, are you sure you will be pleased with the changes he makes? To duck the individualizing responsibility is to take the irresponsible, lazy way. More important, it often means trouble stored up for the future; in other words, *more* work, not *less* in the long run.

BULLETINS: Bulletins are another form of non-individualized communication. In fact, in the hands of an inexperienced or incompetent sales manager, a mimeograph can become a lethal weapon of great destructive power. In the case of some managers, the urge to put a message into *words,* before it has been put into *thoughts,* seems to be almost irresistible. Objectives are either undefined altogether, or poorly defined. There is no ordered plan; the long paragraphs of would-be explanation *obscure* rather than clarify the points; and after reading the headquarters' communication, the salesman in the field often emerges more confused than ever.

Bulletins are a generalized medium, an instrument for *mass* communication, and few managers are skillful enough to draft communiqués which seem to be written especially to the one salesman who is reading them.

If the generalized message in the bulletin gives no hint of the exceptions which must be dealt with, if it does not include these divergencies which have been individually discussed and authorized, then, is it any wonder that the men in the field gain a feeling of confusion, uncertainty, frustration?

Communicate With HIM Specifically

The sales manager can carry the individualization into these bulletins if he tries. A brief note, handwritten at the top:

> Dear Joe—These instructions are subject to the modifications we talked about the other day. They still stand. Good luck!—S.J.H.

What if half a dozen men do need these special notes? Is it not better to take six minutes to write them than to have six men confused and worried by what seems to them a contradiction of instructions?

Selling is a thing of the spirit—the spirit of the *individual*. Yet, how often we are guilty of treating salesmen like mass-produced robots, whose proper lights glow obediently when we push the home-office buttons a thousand miles away! It is not so, dear reader, it is not so! And it was not so with you, when you were a salesman, was it?

The Good Book tells us that man was constructed in the image of his Maker; but the sages of old have told us that a man comes into life over one of seven paths. This must be true, else the diversity we see and with which we must deal, would not exist—and all men would be alike. (See the complete exposition of this concept in Chapter III, "The Seven Basic Types of Men.")

Meetings and bulletins are not the only situations where the individualistic-human concept is likely to be overlooked by the sales manager. The manager's own experience will supply many other occasions where the temptation to "massify" (just to coin a word!) may overshadow the need to individualize.

If the reader is the manager of a large sales force, let us say one hundred men or more, he may be a little puzzled as to how to implement this individualizing concept and put it into practice. "How am I going to individualize my handling of 140 salesmen?" he may ask.

Organize, Deputize, Train, Localize, and Individualize

The answer is: "You, personally, are not going to be able to individualize your handling of 140 men." It is an organizational impossibility. We might say an organizational *monstrosity*, for one manager to manage 140 individuals in any aspects of their operations.

To accomplish his proper objective of treating men as individuals, the sales manager will take four steps:

1. He must organize and deputize, as John H. Patterson, of National Cash Register fame, used to say. That means he must first see the task whole; then, he must break it down into logical parts, delegating certain of these parts to other men, deputizing them to act with authority, and training and motivating them to accept a proportionate responsibility.
2. He must trust his deputies enough so that he is willing to give them permission to MODIFY and LOCALIZE his home-office, staff-built plans and programs.
3. He must train his deputies in the proper methods of modifying and localizing.
4. He must educate them in the techniques of applying the individualizing concept effectively at the salesman's level.

The sales manager who takes these four steps will find that he has set up, not only the machinery to provide all the individualization necessary; but, at the same time, he has put into operation a sound and effective field managerial team.

Avoid Excessive Standardization

However, there is one danger yet to be considered, a threat which will not be present in all companies, but may be found in very large operations. (Observe, this defect is not necessarily a corollary of largeness, but it is most often found there.)

We refer to *excessive standardization of methods and procedures.*

At some point in its history, a small company growing into a large one—and consequently experiencing the problems of rapid growth—suddenly discovers the dangers of uncontrolled diversity in methods and operations. The management gets a picture of every man riding off in a direction of his own choosing; of processes varying from department to department, or even from machine to machine; and in the sales department, a picture of every salesman being a sort of law unto himself, and each district a private principality presided over by a little king, the district manager.

Whether or not they have ever heard of John H. Patterson, his dictum, that "there is one best way to do everything," begins to creep into managment's thinking. And, they suddenly discover the other half of his philosophy—that it is management's responsibility to discover that "one best method" in all important areas of operation and "to make it the universal practice of all." As you know, there is an ancient and respected engineering axiom which says that:

—if you apply *standardized* methods
—to standardized *conditions,*
—you will get standardized *results*

And that end, we all agree, is a desirable objective to achieve.

The old king "diversity" is dead; long live the new king—"uniformity, standardization." Often the installation of the new concept proceeds with a fervor that is almost fanatic, especially if aided and abetted by an overly enthusiastic methods-man or an outside engineer.

Human nature resists the cult of uniformity, of course, but eventually a large degree of standardization is achieved. And, if it has not been overdone, it will have ameliorated, if not wholly eliminated, the chaos that comes with complete diversity. Each man no longer sets his own goals, no longer creates and installs his own methods, nor judges himself (and perhaps others) by yardsticks of his own devising. Of course, standardization succeeds better in some departments than others. Where machines are the chief factor, good results accrue. Where the work is routine and repetitive, still greater improvement is achieved.

Following out the axiom, best results are obtained where conditions can be most completely standardized and controlled.

Fortunately, perhaps, *people* cannot be standardized. Therefore, where people are the dominant factor, progress in standardization is less spectacular. And where the tasks require creative thought, standardization is least effective. Certainly, selling and sales management are areas which call for creative imagination.

But it is likely to be true, nevertheless, that the tidal wave of standardization which engulfs the production, purchasing, accounting, and clerical departments, also inundates the sales department.

When a sales manager finds himself in such a situation, he must first of all recognize that such complete standardization negates the possibility of effective individualization. That does not mean that he wishes to rush precipitately back into the old chaos of complete diversity.

But, it does mean that he must search for a solution that gives his department as many of the benefits of standardization as he can utilize and as many of the freedoms of diversity as he requires for his job of managing human beings.

Classify to Remedy Over-Standardization

One of the simplest ways to achieve these dual benefits is to combine standardization with classification; that is, to standardize salesmen, territories, and procedures by groupings or classes, according to their similarities, rather than to try to achieve complete uniformity.

For example, a pharmaceutical drug manufacturer decides that physicians are its chief source of volume, since without the doctor's prescription, no drugs start to move toward consumption. So, they standardize upon a call requirement of three calls per year, per physician. In practice, their detail men find that this standard, plus their hospital and drug store contacts, gives them too heavy a workload.

A more discriminating analysis shows that all physicians are not of equal value as sources of potential sales. Thereupon, the doctors are *divided* and *classed* into four groups according to one basic similarity; namely, the average number of prescriptions they write per day, week, or month.

> Class "A" physicians are the big "writers"—they are called on twelve times per year, once a month.
> Class "B" physicians are good "writers"—they are called on six times a year, every two months.
> Class "C" physicians are fair "writers"—they are called on three times a year, once every four months.
> Class "D" doctors are over-age, semi-retired, or engaged in research work where no patients are seen and no prescriptions written—they are called on not at all.

Thus, the company escapes both the curse of unlimited diversity and the plague of complete standardization. The classing does it!

A somewhat similar situation exists in any company where, for example, a standard number of calls per day has been set up as a uniform work-demand for all men. System-wide uniformity usually does not conform to the realities of field coverage. Salesmen grumble because, try as they may, they fail to meet the standard. So, the company modifies the standard demand and resolves it into classes which conform more closely to field situations.

Let's say this is an example of a large brewery sales operation with an original average demand of 30 stops per man, per day. The modified demand, revamped into classes, looks like this:

Class	Type of Territory	Number of Stops Per Man, Per Day
A	Metropolitan	40
B	Suburban	25
C	Country	15

Because of the concentration of distribution in big city taverns and package outlets, it is not impossible for their city men to make 40 stops a day. In other words, this group of men can exceed the old standard of 30 stops per day. But the other two groups could never reach 30 stops. Yet, when the monthly stop report is in, on the grouped and classed basis, the whole organization has averaged 32 stops per day, with two fewer salesmen!

Still another example—this, a very simple, but very frequent situation:

A sales manager has 65 territories; seven of these are newly started in areas where this company previously has had no distribution.

Most sales managers—believe it or not!—will total all 65 territories and average them, in order to get their ratios, or average cost per unit of selling, for example. Yet, the *average* figure *conceals* all the essential facts—both good and bad.

The manager needs to classify, to set up 58 *developed* territories in one group, for which he takes off one set of figures, and to set up seven *subsidy* territories into a second group, from which he takes another set of averages. He needs to class, group, consider, and analyze *like* things in groups put together on the basis of their *similarities*.

Including the seven subsidy territories in his figures is likely to lower the average production per man and increase his average sales cost per unit. Lumping both types into one group results in the presentation of a completely warped picture. Standardization by classes remedies the error at once.

It is easy to see that this step—the abandonment of rigid uniformity and the substitution of standardization by groups—is a high-level move that, of itself, accomplishes some measure of individualization. The more you divide, class, and group at top levels, the less individualization remains to be done at the salesmen's level.

Granting permission to modify and localize home office programs and procedures at the level of the salesman is taking another step in the direction of recognizing salesmen as individual human beings.

If these two top managerial steps are coupled with field-manager training that develops a consciousness of the need for individualization, plus a technique for doing that job, then our first injunction—that the sales manager must not forget that salesmen are not only *people*, but primarily *individuals*—can be heeded.

Then, we can join with John Stuart Mill, classical economist and logician, in saying (with one substitution):

> The worth of a sales force, in the long run,
> is the worth of the individuals composing it.

That being so, the concept of handling people as individuals becomes one of the prime necessities of successful sales management.

CHAPTER II

The Roots of Selling Success

"What Makes A Salesman Succeed?"

Ask that question of one hundred sales managers and you are likely to come up with 101 answers.

"The guy with 'guts'—he gets there!"

"If he can CLOSE sales, he will succeed. Nothing else matters!"

"Stick-to-it-ive-ness!—If he has got that, he'll never fail!"

"Give me a man who will *work*—and I will give you a man who will hit the top!"

"Success in selling calls for *personality*—if you can *charm* 'em, you can sell them!"

Those are the kind of answers, dogmatic, single-shot answers you will get from practicing sales managers, if you ask them for the ingredients of sales success.

Strange, but there is not a WRONG answer in the collection; but neither is the *right* answer there! For, success in selling is not a simple growth; its roots are found in many soils; it is nurtured by many waters; it expresses itself in many combinations, each one a little different from all the rest.

In fact, sales success defies complete analysis by any man. After having personally trained an average of 2,000 salesmen per year for fifteen years; after having worked with hundreds of salesmen, one by one, to analyze their personal as well as business problems; after having been, for thirty-six years, the head of a marketing consulting organization, one of whose major activities is the psychological testing of salesmen and salesmen-applicants; we still approach the task humbly and without any dogmatic assurance.

Three Contributing Sources of Success in Selling

In our opinion, there are three groups of factors, three sets of contributions, if we may call them such, in which are found the roots of success in selling.

We cannot tell you which group of factors, or which factor in any one of the three groups, is most important to success; nor which is most likely to forecast failure. We can only say that success in selling is like a three-legged stool— you can't sit comfortably and safely on it unless all three legs are sound and rest firmly on the floor!

In other words, it is not any single factor alone that is important; *it is the sum-total picture.* Explore and microscope each of the three legs of the stool, if you wish, to determine whether there are any invisible splits, or unknown termites in any one leg; but most important of all, make sure that the stool has three sound legs.

For the sake of visualization, let's turn the three-legged stool into a circular pie chart, made up of three sectors, as shown on Diagram 1, opposite. Each portion represents one of the major contributions to success in selling—those contributions made by:

1. TERRITORIES
2. MANAGEMENT
3. SALESMEN

Territories Contribute Geographic Assets

Of these three contributions, we find the territory factors to be the most stable, in the sense that they are least likely to change quickly. The sales territory is a piece of God's geography; it has been there a long time; it is likely to be there long after we have departed. It has its own characteristic topography; within the memory of man that hasn't changed much, and we feel fairly secure in saying that it isn't likely to change much in the future. We don't expect any new mountain ranges to push up from the bowels of the earth, nor any new rivers to cut channels through the land, nor the climate to change appreciably.

Within that area are *people,* the basic essential behind sales potential, particularly in consumption goods and goods for "home and family investment."

There are wholesalers and retailers, essential to the building of a satisfactory distribution picture. For the company selling to the industrial or commercial fields, there are factories and commercial establishments; for those selling to institutions, there are hospitals, schools, and other public service establishments.

Bound up with the habits and customs and loyalties of the people, there is a very valuable asset which contributes mightily to the speed and extent of sales success—that is, the extent to which acceptance of, and demand for, the goods

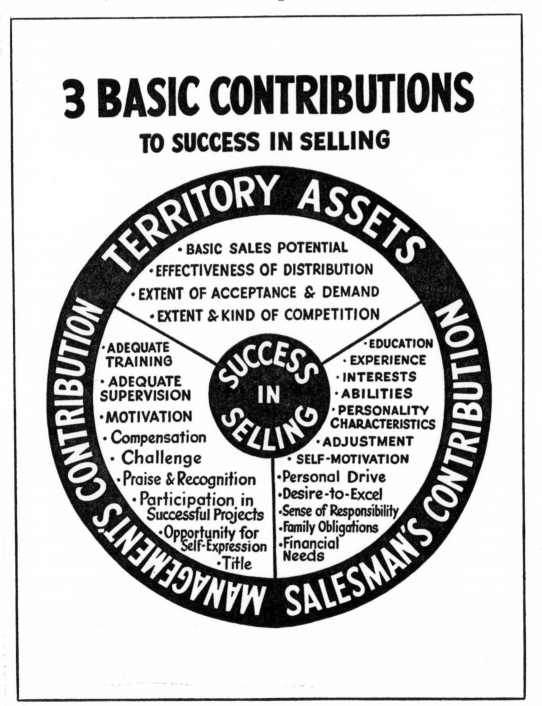

has been developed. "Brand good will" we might call it, expressed in willingness to accept, and even *demand,* a certain brand of merchandise.

Finally, this piece of geography supports some competition. The extent and kind of competition greatly influences the degree of selling success a salesman is likely to have in that territory. These last two factors—acceptance, or demand for our goods, and competition—are largely "things of the spirit" and therefore difficult to identify and measure. But they are there, in some degree, and they are immensely important.

Briefly, that summarizes the first of the three "pieces of pie" in our chart.

Management's Contributions

Second, let us examine the next "piece of pie"—the contributions to total sales success which management *can,* should, and we hope, *is* making.

Training

Management owes a man *training.* It owes him time and effort to acquaint him with the company, its policies, its procedures, its products, its competition, the specific sales resistances and objections which its men usually encounter. Almost every company gives hypocritical lip service to sales education; but very few companies train a salesman effectively, or for a long enough period of time, to really prepare him for his job.

If management fails in this duty, the *salesman* also may fail; but if he does, management will not face the truth and write on the termination interview sheet: "Failed because we didn't do a good training job." If that sounds cynical, let us remind you that we speak from long experience; very few managements have any idea of how much training is essential to equip a salesman for the job he is to hold (we hope!) with them.

Supervision—A Lost Art in Many Companies

The salesman is entitled to competent supervision and enough of it to assure his success in his sales job, provided of course, he is making the essential contributions to success which only he can make. These we will discuss as soon as we have finished with management's contribution.

In many companies—believe it or not—supervision is almost a forgotten function, a lost art! Tight-fisted or short-sighted managements are reluctant to provide adequate field supervision, because they say: "Supervision costs money!" Of course, supervision requires an investment, perhaps even a brief capitalization and amortization of the investment; but if a company *needs* supervision—and what company doesn't?—then the fact is that *doing without it costs more than the cost of providing it!* The difficulty is this: the cost to *provide* supervision is a visible, computable, forecastable figure. But the loss that eventuates from *lack of supervision* is an invisible cost, hard to locate, difficult to compute, and therefore, easy to ignore.

HOW MUCH supervision is a salesman entitled to? How much is "enough"? How long is a string? The answer is necessarily an individual one, depending upon the salesman, the company, and the market situation in the specific territory.

Supervision is partially a continuation of training; this is inevitable. It is partly a process of inspection, and along with inspection, intelligent and compassionate correction. It is partly a process of direct assistance with specific problems which the salesman encounters and which he is not able, at the moment, to handle single-handedly.

Certainly, no salesman is getting "enough" supervision, if his supervisor has fifteen or twenty other salesmen to supervise; or if the supervisor, in addition to his manpower management duties, has a territory of his own where he still acts as a salesman!

Nor can the manager give him sufficient supervision if that manager has the job of training three other new men at the same time. Fresh in my mind, is the example of a Divisional Manager of one large company who was given eleven new men to train in one twelve-month period, although it was generally admitted at management levels that the first year of training a new salesman took a minimum of six weeks of the manager's time. How could this manager train eleven new men (sixty-six weeks' work in less than fifty-two weeks), manage eleven other older salesmen, and run his divisional office? Obviously, he couldn't; he didn't; and both the new men *and the old ones* suffered from this company's failure properly to evaluate the available managerial time and the size of the task.

Obviously, a new man is not getting "enough" supervision—neither enough in time, nor enough in quality—if the manager, supervisor (call him what you will) already has an oversized managerial workload. (Entirely aside from the subject of salesmen's success, here is an interesting and significant statistic on managerial success: In hundreds of studies in many lines of business, one truth again and again emerges—emerges so often, in fact, that we had to recognize it as a basic principle of successful field management. Unless the field manager spends from 75 per cent to 90 per cent of his time WORKING WITH HIS MEN IN THE FIELD, the chances of his having a successful district *are very small.*)

Basic Management Motivation

In addition to supplying the right amount and kind of training and supervision, the company must supply many motivations which spur the salesman on to do his best.

Here are some of the basic motivations which it is management's duty to supply to the total success picture. These motivations contribute largely to success; they can be supplied only by management; therefore, if management fails to supply them, they will not be available and the sum-total chances for success will thereby diminish. (A list of the ten basic needs which supply almost ready-made opportunities for motivation is to be found in Chapter IX, where we also discuss the philosophy, psychology, and practice of managerial motivation.)

COMPENSATION: Management must *pay* its salesmen; pay them enough to live according to their position, enough to give them a reasonable feeling of security, enough to give their wives and families a similar feeling of confidence. Yet, it must not pay them so much as to relieve them of the necessity of earning that pay, or so much that striving is not part of the salesman's own daily drive.

Top managements frequently tell us: "We can't pay more than the going market rate for our kind of salesmen." That, of course, is not indisputably true. If by doing so, and by a combination of other management strategies and tactics, management can get greater volume than their peers, then it may be possible to pay more than the going rate. The thought behind that defensive statement of management is that all businesses of a given kind come up with costs and performances which are pretty much standard. That is largely, but not always, true. Managers who think in original, out-of-the-rut-of-precedent channels very often come up with non-standard patterns that are more effective than those of the run-of-the-mill companies in the same industry.

MANNER OF PAYMENT: Management must not only concern itself with the *amount* of pay, but also with the *manner* and *form* of payment.

We say it softly, but it is true: Managements, as a rule, are notably unimaginative about the psychological effects of their economic decisions. And, most of them are similarly obtuse when it comes to evaluating the psychology of the human being in terms of economic values.

Their point of view, whether spoken or not, is: "What difference does it make about *how* a salesman gets paid, if, in the long run, he gets the same number of dollars on one plan as he does on another?"

Well, the method of payment often makes the difference between enthusiasm and lukewarmness in the work-attitude, the difference between eager drive and lackadaisical performance of his routine duties. It often means the difference between staying on the job or looking around for a new one. It sometimes makes the difference between turning his wife into a full-time, 24-hour-a-day assistant sales manager in the home, or having her complain about the financial aspects of his job.

When you read Chapter IV, on the common weaknesses of salesmen, you will see why the sales compensation plan needs to offset some of those habits of thought and action which are typical of human beings who go into selling.

This is not the place to go into details of sales compensation, but it is not here amiss to point out that the sales compensation dollar, divided into four piles— one for "grocery money" or basic security, a second pile for reaching quota, a third pile for extra pay for over-quota production, and a fourth pile for contests, campaigns and short-term drives—the pay dollar so divided will bring much more out of the human being we call the salesman than will the same dollar paid to him all at once as his total salary, for example.

Which boils down to this: If the company pays enough, and pays it in the right manner, management will be making a partial contribution to sales success.

There are further duties for management to carry out, if it is to make the whole contribution of which it is capable.

CHALLENGE: Management must see to it that the job offers a challenge to the salesman. If he considers his task a "lead pipe cinch", as he might say, then he will not strive as mightily as he otherwise would; and thereby, something of the success-drive is lost.

PRAISE AND RECOGNITION: Management must praise men when they do extra-good work, or get extraordinary results. They must provide opportunities for the salesmen to participate in successful projects; for it is still true, as Napoleon said: "News of a victory is worth a hundred thousand men." Nothing peps up salesmen like taking part in a successful campaign.

OPPORTUNITY FOR SELF-EXPRESSION: Men must be given the chance for self-expression. No man is without his own inner drives toward some kind of accomplishment. If these basic natural urges can be channeled in his work and find satisfactory expression there, then he will feel that his life has been more thoroughly fulfilled, and the job will benefit thereby. It requires a very wise and discerning management to leave room for the individual to express himself; to give him some "local liberty", shall we call it, to apply his own ideas to the building of his own success.

TITLES AS MOTIVATORS: The wise use of titles is also one of management's contributions. So often, a new title is a hollow honor, a cheap substitute for more money, or larger responsibilities. Men see through these hypocrisies and resent them; thus, a step that management intends to spur a man on may return nothing but a scornful curl of the lip from the salesman who says to himself: "How stupid do they think I am to hope that I will not see through this subterfuge?" Even the least educated of men have enough native shrewdness to see through such obviously transparent insincerities. Never count on men being fools—they are wise in areas where you least expect to find wisdom!

A new title honestly bestowed, however, and backed up by increased responsibilities and enlarged opportunities for making money, is a worthy and useful contribution by management to the sum-total of success-possibilities.

The Salesman Contributes Personal Assets

Were it possible for the prospective salesman to view the picture of the first two sets of success-factors which have just been described, and against them to apply the contributions which he can bring to the sum-total pattern of success, we might have fewer misfits and therefore, fewer failures in selling jobs.

For we now come to the third and last of our three "pieces of pie"—the contributions which the salesman makes to the whole.

Manpower Specifications Should Be Written

To be successful, the salesman has to BE certain things, KNOW certain things, and DO certain tasks. Obviously, these three demands ought to be well-defined, in writing, by management, before the salesman agrees to take the job. Often, however, this is not done; both management and salesman fly it blind, to the confusion of both parties. We have long contended that a new employee's first right is to know *what* management expects, *how much* it expects, and of what *quality*. A wise salesman will not walk into a situation where these fundamentals must be guessed at.

Assuming, however, that the manpower specifications have been written by management, and studied and accepted by the new salesman, what are the possible contributions which he brings into the pool of success?

Salesman's TOTAL PICTURE Is Chief Clue to Future Success

He must bring HIMSELF—a bundle of interests, abilities, and personality characteristics—together with his own degree of adjustment to life and to his job. These personal endowments, which are characteristic of this one individual, should have been determined by management in advance of hiring, ascertained by a psychological report based upon a series of psychological tests, filled out by the applicant, and scored and evaluated by an experienced psychologist. (If you are not now using psychological tests, this is not a plea to urge you to do so; we simply know of no other way in which these otherwise invisible characteristics of a man can be discovered and measured!)

Whether or not these qualities and attributes are known by management, the salesman brings these traits to the job; some of them are assets, some may be liabilities. Every human being is a bundle of contradictions; the important thing to study is the total picture. That, and not a random asset or a single liability, is the chief determinant in success or failure.

Unskilled Use of EDUCATION May Be a Handicap

To this job, our salesman also brings his education, or what remains of it. There are occasions—especially in industrial or technical selling where the job calls for a combination of technical knowledge and sales know-how—when we would pray that the man has not retained too much of his academic mood. That is educational treason, we know, but the fact is that few men are so certainly threatened with future failure, as those who believe that knowledge is the OPEN SESAME to sales success. In our experience, we find this truth confirmed again and again.

Let us give you a few examples: Veterinary school graduates are hired as feed salesmen on the ground that their extensive knowledge of animal husbandry will equip them to do a superior job of selling feed. Instead, most of these men become so engrossed in showing off their knowledge—posting chickens to show why they died, diagnosing livestock illnesses and prescribing remedies—that they forget to sell any feed. They are following the customary pattern of intellectual show-offs; they are so busy proving *how much they know*, that they seldom make a sales pitch to sell feed. They soon fail.

A well-known surgical suture company has always employed pharmacists as salesmen. This was a tradition, a dogma which was not to be departed from. During the Second World War, pharmacists were channeled to the armed services and few were available for jobs as salesmen. In the face of dire necessity, this company began—with great misgivings, believe me!—to hire non-pharmacists for their sales force. Gradually, the complexion of the force began to alter, until it was 50 per cent pharmacists and 50 per cent non-pharmacists. At this point, what we call a "success-and-failure" profile was made of the whole sales force. The men were rated by their managers into three groups: the top producers, the middle producers, and the low-level men.

Out of the study emerged this strange, and to the company, inexplicable heresy: All of the men in the low-level group were pharmacists, and all of the men in the top-level group were NON-pharmacists. Once again, the focus of the pharmacist's thinking was his personal technical knowledge; the focus of the non-pharmacist's thinking was getting an order! One group was still showing off its knowledge; the other was getting business. The latter group had no knowledge to brag about. They tried for orders—and got them!

Knowledge possessed by the salesman is not, in itself, a failure factor. It is what is *done* with the knowledge. As an old Buffalo stevedore, "Fingy Conner", who turned newspaper owner and capitalist, once replied when he was criticized for his "vulgar" display of diamonds: "Them as HAS 'em, WEARS 'em!" Rare indeed is the possessor of knowledge who is not moved—like that ex-stevedore with his diamonds—by an irresistible desire to exhibit it. Knowledge, like a slide rule, ought to be kept out of sight in selling and only used when needed; even then, it ought to be carefully disguised.

You wouldn't want to hire a man without the necessary education, of course; but let's hope that the education he brings along is slanted to its proper use and directed to its proper focus in his daily work!

Besides knowledge, the salesman brings work experience.

Similar WORK EXPERIENCE Is Not Always an Asset

If this experience is in the same line of business, it may be useful and save training time; or it may be a liability. In the latter case, the salesman may, in fact, require a thorough course of detraining in the last employer's methods, before you can even START to retrain him in your ways of doing business.

Many examples come to mind. We will choose one which came under our close personal observation for many years. One of our clients hired a man well-recommended by his employer, a Chicago company. From the first, it was obvious that he didn't fit his new company; he didn't think as they wanted their men to think; he didn't operate as their men operated; his ethics and standards were of a different world. His previous employer pursued high-pressure selling tactics; his products were likely to be of indifferent quality; he was a bit careless with the truth; he was seeking immediate volume, not satisfied customers. These previous situations were the direct opposite of those the salesman encountered with his new employer.

If you were speculating about the policies of the two companies, you would have expected the fellow to seize the new situations as advantages; you would have looked forward to a quick change of thinking on his part. But, no such change was forthcoming. In spite of great patience and compassion on the part of the new company, nine years went by and still he had not changed. He *never* changed!

Looking back, in the perspective of time, we would say that all the efforts of many executives to detrain that salesman never moved him a single degree from the habit-patterns which controlled him the day he left his old company. His sojourn cost the second company over $135,000; and in all that time, he sowed not one seed that flowered; he had the touch that withered; and only negative results could be found in his trail. Why did this company keep him? For a strange reason! His immovability was unbelievably granitic; no situation so hopeless had ever confronted them before. One executive after another took him in hand, looking upon him as a challenge to their managerial ability. But, he could not be changed.

This was probably the most extreme case of its kind that we have ever encountered. But it points up the truth that experience, even in the same line of business, is not always an asset. Unless you can eradicate former negative habit-patterns, you're in for trouble. (For this reason, many companies now prefer NOT to hire salesmen with experience in their line of business; they prefer beginner-salesmen, or men from other lines, men who have no hard-and-fast habits that are unchangeable.)

But, good or bad, constructive or negative, the salesman brings with him, willy-nilly, that previous work experience.

Proper SELF-MOTIVATION Makes Management Easier

And finally, the salesman brings with him his characteristic pattern of self-motivation. These motivations are important; if they are of the right sort, they may save you much time and trouble in supervision. If they are not of the right kind, then you inherit trouble.

These motivations include his personal drive, powered by his mental energy, his glandular force, and his physical health. Other of his personal motivations are the products of his ambition, or his desire-to-excel; of his sense of personal responsibility; of his family obligations, or of personal financial needs.

Taken together, these motivations will pretty much determine whether he is a Self-Starter, an Easy Starter, a Dead-Center boy, or one of those Reverse-Gear men who must have a tow or a push to get under way. If he turns out to be a Self-Starter or an Easy Starter, then his contributions will make his sales manager's job of motivation much easier. If the manager believes he is going to be a Dead-Center boy or a Reverse-Gear man, then he should not be hired in the first place. (In Chapter XI, we discuss these four types of salesmen from the standpoint of "enthusability.")

STRIVE FOR PROPER MIXTURE OF SUCCESS FACTORS

This is the total success-picture, so far as we are able to define it. It is not complete, nor is it perfect, but it is much more explicit than is usually to be found.

Success in selling, in our experience, comes from the proper "mixture" of these several contributions. If one important ingredient is missing in the territory, or in management's contribution, or in what the salesman himself brings to the job, that does not mean that the man will necessarily fail on that account. What is missing from one source, often is offset by a compensating strength from one of the other sources.

This endless counterbalancing of liabilities in one sector against assets in one or both of the remaining sectors—a process in which the varieties of combinations seem to be almost uncountable—this automatic interchange of plusses and minuses explains why the patterns of success are so varied, so unstandardized, so hard to analyze, and so difficult to predict even when you have all the facts that can be secured.

To put this present analysis to practical use, the sales manager studies the contributions in each sector, perhaps makes up a check-list for his own use. He may even project his check-list into a rating chart or evaluation blank. He then rates first, his company's territory contributions against the basic contributions in that sector.

Next, he lists and evaluates what *his* management contributes to the management sector, as compared to the established yardsticks. At this point, he has before him a picture of his company's delinquencies in those two sectors where to some extent, at least, he has the power to remedy them.

He may discover, for example, that the company's total sales potential is inequitably distributed, so that some men have much more sales opportunity than others, which means that those with a big slice of potential start off with a better chance of success. He will strive then to revamp territories so as to equalize potential as far as possible; and when he gets into the middle of this task, he will find the possibilities for equalization of potential much more numerous than he had ever realized.

Or, on the contrary, he may find that he has given each salesman a territory too large for him to cover in the ordinary human process of daily work. The salesman's total workload may be out of all proportion to the amount of time he has available to get it done. In that case, the sales manager either classifies his calls and directs his salesman's efforts at calling on the most important customers first; or, he begins a longer-range process of reducing the size of territories and increasing the total number of salesmen, so that adequate coverage in depth is possible.

Perhaps, he finds his sales payment plan archaic and not fitted to today's conditions. It may be a straight commission plan, or a straight salary plan, without selective incentives to spur men to top effort, and with no money left for campaign and contest awards. He sets about bringing it up to date.

He may find his sales training amiss in amount or quality, or both. Perhaps it is being done by district managers, for example, who are already overloaded with too many men, too much paper work, and some executive selling activity which is properly not the district manager's job. As a remedy, the sales manager may supply home office help, or start a regular training program at headquarters to relieve the district managers of at least part of the field-load.

Or, the already-disclosed problem of overloaded field managers may clearly reveal inadequate supervision. New districts are created, fewer salesmen are placed under each manager. Thus, the manager's total workload is lightened, so that he may properly perform the needed tasks.

These are only a few of the many ways in which this analysis of the factors that lead to success in selling may be used by the sales manager to evaluate and overhaul his own situation. He needs only a reasonable degree of objective-mindedness, so that he can face his department's shortcomings realistically. Some improvements, he can make at once; others will have to become longer-term programs timed to the speed of rapid *evolution* instead of instant *revolution*.

But the striving to finish the picture of success possibilities by having available all of the contributions which add to its completeness—that is a striving which never ends.

CHAPTER III

The Seven Basic Types of Men

"Among all the salesmen I've managed, I have never found two who were really alike in temperament, ability, and leanings."

Was there ever a sales manager of mature experience who, in the contemplative lookings-back of his riper years, has not been struck by this picture of seeming diversity, this apparent absence of identical duplicates in the human family?

Yet, if we turn to any of the lower kingdoms of nature, we find a similar variety. De Tournefort, in his classification of plant life, listed eight thousand *species,* each, no doubt, including thousands of individuals, none of which were really identical in the truest sense of that word. In mineralogy, anthropology, zoology, and other natural sciences, we find an equally bewildering multiplicity of non-identical individuals. In fact, this question of endless variety has puzzled and challenged philosophers and scientists from the time of Aristotle to the present day, and the continuing efforts of many great and orderly minds have been in the direction of classing the great mass of individuals in the several kingdoms into a few groups, so limited in number as to be comprehensible by the human mind.

Manager's Need for Classifying Individuals

When the sales manager considers the human being as a functional whole within the framework of his suitability for sales work and his manageability as a member of the team, this same question of multiplicity of individual patterns plagues him, too, in a very practical way.

Therefore, out of that chaos of multiplicity, let us endeavor to bring some order by using the age-old method of classing all individuals into a limited number of groups—seven in our case—and then familiarizing ourselves with the typical characteristics of each group. This process has the effect, let us say, of "shaving off the numberless random 'whiskers' of extreme variety", and of forcibly fitting all individuals into one or another of the seven basic types.

This scheme is not of our invention. In its original form, its lineage is ancient and distinguished. The sages of old Egypt and the Rishis of Vedic India, while they had no need to hire salesmen, did wish to understand themselves and their fellow men.

For that purpose, they classed human beings into seven basic types according to the life trend or predominant "drive" of the individual. They further divided each of their groups into seven sub-groups, making forty-nine classes in all.

Grouping Men by Life Trends

In the modernized form of the scheme, as it is presented here for the practical daily use by the sales manager, some of the complexities have been eliminated; and we will work with but two dimensions—the BASIC LIFE TREND and the MODIFYING LIFE TREND.

The validity of this method of classing men is based upon a simple concept: that men come into life with a basic drive or pattern of motivation, modified in a greater or lesser degree by a secondary trend. These drives, or trends, strangely enough, do not change substantially throughout life. The GOALS sought by each individual, the PATHS he pursues, the METHODS he uses, the BEHAVIOR PATTERNS he exhibits—over the long pull, these are more likely than not to manifest consistently in accordance with the basic trend. Skills may change, but the basic personality traits are modified but little by time and experience.

Therefore, *if the manager can identify the basic drive and the modifying trend of a man, he can predict his future direction!*

This approach requires facts as the basis for appraisal as much as does any other method. Personal acquaintance with and observation of the man in action is a valuable source of such information. But, in the case of applicants previously unknown to the manager, he can obtain much of the needed data from the customary sources—from the personal history record, which should include a job history; from interviews, usually more than one; from previous employers, such facts being secured preferably by personal, face-to-face inquiry. A detailed, independent, personal history report, sometimes called a character-and-credit report, is also useful if made by an outside reporting agency. However, routine information supplied on mimeographed inquiry forms is of little use in this system of appraisal.

This seven-types method is really a *personal* form of appraisal, and if he is to use this approach successfully, the sales manager must get his impressions firsthand; not solely at second hand, from interviewers' reports. For this reason and many others, this scheme does not supersede, nor is it a substitute for the formal reports of a trained personnel psychologist.

Use of Key Chart

In the discussion which follows, each type is described not only by its characteristic traits, but often one type is compared to and contrasted with other types.

The reader will find it helpful, therefore, to refer to the summary chart on page 25, entitled "Key to the Seven Basic Types of Men", even before starting on the description of Type One. For the Key Chart gives three kinds of summary information about each type, namely:

1. It describes the traits, qualities, attributes, "drives", which characterize each type and distinguish that type from the other six.
2. It lists typical occupations in which individuals of each type are predominantly found.
3. It supplies the names of two well-known people whose trends are characteristic of the type.

Once the reader has full information about each of the seven types, we will discuss several ways in which *groups*, as well as the individual manager, can use this appraisal, ways which combine the entertaining features of a game with the more serious purpose of learning to appraise ourselves and others more accurately.

One word of warning should be given, however, before the reader begins to acquaint himself with the characteristics of each of the seven types. No man is a "pure" type. All of us are mixed types, combining, in the case of an ordinary person, the major drive of a basic, and the lesser energies of a modifying life trend. In fact, in certain cases, when typing unusual men and women, we are sometimes compelled to depart from our simple two-dimensional pattern which has proven adequate for the normal type of human being, and to analyze the outstanding individual in terms of three, and in one case (Franklin D. Roosevelt), four dimensions. Why is this departure essential? Because the recorded and historic words and actions of these exceptional individuals, as they respond to

KEY TO THE SEVEN BASIC TYPES OF MEN

NO.	TYPE	QUALITIES WHICH CHARACTERIZE AND DISTINGUISH THE TYPE	LIFE TREND AS SHOWN BY MAJOR LIFE ACTIVITY	TYPICAL INDIVIDUALS
1.	THE DYNAMIC DRIVER	Man of power, purpose and determination. One-pointed. Intensely focussed on personal objectives. Ever goal-conscious. Self-centered. Unyielding. Uncompassionate. "The world is my oyster!"	Military leaders, statesmen, explorers, "empire-builders," industrial "giants."	"Captain Eddie" Rickenbacker* John D. Rockefeller*
2.	THE HUMAN SERVER	Humanitarian. Puts others first, even when it means sacrificing own interests. Sensitive to others' suffering. Strongly sympathetic, even empathetic with the poor, ill, underprivileged. Concerned about their burdens.	Physicians, nurses, social workers, teachers, preachers, missionaries, some detail men.	Dr. Jonas Salk* Dr. Albert Schweitzer*
3.	THE ACTIVE ADAPTER	Compelled to reach objectives by flexibility of action. Practical, realistic, tactful. Adapts himself to conditions and pressures. Seizes, capitalizes opportunities. Adjusts to others' ideas. Action, not ideals, his goal.	Diplomats, politicians, legislators, promoters, "merger-makers."	Andrew Carnegie* Winston Churchill
4.	"BRIDGE-BUILDER"— HARMONIZER	The opposite of an extremist. The "middle-of-the-road" individual. Sees both sides in an argument. Reconciles opposing ideas. Not only a moderate himself, but works toward making OTHERS moderate.	Negotiators, mediators and arbitrators in labor and other disputes.	Dag Hammarskjold* William Howard Taft*
5.	THE ABSTRACT THINKER— PURE SCIENTIST	The high-level, logical thinker. The reasoner, who thinks abstractly, in terms of laws and principles instead of concrete examples, such as is the habit of the lower-level, ordinary thinker.	Mathematicians, logicians, pure scientists, advanced physicists.	Thomas Edison* Nikola Tesla*
6.	THE ENTHUSIAST— THE DEVOTEE	The single-purposed enthusiast. Interprets all things in relation only to his favorite belief. Not "self-focussed", but centered on an external idea or "cause" which seldom benefits him financially. Will sacrifice self and all others to his consuming objective.	"Fans" of any kind—baseball fans, flying saucer fans, single-pointed devotees of any "cause."	John Wesley* Woodrow Wilson*
7.	THE MAN OF "LAW-AND-ORDER"— THE RITUALIST	A perfectionist in physical things. Sees plan, order, balance, number and precision in everything. Finds beauty, rhythm everywhere. Likes formal ceremonials, ordered rituals.	Architects, engineers, builders, poets, priests, musicians, dancing masters, Masonic leaders.	Johann Sebastian Bach Frank Lloyd Wright*

*Analyzed in text

the life pressures of great events and large responsibilities, cannot be wholly understood and explained within the two-dimensional framework used for the everyday man or woman.

Roosevelt, for example, clearly exhibits three basic drives instead of one; and a modifying trend besides.

John Wesley, the evangelist and founder of Methodism, another example, shows one clear-cut basic trend, but two unmistakable modifying trends.

And while the life patterns of these two men, Roosevelt and Wesley, differ entirely, both are exceptional human beings, and neither could be adequately analyzed or described within the limits of the two-dimensional scheme.

But it is not solely the recognized geniuses and leaders of world thought who exhibit a multi-trended life pattern. Now and then, one of the lesser, unhistoric men and women treads the path to greatness without becoming great, because time and chance do not cooperate. A seemingly simple man, for example, a custodian, let us say, of a small-town school building, may also exhibit the signs of a broad multi-typed life trend; but who is there to type him or who to discover or herald his intrinsic greatness? Perhaps, he holds his job through a long succession of cranky and critical school boards, because of his Type Three adaptability; he studies physics at night and uses the school physics laboratory for his experiments, thus demonstrating his Type "Five-ness"; one sad day, when a flash-fire threatens hundreds of young lives in the school he serves, he exhibits a previously unshown strain of Type One courage; and a half hour later when he calms the hysterical and helps to bind up the raw wounds of the unlucky, his Type "Two-ness" comes to the fore in the demonstration of his great human compassion. But how is the confined light of his little life to project the true picture of his many-faceted personality upon the great screen of public attention and recognition?

And thus it comes about that we seldom discover in these "mute inglorious Miltons", the great potential breadth of being, that "heart once pregnant with celestial fire, those hands the rod of empire might have swayed", those thoughts that might have "waked to ecstacy the living lyre."

For these take "the noiseless tenor of their way" and are lost to history. It is true, indeed, as Thomas Gray wrote in his "Elegy"—

> Full many a flower is born to blush unseen,
> And waste its sweetness on the desert air.

But this does not reflect a defect in the classing system; it relates to an entirely different subject—the pattern of *destiny* in human life—and this we know not how either to *type* or to *predict*.

Furthermore, if we were to include additional facets in our classing scheme, we would only complicate it and make it more difficult to understand and to operate. Usually, two dimensions can encompass all the knowledge the sales manager will have about an individual; furthermore, these dimensions are sufficient for his practical purposes.

But examples of the multi-trended lives of familiar figures *do* help us to understand the types, the typing process, and the individual being typed. And these exceptional examples in no way handicap us in our daily use of this typing scheme in its practical applications. For a type runs true to the characteristics which comprise it, whether it is combined with a single modifying type, in the case of an ordinary person, or brought together with two or more further dimensions, in the unique and towering pattern of some extraordinary individual.

Therefore, in attempting to class a particular person, the beginner will do well to run him through all seven of the "screens" before trying to reach any final decision as to major and modifying trends. As a result of this process, some tentative "typings" will emerge. These should be re-scanned to verify their validity and weighed to assay their relative "weight" in the total picture of the individual's personality. Ask: "Which of the seven trends seems to dominate his life? Which seems subordinate?"

The answers to these two simple questions will bring the evaluator closer to his decision. Some further testing against the characteristics of other types, the bringing in of additional "evidence", and lo!—the decision almost *"makes itself!"* Later, as practice matures the skill, the series of sequential screenings can be speeded up; in time, the appraiser may be able to arrive at his final judgment without a deliberately-conscious process of seven screenings. But even though a skilled rater eventually arrives at his conclusions through a flash of intuition, it will be found safer to test and validate the result by continuing to run it ploddingly through the sorting screens of the seven types.

Type One—The Dynamic Driver

This individual is the embodiment in human form of the most primitive of human urges—the will to be, to live and experience life, to act, to express itself in action. He is dynamic, driving, sometimes ruthless in his aims and methods. His reach often exceeds his grasp; but as Browning says, if this is not sometimes true, "what is Heaven for?" (For the individual whose life trend includes the tendency to *adjust* his reach to *correspond* with his grasp, we must look to the Type Three man, to be described in detail later on.)

The Type One man's hunger for his chosen work is voracious; his desire to accomplish his usually self-centered goal, knows little or no restraint; he recognizes no obstacles—and if the obstacles which do fall across his path happen to be other human beings with their own plans and purposes, there is almost sure to be a collision. It is in such situations that the fangs of his Type One ruthlessness are bared, and unless the obstructing obstacle is elastic and adaptable (as a Type Three man naturally is), we are likely to see the human equivalent of the "irresistible force meeting the immovable body." Is it not fortunate, therefore, that there are no "unmodified" Type One men?

Let us now discuss the modifying trends as well as the basic Type One "drives" of a few well-known individuals.

"Captain Eddie" Rickenbacker, A Clear-cut Type One

"Capt. Eddie" Rickenbacker, the driving dynamo behind Eastern Airlines, can be classed as a predominantly Type One individual. His daring when he undertook this enterprise in its early days, his persistence in hanging on through initial difficulties, his far-reaching embrace of a great network of air routes and, his tenacious battle for the right to purchase smaller lines when they were for sale—all characterize him as a strong Type One.

His single-pointed purpose was demonstrated again when he and a group of companions, during World War II, found themselves adrift in mid-Pacific without a visible chance of rescue. His will did not falter; and after a series of almost miraculous occurrences, the group were rescued from starvation and death. His *will* was that of a Type One individual, but his *faith*, his *prayers*, his *firing* of his companions with *hope* and the urge to strive on—these attributes were those of Type Two men. If you will refer to the Key Chart on page 25, you will observe that theoretically, Type One recognizes no purpose but his own, no means other than those of which he is himself master. But the Type Two individual recognizes others first and works through them as means, rather than solely through himself. Thus, you can understand why Rickenbacker's modifying trend is that of a Type Two individual.

Cecil Rhodes, Evolving Empire Builder

As a further example of the basic Type One man, let us cite Cecil Rhodes, the young Englishman whose doctors sent him to South Africa at age 20, supposedly in the last stages of tuberculosis with only six months to live.

He worked for a while in the diamond mines, recovered from his malady, and lived to become the diamond king of the world. Half a continent (Rhodesia) was named after him; and it would not be inaccurate to say that, at the peak of his power, he was more influential in the world than were the chief ruling kings and princes of the time.

When his great part in the world's affairs was about to be ended by the death he had so long defeated, his last words, as he turned his face to the wall, not in fear but almost in despair, were a characteristic and typical Type One utterance: "So little done—so much to do!"

But, Cecil Rhodes, as is true of all men, was not a pure type. His Type One drive (fortunately for him) was modified by some Type Three traits, and these two (One and Three) generated more than a modicum of Type Two force within the man.

His actions give us the facts to support this analysis. For example, he seized numerous opportunities which were not in the direct line of his personal planning, but called for adapting himself to other men's plans. This is a Type Three modifying trend. One of the chief examples of this Type Three trend was his joining with Barney Barnato, his most powerful rival, to form De Beers Consolidated, a company which still controls the diamond supply of the world. Had he been all Type One, he would have fought Barnato to the end, until one or the other was destroyed. But his Type Three trait of adaptability acted to *modify* the one-pointed drive of his Type One nature, with the result that he became a more poised man, an individual with balanced judgment, shrewd as well as powerful, aware of obstacles and finding his way around them, using other people to help him reach his objectives, instead of being unaware of their existence, or riding Juggernaut-like over them.

Rhodes is also an example of another very interesting phenomenon—a result which arises out of the interaction of the Type One and Type Three forces in a single individual. When both the Type One and Type Three forces become strongly active—and balanced—in a man, the combination *begins to generate a strong type two force,* the typical trend of the humanitarian.

This trend took clear expression in the will of Cecil Rhodes, in which, among other things, he established a large fund for the now-famous Rhodes Scholarships. This fund provides the financial means to send to Oxford University each year more than thirty young men from the British Empire, and an almost equal number from the United States.

His will states the purpose in what are certainly Type-Two phrases: ". . . to create in American students an attachment to the Country from which this nation originally sprang, without weakening their 'sympathy for their own.' "

John D. Rockefeller, Evolving Industrialist

In the industrial field, John D. Rockefeller, Sr., is a similar example. Like Rhodes, starting out as a Type One dynamic driver, life taught him, also, the uses of adaptability, the Type Three trait; and before his death, the interaction of the Type One and Type Three traits had evolved into many Type Two characteristics. He publicly began giving away shiny new dimes to children. Today, his own children are the benefactors of activities which give aid to the difficulties of their less fortunate fellow men, a definitely Type Two undertaking on a world-wide scale. In a corporate way, the germs of this Type Two trend became visible within the Rockefeller empire long before the shiny, new dimes era of the elder Rockefeller. After a bloody strike had taken place at one of the Rockefeller properties in the West, action was initiated to see to it that no such conflict would ever again transpire in any Rockefeller-owned enterprise. Out of the steps taken to avoid a repetition of the so-called "Ludlow Massacre", there grew a professional industrial relations organization which was a pioneer in that field and which formulated some of the earliest definitive thinking embodying and activating the Type Two idea in employer-employee relations.

Can we not sum up the Rockefeller example by saying that in his case, a predominant Type One individual was balanced through life experience, by an expanding Type Three trend to adaptability, which taken together with the Type One force, evolved into an ever stronger and stronger Type Two thinking. Interestingly enough, the Type Two traits are being practiced by the second and third generations and appear to have become the predominant life drive of several of Rockefeller, Sr.'s offspring.

TYPE TWO—THE HUMAN SERVER

Those men and women whose basic life trend classifies them as Type Two are best described by the broad term—*humanitarian*.

Whereas Type One individuals are predominantly *inward*-thinking, self-centered, and theoretically unaware of others, Type Two folks are *outward*-thinking, with a keen awareness of other people and a deep concern for others' well-being.

Let us cite an unusual, but highly-fitting parallel. The authorities on animal husbandry tell us that a dairy cow, for example, in the process of carrying out her natural function as the mother of her calf, will literally "suck" out of the marrow of her own bones the life- and body-building substances needed for a healthy offspring, in the event that her feed ration does not provide these vitamins, minerals, and proteins in proper amount and balance.

In a like manner, but in varying degrees, depending upon the indwelling intensity of the Type Two trend, this type of individual will deprive himself to aid others who appear to him to be in need. Most of us have used the expression: "He's a fellow who will give you the shirt off his back if you need it!" That phrase well describes the highly dedicated Type Two individual.

As in all other typical patterns, the Type Two influence is modified by other trends even in the predominantly Type Two man, so that we seldom encounter any person in this group who even approaches the pure type; but wherever you discover a man manifesting a strong empathy with his fellows, especially those whom he feels to be less fortunate, you can confidently label as Type Two the driving force behind his thinking and his actions. If he has an extraordinary capacity to look outward, to include others in his thinking, and to identify himself emotionally with what he considers to be their problems, he shows further evidence of Type Two characteristics.

The fifteenth century physician, psychiatrist, herbalist, pharmacist, chemist, and alchemist, Theophrastus Bombastus Von Hohenheim, better remembered by the name Paracelsus, which he bestowed upon himself, once said: "The difference between a physician and the rest of men is this, that the others need think only of themselves, while the physician must not only care for himself but for others. His office consists of nothing but compassion for others. . . . No one requires greater love of the heart than the physician (for the) art of medicine is rooted in the heart."

Paracelsus was surely describing the Type Two humanitarian, the man of compassion, of regard for others.

In the second article of his "Vow of the Physician," he has the doctor's pledge . . . "to love the sick, each and all of them, more than if my own body were at stake." That is the very keynote of Type Two.

And, we do find many physicians among Type Two individuals. If the physician is the laboratory-frequenting research medical man, he is likely to exhibit a strong modifying Type Five (pure scientist) trend. But the personal practitioner, the "bedside" physician who achieves great personal popularity as well as professional success, is likely to be heavily trended as a Type Two human being.

In this group also, we find nurses, social workers, teachers, ministers, missionaries, and sometimes pharmaceutical detail men, those salesmen who call upon prescribing physicians to stimulate the writing of prescriptions for their company's drug products.

Experience with the sales managers of detail men in the ethical drug business has given us an interesting sidelight which we ought to recount here, because it illuminates an important aspect of "typing" men.

How a Specific Type Two Classification Can Help the Manager to Avoid Misleading Generalities

Frequently, we have suggested to pharmaceutical drug company sales managers that they especially consider as applicants for detail jobs, the frustrated "pre-med" or full medical-course students who were compelled to quit school unexpectedly because of a sudden change in family finances, such as that caused, for example, by the father's death.

In several cases, after the sales manager had studied his hiring records and found that early-quitting medical students did not turn out to be better-than-average detail representatives, the soundness of our recommendation was challenged. After this occurred two or three times, we suddenly realized that we were at fault. We had not taken pains to disclose to our sales manager friends that our recommendation applied only to applicants exhibiting a major Type Two life trend.

In other words, the youngster who goes into medicine because of a strong Type Two life trend—that is, because he is "at heart" a Human Server and is, therefore, moved by a strong drive to associate himself emotionally with the ills of others and to help alleviate them—finds a "substitute satisfaction" in calling upon doctors and aiding them in their problems of patient medication. We might almost say that in this work such a young man finds a vicarious fulfillment of his life urge. He brings to the detail man's job a special "built-in" drive toward success. Consequently, our recommendation should have read: "Pre-med or full medical course students who are compelled to quit school before completion of their studies and training make better-than-average detail representatives IF THEY ARE BASICALLY TYPE TWO INDIVIDUALS!"

In the case of a NON-Type Two medical student, the situation differs at every stage. His basic trend is not toward human service. As a result, the practice of medicine does not especially serve the ends of his basic life drive. In fact, another occupation might easily offer him more opportunities in his particular direction.

Quitting medical school early, and the consequent fact that this eliminates the possibility of his becoming a physician, at most, inconveniences him, costs him some time, compels a reshuffling of plans; but does not dam up any basic trend, nor remove the one particular channel for expression which his heart is "set on."

Consequently, for this non-Type Two youngster, getting a job as a pharmaceutical detail man is not likely to forward any basic life drive or open up any "cherished-before-all-others" life opportunity. To him, detailing is a job, just a job, a way to earn money, neither better nor worse than many other jobs.

It is not difficult to see why our omission of the Type Two qualification made our recommendation only partly valid, and therefore, largely misleading.

This analysis has been given in considerable detail because it shows the danger of generalizing about the success-possibilities of a certain class of applicants, such as the forced "quits" among medical students, unless that generalization is tested to determine whether it is equally true of each of the seven basic types of men. This is another way of saying that classing men into one or more of the seven types usually provides a grouping more significant than that of other more random methods of classing.

Dr. Albert Schweitzer, An Unusual Expression of Basic Type Two

In our chart, as two typical individuals of the major Type Two life trend, we list Dr. Albert Schweitzer, famous humanitarian, and Dr. Jonas Salk, developer of the Salk polio vaccine. Let us first discuss Dr. Schweitzer, who is a many-sided man, but none of whose activities stray far from the Type Two path.

He is a physician and surgeon, an organist and top authority on the music of Bach, a theologian and preacher, and in his most famous role, the founder, director, and moving spirit of a hospital for the black-skinned natives of the province of Gabon, in French Equatorial Africa.

Here in the hot and humid jungle of this Lambarene region, he pursues his almost single-handed way. He tends the patients personally, performing the surgeries, diagnosing, prescribing for, and personally administering to the minds and bodies of native men, women, and children who are little more than aborigines in their development. He turned his back on fame in the world of men, fame which he could have achieved in many fields, to serve an unevolved and almost forgotten people.

In Dr. Schweitzer's early life, there are a great number of signs to foretell that his basic life path was to be that of a Type Two humanitarian. Let us cite a few:

1. In 1896, when he was twenty-one years old, he determined to live for science and

art until he was thirty; thereafter, to give his talents to the direct service of humanity.

2. In 1899, when he took his doctorate in philosophy, his thesis was written on the Religious Philosophy of Immanuel Kant.

3. On his thirtieth birthday, true to his pledge to himself, he decided to study medicine and go to Africa.

4. For his medical degree (1912-1913), he wrote a thesis on "The Psychiatric Study of Jesus", still a famous little book with an arcane flavor, touching upon the inner urges, tensions, and drives of the Master of Nazareth, which at the time of its publication (1913 in German), invaded the very holy of holies of the psychiatrists.

5. On March 26, 1913, the Doctor and Madam Schweitzer sailed from Bordeaux for Africa. The surging Type Two life trend was now fully launched; all that had gone before was preparatory.

6. For a London publisher, he had written a book with the decay of civilization as its central theme. In 1915, he recalls, he awoke from a sort of stupor, suddenly finding himself in search of an affirmative attitude to express his life purpose. He tells it . . . "Lost in thought I sat on the deck of the barge, struggling to find the elementary and universal conception of the ethical concept which I had not discovered in any philosophy . . . Late on the third day, at the very moment when, at sunset, we were making our way through a herd of hippopotamuses, there flashed upon my mind, unforeseen and unsought, the phrase 'Reverence for Life.' The iron door had yielded; the path in the thicket had become visible. Now I had found my way to the idea in which affirmation of the world and ethics are contained side by side!"

Here is the Type Two man is his finest flowering, his not the task of "talking about the religion of love," as Dr. Schweitzer had said, "but . . . as an actual putting it into practice."

It is difficult to name any other living man who so completely fulfills the requirements of the Type Two individual.

Certainly, Dr. Schweitzer is an *humanitarian,* on such a grand scale that, alongside him, ordinary men and women seem hardly to deserve the description.

Certainly, he puts others first, even when it means sacrificing his own interests. Surely, he is sensitive to others' suffering, so much so that he has sacrificed the kind of life to which other men aspire, in order that head, heart, and hands might be dedicated and devoted to the service of the suffering. And he is markedly sympathetic, even empathic with the poor, the ill, the underprivileged; for he has chosen to aid the most extreme examples of these types.

Compassion for others, which is the basic attribute underlying all Type Two traits, certainly is the key to Dr. Schweitzer's thinking and actions. His creed— "reverence for all life."

In fact, Dr. Albert Schweitzer is so emphatically Type Two that we find it difficult to discover his *modifying* trend or trends. It is, of course, the Type One dynamism and drive, coupled with a terrific capacity for adaptability in the Type Three area.

For example, his wife cannot live for long periods in the tropical climate of central Africa; hence, the Doctor must sacrifice many of the satisfactions of normal family life in order that his Type Two objectives may be realized. In this as in many other ways, we see evidences of his Type Three qualities of adaptability and adjustment.

In summing up our analysis of this famous man, we find he is a major Type Two, with a predominantly Type One modifying life trend, coupled with a strong Type Three capacity for adaptability, or adjustment to the obstacles and necessities of daily life. In other words, this modern St. George, who battles the dragons of disease, ignorance, and want in one of earth's forgotten places, cannot be adequately pictured or analyzed on less than a three-dimensional scale. His basic Type Two humanitarianism is implemented and activated by a strong Type One drive and determination; and this, in turn, is modified and *modulated* by a Type Three highly practical, common-sense adaptability.

Dr. Jonas Salk, Humanitarian-Scientist

Our second example of a Type Two individual is Dr. Jonas Salk, the discoverer and developer of the early polio vaccine. He is a dedicated scientist, whose humanitarianism is exhibited to us in a less personal way, perhaps, than that of Dr. Schweitzer. However, as a compensation, Dr. Salk's discovery has been of service to many millions who may not even know his name, whereas Dr. Schweitzer's dedication has aided only a comparatively few, if we except the world-wide power of his example.

And what is Dr. Salk's modifying life trend? Can it be other than that of the Type Five man, the logical thinker, the pure scientist?

Yes, Dr. Salk is major Type Two, modified by Type Five. His modesty in public appearances, his channeling of financial awards and honorariums back into further research, his disinclination to seek the limelight of public fame—these are traits typical of the Type Five scientist.

Dr. "X", Scientist-Humanitarian

Perhaps it will help the reader better to understand the endlessly-diversified combinations of life drives, if he will consider that in the case of another scientist, Dr. "X", let us call him, his basic life trend might have been that of the Type Five scientist, with the Type Two humanitarianism as the modifying drive. In Dr. "X", our hypothetical scientist, science comes first, and his humanitarianism is only a secondary, modifying trend. In brief, the extent to which the attributes can be combined—shuffled and reshuffled—is almost endless.

Need for Type Two Salesmen

Furthermore, on only cursory examination, a sales manager might be moved to say that there is not much place for this Type Two man in selling. But that is not true; for wherever there is a need for a *simpatico* between the salesman and the customer, wherever there is a human service aspect to the sale, wherever the salesman must feel *with* his prospect, the fellow with the Type Two trend is likely to prove very useful.

We have already mentioned the detail representative of the ethical pharmaceutical company as a good example of the proper use of the Type Two individual.

We might add, as other examples, the hearing aid salesman, the salesman selling major orthopedic appliances direct to the patient, or the salesman selling health insurance. In short, in almost any sales operation where it is helpful for the salesman to be able to stand imaginatively in the other fellow's shoes and feel as if he *were* the other fellow, the predominantly Type Two man is likely to be a better-than-average representative.

TYPE THREE—THE ACTIVE ADAPTER

When one of Napoleon's aides excused the loss of a battle by an enemy commander on the grounds that "circumstances were against him," Bonaparte, with characteristic confidence, replied: "Circumstances?—*I make them!*"

Napoleon, of course, was a predominantly Type One military leader, but his modifying trend was certainly that of the Type Three individual, he whom we designate as the "active adapter." And the Little Corporal's rejoinder about circumstances was a true reflection of his Type Three thinking. Does not our key Chart describe the active adapter as one who adapts himself to conditions and pressures; seizes, capitalizes opportunities; *action*, not *ideals*, his goal. In other words, by virtue of his quick intuitive discernment, the fluidity or flexibility of his planning, and his natural capacity for translating thinking into action, Napoleon so effectively capitalized upon circumstances that he could claim with much truth that he *made* them.

Adaptability is the first key to understanding the life trend of the Type Three individual; the second key is *action*. For the Type Three operator is not of a contemplative nature. He may be an extremely competent thinker, but thinking is not, to him, an end in itself; it is only the means to an end, and that end is—ACTION!

We have all met the fellow who is an excellent planner, but to whom planning is the destination itself, not a road map by means of which to reach that destination. This Type Three chap is the very opposite of the planner, the dreamer, the idealist, the visualizer. Recall what the Chart reveals—*action*, not *ideals*, his goal! In fact, we may find the Type Three individual incapable of the plodding patience needed for planning—"to hell with the blueprints—let's get some action!"

Andrew Carnegie, Industrialist-Adapter Evolving

Andrew Carnegie, the steel master, is an excellent example of the individual whose major life trend was Type Three.

Carnegie, it will be recalled, was not only a pioneer industrialist who built a gigantic empire in the steel business; he was probably the first man in this modern world to amass a personal fortune of over a billion dollars. And then he began to build and endow public libraries. Carnegie libraries became a part of the fabric of the intellectual and cultural life of the American community and even today, the Carnegie Institute of Washington, D.C. is a factor in those philanthropies which touch the aspiring side of men's striving.

Let us examine one or two of the revealing recorded incidents of Carnegie's life. This will give us some ideas as to whether our analysis of the steel master is accurate.

Back in the days when Carnegie was a young man holding a humble job as telegraph operator for the Pennsylvania Railroad under Colonel Thomas A. Scott, an incident occurred which clearly reflected upon the veil of the future the life trend of this man of steel. In *Succeeding With What You Have*, Charles M. Schwab, one of Mr. Carnegie's boys, provides the details:

One morning a series of wrecks tangled up the line. Colonel Scott was absent and young Carnegie could not locate him. Things looked bad.

Right then Carnegie disregarded one of the road's strictest rules and sent out a dozen telegrams signed with Colonel Scott's name, giving orders that would clear the blockade.

"Young man," said the superintendent a few hours later, "do you realize that you have broken this company's rules?"

"Well, Mr. Scott, aren't your tracks clear and your trains running?" asked the young telegrapher.

Colonel Scott's punishment was to make Carnegie his private secretary. A few years later, when the colonel retired from office, he was succeeded by the former telegrapher, then only twenty-eight years old.

Upon another occasion, during a depressed period in American business, the Southern Pacific was about to place a big order for steel rails. Competition was tough, and price-cutting was the chief sales argument. Carnegie needed the business for his mills. He telephoned Collis Potter Huntington who *was* the Southern Pacific as far as the rail order decision was concerned. He reminded the Westerner of the many past occasions when it was the credit which Carnegie had extended that had kept Huntington's head above water.

"What price have you been quoted?" asked Carnegie. Huntington told him.

"We will meet it," said Carnegie, "but I want the business!"

And he got it!

Observe the Type Three traits revealed in this transaction—practical, realistic, tactful; adapts himself to conditions and pressures; seizes, capitalizes opportunities.

Compare Carnegie's action with these specifications. He needed and wanted the Huntington business so he took the practical, the realistic, step—HE ASKED FOR IT!

His earlier credit leniency had put Huntington under obligation; Carnegie seized the opportunity and capitalized that obligation.

But he did not push his rights too far; he was tactful, realistic, and quickly adjusted his thinking to the practicalities of the situation. He did not expect Huntington to go so far as to pay him *more* than others for the rails—that would not have been realistic. He met the competitive price but did not cut it. Once the price was even, he relied upon the weight of the obligation to tip the scales of the sale in his direction.

Like Napoleon, by the shrewd practice of *adaptability*, Carnegie capitalized upon circumstances, even unfavorable circumstances.

Beneath the surface of these clear-cut Type Three characteristics of Andrew Carnegie, however, there was a strong undercurrent of Type One tendencies—granitic purpose, determined will, one-pointedness, goal-consciousness. He was an empire-builder who assembled an industrial domain which still survives in great vitality. Today, we have other giants which exist alongside the Steel Corporation—A.T.&T., in communications; Du Pont, in chemicals; General Motors, in the automotive field. But, in that day, steel was the supreme giant. Only a man with some Type One drive could have developed and unified the steel industry. Carnegie had the advantage of being a basic Type Three individual first, these traits being modified by Type One trends.

And when the Type One and Type Three qualities had done their respective jobs and achieved their common objective, a metamorphosis such as that which touched John D. Rockefeller, at a later date, took place in Carnegie. He became America's first great philanthropist, placing his funds in the hands of a publicly-administered foundation out of his personal control. He chose libraries as one of the chief avenues of his humanitarianism and, brought almost to the doorstep of the humblest citizen everywhere in the land, the gift of available knowledge as found in books.

Strange, is it not, how frequently the interaction of the energies and drives of Types One and Three eventually meet in the center, as it were, and generate new and powerful Type Two trends and traits which operate to present to the world an almost different human being with new purposes and new ideals, a man whom the world believes it has never met before?

And yet, this seemingly inexplicable process repeats itself, time after time, in the lives of men great and small. Nature requires only that both types of drives be present and that the generating drives be fairly well balanced in "horsepower."

And then—"abracadabra!"—the mystic alchemical transmutation takes place; the new man appears. And as a consequence, humanity, in one way or another, reaps where it has not sown.

Type Four—The "Bridge-Builder"—Harmonizer

The pattern of the individual who is motivated by a Type Four life trend is best described by the phrase "middle-of-the-roader." Just as the Type Four spot is the mid-point in the list of the seven types, so also are the characteristics of this type of individual typical of the man of moderation. Just as the "middle path" of the Buddhists, or the "middle pillar" of the ancient Kabbalists, refers to the wise balance or equilibrium in life, so does Type Four exemplify a similar central point between the two extremes.

The Type Four individual sees the virtues and faults of both sides in an argument. He is the *reconciler*, the *mediator*, the individual who *builds a bridge* between opposing points of view. He partakes to some extent of those qualities which are usually inferred when reference is made to *"the judicial temperament."*

Predominently Type Four men and women are peculiarly suited by their life drive to be negotiators, mediators and arbitrators in labor disputes, or magistrates and judges in courts where differences of opinion must be argued out and settled.

Like the individual in every other type, the Type Four man has "the defects of his virtues." Should he be in the legal profession, for example, he is not likely to be the fiery public prosecutor, passionately pursuing the prosecution of a public criminal; nor a second Clarence Darrow, defending with his own passionate fire, the innocence of a famous defendant. The quiet seat upon the bench more naturally fits the life trend of this type of man. The blindfolded figure of Justice with the balance in her hand is one familiar symbol of the Type Four trend.

In business, this man is not the enthusiast; he lacks, for instance, the one-pointed, one-sided drive of the dynamic Type One individual, such as Cecil Rhodes; or the passionate devotion of the Type Six man. But he also possesses the virtue of avoiding the excesses common to these two types.

Mark Sabre, A Novelist's Creation of a Genuine Type Four

The character of Mark Sabre, as sketched by A. S. M. Hutchinson, in his novel *If Winter Comes,* gives us a very good picture of the Type Four man.

Sabre was talking about himself to Nona, the one woman in whose presence he seemed to be his most effective self. Here, in his own words, is his analysis of himself, and with it a sort of yearning to possess some of the drive of the Type One or the fiery devotion of the Type Six individual.

> ". . . I've got the most infernal habit. . . . I've no convictions; that's the trouble. I swing about from side to side. I can always see the other side of the case, and you know, that's absolutely fatal."
> "Fatal to what, Marko?"
> "Well, to everything; to success. You can't possibly be successful if you haven't got convictions—what I call bald-headed convictions. That's what success is, Nona, the success of politicians and big men whose names are always in the papers. It's that: seeing a thing from only one point of view and going all out for it from that point of view. Convictions." (He meant, of course, the headline-making Type One men!)
> ". . . you know, you can't possibly pull out this big, booming sort of stuff they call success if you're going to see anybody's point of view but your own. You must have convictions. Yes, and narrower than that, not convictions, but conviction. Only *one* conviction—that *you're* right and that everyone who thinks differently from you is wrong to blazes. . . . and I'm dashed if I ever *think* I'm right, let alone conviction of it. I can always see the bits of right on the other side of the argument. That's me. Dash me!"

Where can we find a truer delineation of the extreme Type Four individual who sees the equities on both sides of the argument to the point where his normal human urge to act in one direction or another is cancelled out by the equal balance of the opposing forces.

And yet, in this Mark Sabre, we catch glimpses of his admiration for what he terms the "booming sort of stuff they call success"—the dynamic, driving Type One individual or the politician, usually a Type Three; or as the reader discovers later in the book, his sympathy for the enthusiastic, almost fanatical activities of the "women's rights" group who were engaged in a typical Type Six activity. In short, Sabre recognized the defects of his Type Four trend and he longed for the drive, the expression in action of those compulsions which characterize Types One, Three, and Six.

Of course, not many Type Four individuals are so delicately balanced as to be reduced to complete impotence in action; but an understanding of the dead-centered dilemma which distinguishes this type helps us also to fix in memory its characteristic trends.

William Howard Taft, Ineffective President—Celebrated Jurist

On the Key Chart, we list as one example of Type Four, William Howard Taft, ex-President of the United States and former Chief Justice of the U.S. Supreme Court. It was as Chief Justice that Mr. Taft most clearly demonstrated those qualities of even-handedness which placed him in the Type Four classification.

It is very revealing to recall that Mr. Taft as President was regarded as a relatively ineffective executive. One of the complaints about him which was echoed by so many of his White House associates and friends was his *lack of decision.* To him making a decision seemed to be a painful process; he constantly procrastinated, dillydallied, and put off decisions on national matters of great importance; he kept others unintentionally on the anxious seat, waiting for him to give the decisive word. This trend, in our opinion, contributed largely to the break between himself and his close friend Teddy Roosevelt. T. R. was the personification of driving action—a strong Type Three, modified by a Type One drive. Is it not easy to understand why Roosevelt could not put up with Taft's inborn indecision?

It is easy also to see why Taft, living under a strong Type Four life trend, "found things even that were wide apart." And lacking the one-sidedness of the Type One advocate, or that of the Type Six devotee, he found it difficult to make "fine-haired" presidential decisions.

Strange, is it not, that the very traits which made him a poor executive, equipped him to be an outstanding jurist?

Dag Hammarskjöld, A Treader on the Razor's Edge

Our second example is Dag Hammarskjöld, Secretary General of the United

Nations. In all the world, what job more than this demands the qualities of the Type Four man? For this task calls for *un*self-centered middle-pointedness, instead of the self-pointed inlooking of Type One; it requires the capacity to see and understand opposite points of view, instead of the single-purposed, passionate devotion of Type Six, shortly to be discussed.

It seems natural to call Hammarskjöld a *diplomat,* but he is not a diplomat in the customary narrow and nationally-partisan sense of being the representative of a single nation, having that nation's interests first at heart. He is a diplomat in the larger, world-wide sense, representing the peaceful unity of *all* nations, and as such must be the living embodiment of Type Four characteristics.

But he has enough of the Type Three action and adaptability traits to make his Type Four approach dynamically effective.

The Type Four individual who lacks some of the characteristics of Types One, Three, or Six is likely to experience Taft's difficulties—inertia fixation, lack of action. To genuine Type Four people, equally-balanced forces do not call for further action. With them, *achieving the balance in itself is the major objective!* This is at once their chief virtue and their outstanding fault.

TYPE FIVE—THE ABSTRACT THINKER—PURE SCIENTIST

The sales manager having behind him a good deal of experience with people has learned that the proportion of abstract thinkers in a sales group is relatively small. Has he not struggled constantly in his sales training activities, for example, to convert abstract concepts into concrete pictures so that the average man can comprehend the teaching?

If he happens to have had experience in managing a sales force selling intangibles, for example, he has observed how many salesmen who succeed in selling *tangibles*—that is, physical merchandise which can be seen, touched, tasted, smelled, or heard—are failures when they attempt to sell *intangible* services such as life insurance, accounting, consulting, and research.

Why?

First, because they are not themselves abstract thinkers, and therefore fail to understand the intangible service they try to sell. Second, their prospects, like themselves, are non-abstract thinkers, and are therefore, unable to visualize the service and their need for it, until the intangibilities have been reduced to concrete "physical-ities."

But the Type Five individual is that *rara avis,* the abstract thinker. He is the reasoner, the individual who thinks in terms of *causes,* not solely in terms of *effects,* as is true of the ordinary individual who is a *concrete,* not an abstract *thinker.* The Type Five man can think in symbols, in terms of basic laws and principles. Perhaps we can call him the syllogistic thinker, possessed of the mind to pursue a proposition to its logical conclusion, even though this means following a not-always-visible trail.

In this group, we find the pure scientist; the researcher whose drive to investigate arises almost entirely from a desire for knowledge; the high-level "dreamer", as he will be called by some, who reaches into those higher mental levels unknown to most of us, and comes up, for example, with a new invention in electronics, a new discovery in medicine, or a new concept in physics.

Obviously, we are not likely to find many of the more conspicuous Type Five individuals in the field of selling, unless it be in some of the new nuclear industries where high-level scientific knowledge is essential; and even then, such an individual is more likely to be an *engineer* than a salesman.

In this, as in all other classes, it is true—as we constantly remind you—there are no pure types. This means that Type Five men, having other types of modifying trends, *will* be found in selling. Or, the reverse may be true. They may be men whose major life trends are found in other types, but whose modifying trend will be Type Five. The sales manager will seldom hire men in the higher levels of this Type Five group; but he may from time to time employ men who are abstract thinkers, who are logical in their thinking processes, and capable of meeting on their own intellectual level prospects and customers of similar trends of thought.

Let us see if we can bring the more common manifestations of the traits of this Type Five individual into focus here. Shall we choose a salesman with a Type Three basic life trend (that is, adaptability and action) coupled with a Type Five modifying trend?

This is the man who is continually plying his trainer, and later, his manager, with questions. *How* does it work? *Why* does it work that way? *Why* didn't they do it this way?

Because he is essentially a logical thinker, he will be worried and frustrated by the seeming illogicalness found in selling situations which are so often charged with emotion. Certainly, he will not understand them, without outside education in the principles of psychological motivation and persuasion. The sales engineer often exhibits such Type Five traits. For example, if a piece of equipment is well designed and gets the results claimed for it, he will find it difficult to understand why the prospect doesn't buy it. The fact that the buyer is content with his less efficient machine, that he is motivated not by logic, but only by emotional fear and loss appeals, will confuse the orderly thinking of the Type Five engineer—for to such a man, effect must follow cause as night follows day and to him, logic, not emotion, is the prime mover in selling.

Type Five at the Genius Level

An outstanding example of the basic Type Five trend is Albert Einstein, one of the greatest abstract thinkers of his age. As a result of his remarkable gift in the area of abstract thought in the field of higher mathematics, he postulated great axioms, many of which were found to be true and demonstrable on the concrete levels of the physical world. He spoke of the curvature of space and the space-time continuum; and his classic formula $E = mc^2$ reconciled the views of the scientists and the philosophers, proving that in the end, both were talking about the same thing.

Einstein is cited as an example of the Type Five life trend, because he was so completely characteristic of the traits of this type of abstract thinker and scientist. But the example will be misleading unless the reader, with a little assistance from myself, is able to visualize these same basic traits, greatly diluted in intensity, manifesting on a much lower level in persons of less conspicuous genius, or of no apparent genius at all.

Type Five at the Level of Ordinary Men

Such persons need not be scientists, or mathematicians, or even technically-minded or technically-trained. You can identify them by the fact that they have the habit of orderly and sequential thought; they observe effects and search naturally for causes or, seeing causes, they seek for effects. In short, they pursue the partial equation until they can view it completed. They are searchers; they are not content until the solution is found.

As previously mentioned, good sales engineers often exhibit Type Five trends, usually as the *modifying*, not the *major* factor. Where the job requires the man to do survey work, investigate prospect or customer conditions and needs, the Type Five traits—to pursue the cause to its effect, or the effect to its cause, or to "complete the equation"—are attributes of much value. In a job where such extensive knowledge is not necessary in order to complete the sale, this tendency to pursue facts to the end may turn out to be only a time-waster! A lawyer friend of mine once said: "I never try to prove more than I need—to win the case." A similar philosophy is equally wise for the salesman: "I never try to get more facts than I need—to close the sale."

Two Inventors, Variant Expressions of the Same Life Trend

Two other examples of the Type Five life trend as the factor shaping the lives of men are to be found in two great inventors, Nikola Tesla and Thomas Edison. They were both creative geniuses; yet the channels of their thinking were wide apart, so wide indeed, that it literally forced them into different paths, where each carved his own enduring, but peculiar niche in the scientific hall of fame.

For a little while Nikola Tesla worked for the Edison enterprise, but not directly for Edison himself. Edison had a contract to install a telephone system in Hungary in the early 1880's, and it is easy to understand how the wide-ranging genius of the budding Tesla was of great value to the Edison Group. The story goes that Tesla was aware of his worth; he approached Edison's Paris manager with a request for a raise. He failed to get it. That was a minor matter of course, one that probably never came to Edison's attention.

But there was already vibrant in the hidden time-folds of the future, a larger and much more fundamental disagreement between these two great minds in the then new field of electricity. Edison was an advocate of the single-directioned direct current; Tesla, on the other hand, was convinced that alternating current was the best form of electric power for the future.

As history shows, Tesla was supremely right; Edison wrong. Today, the commercial generation of direct current has all but disappeared from the American scene. But to those of us who had no part in the conflict, it is hard to understand how fierce was the battle between the direct current and alternating current schools of thought.

Tesla, in fact, can be said to have been the father of alternating current; he invented and developed the a.c. generators installed at the first hydro-electric plant in the United States, at Niagara Falls.

Tesla conceived, designed, and developed the heavy transformers which stepped up the voltage and made the long-distance transmission of alternating current so much more economical than direct current, the transmission range of which is limited. Later in life, Tesla turned to high-frequency electronics, and made many contributions to this newer field.

While all this makes an interesting side light to history, it is still more interesting to observe the surprising differences in the two men's application of their Type Five drives.

In the case of Tesla, it is said that his power of abstract thought was of such a high order that not only was he able to intuit the new concepts and principles which he incorporated into his revolutionary inventions, but he was able to visualize down to the smallest part what, to other men, would have been the "drawings" of their inventions. Tesla, however, built his models from his "mental drawings", without troubling to put them on paper.

Thomas Edison, as much a Type Five as Tesla, exhibited his life trend in a different manner. He did not manifest the exceptional capacity for intuitive conception and visualization which characterized the creative activities of Tesla. Edison was a more down-to-earth scientist, operating on practical levels more understandable to ordinary mortals.

I met him first in his laboratory-shop in East Orange, where, surrounded by twenty or so young Japanese laboratory assistants, and clad in vest and white shirt, his hat still on his head, he was inquiring of his foreman about a delivery of copper sheeting from nearby Newark.

Behind this commonplace exterior, Edison had the Type Five scientific curiosity, although curiosity is not the perfect word to describe this mental tendency to probe and pursue a problem to its solution. Let us say that once having gotten hold of a "string of knowledge," he seldom let go until he had followed it to its other end.

This "never-let-go" tendency could be seen to the very end, in Edison's espousal of his direct current philosophy. But it was more constructively visible in the persistence of his earlier efforts to perfect the first incandescent electric light.

Nelson C. Durand, one of his early office boys, who became an important vice president, told me the story.

For the filament of his lamp, Edison needed a fibre strong enough to be carbonized and retain its form; one which would conduct electric current, yet, which would at the same time offer sufficient resistance to produce heat to the level of light without being consumed. Among others, he sent James Recalton, a school teacher, to Japan, where the New Jersey pedagogue pushed a handcart through the bamboo forests, selecting hundreds of samples which were sent back to the laboratory for experiment. It was one of these samples, so laboriously collected, that provided Edison with his first usable lamp filament, and thus made it possible for him, in turn, to give the world the electric light.

One, a genius-scientist, with a high-level capacity for intuition and abstract thought, a modern Prometheus who, reversing the ancient role, seized and bound the gods, and tapped their transcendent powers; the other, a genius, too, but operating on lower levels, seemingly nearer to the ordinary man, practical, sometimes almost plodding in his methods. Such were Tesla and Edison.

Yet each expressed, in his own unique and individual way, the powerful characteristics of that life trend which we call Type Five—the trend which characterizes the scientist, the man of abstract thought, the individual of exceptional knowledge. We know of no two examples which so well exemplify the great variety which nature sometimes introduces within the framework of a single type.

TYPE SIX—THE ENTHUSIAST—THE DEVOTEE

The man or woman with a pet "cause", the religionist, the proselytist who would convert all others to the belief of his choice, the professional feminist—these are extreme examples of individuals who fall into Type Six. This group is characterized by their single-pointed devotion to a "cause" which is usually unselfish and not related directly to their personal welfare, except insofar as they eventually make the project of their choice a personal one.

It is characteristic of Type Six individuals to be one-*pointed*, even one-*sided* in their enthusiasms. They often have the intensity and single-mindedness of purpose seen in the Type One dynamic driver, with this difference—that the Type One individual drives toward the objective of his own selfish interest to express his own will and desire, while even the most extreme Type Six will usually have attached himself to a cause or movement of which he was not the originator. In other words, the Type Six drive is not for personal ends, but for objectives arising outside of the individual.

Words like *adherent, advocate, devotee, enthusiast, proselytist,* and *protagonist* help to convey some idea of the essential nature of the Type Six person. In extreme situations, the word might easily be *fanatic*. But the other less emphatic names are more descriptive of the usual Type Six individual.

There is a temptation to refer to this group as *idealists*. Certainly in this classification, the proportion of idealists would be high. But idealists are not limited to this type; they are to be found in all types.

Woodrow Wilson, Visionary Devotee

Illustrative of Type Six, our most famous example is Woodrow Wilson. His pet cause, it will be remembered, was the League of Nations, the aborted predecessor of today's United Nations. An international union, worthy as it was, in President Wilson's mind was first an ideal; as his political enemies opposed him, this fierce determination turned it into a *cause célèbre,* a personal passion, which as history relentlessly records, unfortunately turned into an obsession. In the end, the very fire of Wilson's dedication consumed the one man (himself) who could have been the League's ablest advocate had he been moved less deeply by the flame of the devotee, and more wisely by the adaptability which is characteristic of Type Three or, by the moderation common to Type Four.

But Woodrow Wilson was not, of course, solely Type Six. He manifested a good many Type One traits of dynamism and drive. In fact, it would not be amiss to inquire whether or not the intense Type "Six-ness" of his latter days did not grow out of his *frustrated Type One trends!* There was a good deal of Type Five in the ex-President, too, for was not the first half of his life spent in the scholarly pursuit of knowledge, much of it very largely in the realm of the abstract, an activity which is characteristically Type Five. The ruthlessness with which he tossed the politicians out of power once he became Governor of New Jersey exhibits his Type One drive plus his idealism.

The man whose intellectual oratory gave us such long-lived phrases as "the world must be made safe for democracy" and "there is such a thing as a man being too proud to fight", certainly revealed himself as an *idealist* and a *thinker* who conceived of freedom more in terms of a high level abstract concept, than in terms of practical and achievable national objectives. In fact, he publicly confessed to his idealism, when in a speech at Sioux Falls, S. D., in the Fall of 1919, he said:

> Sometimes people call me an idealist. Well, that is the way I know I am an American. America is the only idealistic nation in the world.

But his idealism was largely mental, revealing the Type Five thinker applying his abstract concepts to the field of statecraft and politics, but lacking in the Type Three qualities of adaptability which would have brought him to compromise on lesser issues, and thus to secure a half a loaf if he could not get it all. Getting action in the field of politics almost always calls for flexibility. Had Wilson been willing to yield a little on his crystallized mental concepts, he would have gotten the action his stubborn idealism prevented.

John Wesley, Go-getter Devotee

Another outstanding example of the Type Six enthusiast and devotee is John Wesley, the founder of the Methodist Church. It is estimated that during his lifetime (1703-1791), he preached perhaps fifty thousand sermons, beside completing an enormous mountain of literary work. History tells us that as many as thirty thousand persons came together at one time to hear him preach, some arriving on foot, many carried on the backs of friends, others on litters, in pushcarts, hay wagons, donkey carts, and by every imaginable means of transportation. These devoted followers waited hours, some throughout the whole of the previous night, to hear Wesley's words.

When, upon one occasion, he was asked the secret of the oratorical power with which he drew these crowds, he gave a reply, characteristic, indeed, of the Type Six individual: "I just set myself on fire—people come to watch me burn!"

John Wesley had within himself this "fire of the Gods", as the Greeks called it—enthusiasm, that internally-generated magnetic fire which draws people almost unknowingly to its warmth; and with its help, he became one of the greatest evangelists of all time.

Recalling his tremendous physical drive as expressed in his countless sermons and teachings and writings, we might suspect him to be better classed as a Type One dynamic driver. However, we return again to our Type Six classing when we remind ourselves that he began his work in the church as a conservative High Churchman, and that it was only after his meeting with the Moravian missionary, Peter Böhler, that his new evangelism took fire. Thus, it was another's spark which touched the tinder of his genius and set aflame that almost Godlike enthusiasm which was the lodestone of his hold upon the hearts of the men and women who heard him.

The characteristic Type Six qualities are everywhere evident in Wesley's acts. He was the typical enthusiast, centered on a cause sparked from the outside, sacrificing himself, his life, his former position in the Church, to a single consuming objective.

His literary labors alone are said to have brought him an income of more than thirty thousand English pounds, every penny of which he distributed to charity during his lifetime. This marks him as a humanitarian, having a good deal of the characteristic life trend of the Type Two. But what is a Type Six, if not a reflected and modified image of a Type Two, his dominant traits heightened, and emphasized, and carried almost to the point of fanatacism?

However, his Type "Two-ness" was not his chief modifying trend. Chambers's *Biographical Dictionary* says . . . . "the most striking feature of his life as a theologian was his readiness in the last resort, whatever it cost him, to adapt his creed to indisputable facts." There we have it—*adaptability!*—the most characteristic of all Type Three attributes. "Whatever it cost him", he was *adaptable*. If we accept this as "the most striking feature of his life as a theologian", we must conclude that his chief modifying trend was that of the Type Three individual.

Imagine this Type Six human being—devoted, enthusiastic, physically powerful, housing a great new blaze sparked by Böhler's thinking, and yet, a man born with a capacity for wise adaptability to opposition and obstacles. Wesley was not the customary dogmatic, crystallized theologian, willing to risk all for the sake of some obscure or unimportant point of dogma or doctrine; rather, was he flexible, adaptable, willing and wise enough to modify the means to gain the end.

Such, so history tells us, was John Wesley, founder of one of the largest Protestant sects, evangelist, enthusiast, devotee, a Type Six human being, lucky to have been born with the strong Type Three characteristic of adaptability. This saved him, no doubt, from being called a fanatic and led him into the broad paths of an historic success, a success which his own acts would have denied him had he been a pure Type Six who, like the unfortunate Woodrow Wilson, would have been unable to "roll with the punches!"

Risks of the Type Six in Business

In business, the enthusiasms of the Type Six man may be the source of much satisfaction to his sales manager, provided the man's "devotee-ism" can be successfully tied up with his job objectives. In such a case, his sales vehicle is largely propelled by a great and powerful energy—*enthusiasm*.

But if that enthusiasm is channelled into some activity outside of his job, it can be the cause of difficulties innumerable.

I recall an interesting case of this kind with which we had to deal in our own business. One of our able account executives, whose job was to call upon clients and advise them in connection with their marketing problems, suddenly discovered a forty-year-old method of "character" analysis, based upon the examination and "diagnosis" of facial contours, bumps and depressions, an activity having nothing whatever to do with our business. Within him, the subject evoked a deep and immediate response. He took an evening course; was soon made an associate evening instructor; and within six months, this project literally became his consuming passion. Its hold upon him, the complete manner in which it engaged his attention, both in his office and away from it, was hard to understand. He talked incessantly upon this pet subject, even to clients; and thereby was compelled from lack of time, to exclude consideration of their pressing affairs. Soon his clientele began to complain; they were irritated partly by his "evangelism", partly by his neglect of their affairs. A different executive was assigned to one client after another; and we finally "allowed" his outside enthusiasm to "magnetize" him right out of our employ into the work into which both his head and heart had been ensnared. His Type Six

For our example, let us take a noted and controversial figure—Frank Lloyd Wright.

Frank Lloyd Wright, A Panorama of Type Seven

Architect extraordinary, Wright was the chief idol-smasher of his profession. Born to an endless flow both of ideas and words, he never ceased to challenge the safely entrenched great of the architectural world with new concepts both of design and construction in their own field. He was a phenomenon, both professionally and personally—a modern combination of some of the talents and tendencies of Leonardo da Vinci, Salvador Dali, Bernarr Macfadden, James McNeill Whistler, and Harold Ickes.

Wright began the practice of architecture in 1893, at the age of twenty-four. In New York, in 1953, he sponsored an amazing personal exhibit which he labeled "Sixty Years of Living Architecture"; and that meant, of course, Frank Lloyd Wright's living and Frank Lloyd Wright's architecture.

At Wright's Taliesin, in Spring Green, Wisconsin, he operated a school of life and art where students paid for the privilege of doing the drudgery of his drafting room, and where the dynamic drift of his restless mind found new envoys to preserve his thinking for the future.

He was a profound and work-centered egotist, making no pretense of leaving the praise of his work to others.

Years ago, he designed the Imperial Hotel in Tokyo, in the midst of Japan's earthquake zone, resting that great structure on what is literally a "floating foundation." The concept was new and revolutionary, but when the 1923 earthquake came, his hotel rode through the tremors unscathed, while the conventional skyscrapers of the traditional architects crumpled like leaves. In a single day, his radical design was vindicated, and his fame as a sound, courageous, and original designer was assured.

Here is the restless innovator, the scorner of precedent, the daring adventurer in his own field.

How do we type this unusual, we might almost say, erratic genius?

As an architect—and everything points to the fact that he was first the architect who channels all of his other talents into his art—his basic life trend was certainly Type Seven. Spatial relationships, law, order—these were the chief material of his thinking. And rhythm, as expressed in stone and steel, was breathed like the breath of life itself into every design.

His modifying trend was Type One, that of the dynamic driver. And so dominantly did this urge crash through his acts and speech that the evaluator, having placed him in Type Seven from the standpoint of his basic drive, might begin to ask himself whether or not Type One was Wright's major life trend. John Lloyd Wright, also a famous architect, once described the Type One in his father: ". . . he is a genius who has always been obsessed by an insatiable craving to conquer everything in the world of architecture there is to be conquered. And he has the gigantic ability to match the insatiable craving."

In that quotation will be found the reason that we typed Frank Lloyd Wright first as a basic Type Seven, with a modifying Type One drive. His son remarked that his father's craving to conquer was limited to "the world of architecture." Therefore, since his drive in the general Type One direction lay within the architectural field, we considered his modifying Type One expression as the motive power, the propellant, to use a modern missile phrase, behind his basic Type Seven artistry. In short, he was Type Seven in his basic interest; Type One in the drive behind it.

We recall that Type One and Type Seven are often found together; and when they are, the result usually is an extraordinary human being. And, that Wright was; for like Franklin D. Roosevelt and other men of exceptional attainment, the customary two dimensions—one basic life drive and one modifying trend—did not measure and express all there was to Frank Lloyd Wright.

He also revealed an extraordinary Type Six trend, which made him a truly three-dimensional individual. As the reader will recall, Type Six is characterized by the designation "devotee", the single-pointed enthusiast, whose "cause", if carried by him to extremes, finds him labeled a *fanatic*. On the subject of his own innovations in architecture, Wright closely approached the mood of the fanatic. His thinking was ahead of his time; he smashed with unconcern, almost with glee, the cherished idols of architectural precedent. He was as opinionated as Whistler, and as much of a poseur and showman as Salvador Dali.

Yet, all this amazing and variegated life activity revolved around architecture; that was his real love. In a letter to his son he wrote: "I am afraid I never looked the part (of a father), nor ever acted it. And yet a building was a child. I have had the father-feeling, I am sure, when coming back, after a long time, to one of my buildings."

From the evidence, it seems that we must conclude that his architecture was not only his first, but also his only true attachment! And so, Frank Lloyd Wright was a basic Type Seven architect, backed up by a terrific and unusual Type One dynamic drive, with a devotion to his art that fringed almost upon the fanatical.

Such intense focusing upon a single art burns away the common dross and leaves a genius—innovator and dogmatist of the new (a strange combination!), egotist, intolerant toward the arts and opinions of others, respected and passionately disliked, revered and hooted at in the self-same hour! When the Divine Alchemist compounds in one human crucible the power of Type Seven, with the drive of Type One and the fire of Type Six—He expects nothing short of the artistic conflagration which was the lifelong spectacle that was Frank Lloyd Wright.

The Exceptional Man of Many Types—Franklin D. Roosevelt

We have seen in our analyses of Rockefeller and Rhodes, for example, that these great lives tended to push out beyond our simple two-dimensional framework which consists of one basic and one modifying trend. Each of these men combined a basic Type One with a modifying Type Three, out of which union his life experience generated an intermediate Type Two trend which eventually became so intense that, in the latter part of his life, it assumed the power of a true basic drive.

Andrew Carnegie, on the other hand, began with a basic Type Three trend, coupled with a modifying Type One drive; and again, this pairing eventually gave birth to a Type Two humanitarian trend that dominated his later life.

In this group, we find that each is an example of a man in whom a strange metamorphosis occurred, a sort of mystic birth of whole new congeries of qualities—those of the Type Two, the human server.

Among our examples, there is another group, consisting of Wesley, Wright, Wilson, and Schweitzer, in which the departure from the two-dimensional concept takes a different form. These men, it will be recalled, exhibited not one, but *two modifying* trends.

We have one more example—a human figure of such extraordinary attainments that we find within this one inclusive personality not one, but *three basic life trends*—plus one modifying trend!

Such was former President Franklin D. Roosevelt. It will be recalled that, in his time, few people thought about him calmly; to his partisans, he was a god; to his detractors, Satan incarnate. In the process of typing this unusual man, we shall begin to see why this was true.

First, let us examine his qualities to determine whether our seven types analysis can encompass and accurately classify all of his attributes. To arrive at an estimate of those qualities, "let's look at the record", as Roosevelt's one-time champion, Al Smith, would have said; that record as set down by Rexford G. Tugwell, in his penetrating biography, *The Democratic Roosevelt.*

Tugwell is a shrewd and perceptive observer and a clear and forceful word artist. He is biased by his experiences with F.D.R., to be sure, but that need not hamper us in using his evidence, because the very process of classing an individual into one or more of our seven types is, in itself, an act either of favoritism or of prejudice. And is it not true that the better we know the person we are classing, the more subjective are our decisions likely to be? But this is no fault of the "system", but the fault of almost all raters who, as human beings, are seldom able to be completely objective in their judgments.

Tugwell wisely interprets Roosevelt chiefly in terms of his *behavior,* his acts rather than his thoughts. When he probes into the ex-President's thinking, it is with commendable reserve, and with a signal clearly given in advance which warns the reader that the author knows he treads upon speculative ground.

Let us begin our typing process then, based upon the facts as evidenced by Mr. Tugwell.

An Irresistible Force, Basic Type One

". . . (Roosevelt) was certain of a commanding destiny . . . He considered himself appointed to be a leader . . ."

But F.D.R. not only entertained these concepts *mentally,* he moved powerfully to implement them.

Tugwell writes:

> The *ferocious drive* behind this progression toward destiny . . . consists in an *impulsive urge* so deeply seated and so *primitively energized* that it *activates and controls every other impulse* . . . The most persistent as well as the most astounding feature (of Roosevelt's career) is this *fierce flame burning at its core.*

Reading that paragraph, we might almost be convinced that Tugwell had been a lifelong student of our seven-basic-types philosophy, for where will we find a more accurate delineation of the Type One individual?

Observe the italicized phrases: *"ferocious drive, impulsive urge, primitively energized, activates and controls every other impulse, this fierce flame burning . . ."* We might almost say that the former Columbia Professor gives us a better listing of Type One characteristics than we have in our own Key Chart!

And, Tugwell gives us more evidence:

> The head of steam it (that is, the "drive") generated allowed its containing vessel no rest even in invalidism, much less in seeming defeat; it drove his

turbines with a merciless impatience. *Its source was certainly an original force which is shared very unequally among men.*

With this evidence before us, we have little difficulty in deciding that Mr. Roosevelt's basic life trend falls within the outlines of Type One. Then, as if to clinch our decision, Tugwell adds:

> . . . Hitler, Mussolini, and Stalin, as well as Churchill, had the same kind of fire in their vitals. All these were Franklin's rivals for world leadership; he knew them as such, and they knew him for what he was. Churchill accepted subordination; the others were crushed.

It is true that Hitler, Mussolini, and Stalin were Type One individuals; it is true that they had something of the "same kind of fire in their vitals." But this fire of the dictators was an evil fire, originating in the lower cesspools of the Type One trend, not in those higher levels from which Roosevelt derived his drive. As for Churchill, he was more dominantly Type Three than Type One, and Tugwell's narrative unwittingly proves it—*"Churchill accepted subordination . . ."*

In other words, as our Type Three study has shown us, *Churchill was adaptable;* he would not play the part either of the irresistible force or the immovable body. But the others—Hitler, Mussolini, Stalin—the granitic Type One antagonists of F.D.R.—they could not change; adaption was not in their characters; and when the *force*, which was Roosevelt, met these bodies, they were "crushed!" Such ends almost always the battle of Type One Titans!

Does it not seem almost inevitable, therefore, that we must class the life trend of Franklin D. Roosevelt as that of a basic Type One?

But wait! Not all of the evidence is in. Let's record our Type One decision only *tentatively!*

High Champion of the Underprivileged, Basic Type Two

Tugwell continues; and we begin to ask: "Can this be a basic Type Two individual who emerges from the present evidence?"

> (Roosevelt) had a weakness (does he not mean an "empathy"?) for struggling humanity *which rose to a feeling of responsibility.* Those who were oppressed and suffering touched a spring of indignation in him which welled up persistently. It is one clue to his whole life's orientation. It explains what he always did with power after he achieved it. He was forever turning to the righting of wrongs, the correcting of injustices, the recovering of the disadvantaged, the placing of the poor in a better position.

Again we stand amazed at the accuracy, the goal-fitness of Tugwell's words as an almost perfect listing of the attributes of the Type Two human being whom we call an humanitarian. In our description, we say he is sensitive to the suffering of others. Tugwell says Roosevelt "had a weakness for struggling humanity!"

We say that the Type Two man is strongly emphathetic with the poor, the ill, the underprivileged. Tugwell says of F.D.R.—"Those who were oppressed and suffering touched a spring of indignation in him which welled up persistently."

We describe the Type Two human being as one who is driven by his basic inborn life trend to lighten the burdens of the less fortunate. Tugwell says of the ex-President: "He was forever turning to the righting of wrongs, the correcting of injustices, the recovering of the disadvantaged, the placing of the poor in a better position."

As described by Tugwell, Franklin Roosevelt fits so well into the pattern of Type Two characteristics that we are moved to reverse our previous decision to class him as a clear-cut Type One, and to move him into basic Type Two.

However, before doing so, we must not overlook the highly interesting *interweaving of types* as revealed, perhaps unwittingly, in these lines.

Tugwell says the underprivileged groups "touched a spring of indignation" in F.D.R. Observe here how his Type One driving power, that often ferocious, relentless characteristic which is frequently found in Type One individuals, helped to convert the almost equally controlling Type Two humanitarianism into prompt remedial action. Tugwell's action-implying verbs tell how what might have been no more than the armchair sympathy of a wealthy man for his less fortunate fellows was turned into specific actions for their immediate benefit— *righting* (of wrongs), *correcting* (of injustices), *recovering* (of the disadvantaged).

It is interesting to observe that without this linking of his Type One drive with his Type Two idealism, the empathetic and indignant dreams of the President *might still be dreams*. So important to the progress of the race is this combination in our leaders of empathetic vision and driving action!

But, hold that impulse to class his basic life trend as Type Two; there is still more evidence—yes, and we may almost say *contradictory* evidence—to be considered.

Flexible Strategist About Means, Basic Type Three

> There never was a prominent leader who . . . was more *flexible about his means* . . . That elaborate adjustment to public tolerance, that delicate, almost mincing approach to departure from the accustomed, that devious hinting at and suggesting of something new and needed . . . that was politics—its very essence.

... His strategy was based on the manipulation ... of the vast imponderables of democratic life. It was calculated in the end to bring about the conditions he judged worth working for and sacrificing to establish.

In the above quotation from *The Democratic Roosevelt*, the author describes F.D.R. as being *flexible about means* and having that *delicate approach to departure from the accustomed*.

Read the description of the Type Three man on our Key Chart:

Adapts himself to conditions and pressures. Seizes, capitalizes opportunities. Adjusts to others' ideas. *Action*, not ideals alone, his goal!

Here is our picture of the Type Three Active Adapter. He is the practitioner of adaptability. The practical man who ever keeps his eyes on his main objective, who will yield on a minor issue in order to insure action on the major end in view. (Something which Woodrow Wilson could not do!)

Tugwell insists that this picture, too, is that of Franklin D. Roosevelt, nestling comfortably, as we now are aware, not only in the matrix of the Type Three Active Adapter, but also in the mold of the Type One Dynamic Driver and in the chrysalis of the Type Two Human Server. Here we see before us one individual, extraordinary in his endowments, manifesting three clear-cut basic life trends. Among the notable men analyzed in this chapter, no other can lay claim to having driven a three-horse team down the broad roadway of his life.

Reconciler of Viewpoints, Modifying Type Four

But the end is not yet, for Author Tugwell leaves us to ponder over another significant characteristic—not a basic trend perhaps, yet certainly a tendency too pronounced, too much a part of his thinking and actions to be ignored.

He was a political man ... he believed in getting things done with full, if not always complete, consent. (So far, this is still a Type Three characteristic.) Getting this approval very often required *compromise. He took what he could get for what he had to give.* He thus subordinated the important to the necessary, trusting his judgment to yield a public profit.

In this quality, we find the characteristics of our Type Four—the Bridge-Builder and Harmonizer. The traits of the compromiser are clearly present here, the tactics of the man who willingly gives up a little to gain a lot.

Roosevelt's Type Four traits were probably not powerful enough to describe his basic life trend as were his Type One, Two, and Three characteristics; but certainly the ability to compromise colored his thinking and constituted no little part of the *means* by which he often was able to reach his objectives. Looking at our list of Type Four characteristics, we read phrases like moderate, middle-of-the-road, works toward making others moderate; and we find we must grant to the man from Hyde Park, at least a modicum of Type Four traits. We can hardly say he justifies a full-scale basic Type Four rating. Perhaps, we should say that his Type Three adaptability-action characteristics borrowed from time to time some Type Four qualities to further the ends he held so dear.

So, all in all, what have we in this man Roosevelt?

1. We have a world leader, a statesman, the top man of a great government . . .

   (In these occupations, throughout history, we find a predominance of Type One Dynamic Drivers.)

2. . . . who was, at the same time, a natural born humanitarian, a leader of great social vision, the head of a powerful government who was himself deeply *simpatico* with the underprivileged . . .

   (Certainly, a clear-cut Type Two Human Server.)

3. . . . living in an age characterized by widespread social and economic change, who shrewdly and opportunistically used the turmoil of his times and the prestige and power of his office to force the activation of his concepts and their inclusion into the fabric of Congressional action.

   (This is the Type Three Active Adapter.)

4. And who, in a much lesser way, flecked his Type Three action with golden touches of tact and compromise (even to the point of disingenuousness) in his reconciling points of view opposite to his own, always to the end, however, that his Type One drive could satisfy itself by getting Type Three activity in the direction of his predominant Type Two social and economic ideas.

   (This willingness-to-compromise is a Type Four characteristic, but we must observe and emphasize the peculiar direction of its use—chiefly as an instrument for getting action for his Types One, Two, and Three drives.)

It is interesting that Tugwell found Franklin D. Roosevelt's behavior patterns to be *simple*, while Frances Perkins called him *complex*. Perhaps it is because Tugwell has been able to search out the causes, the roots of his acts; while Mrs. Perkins saw only the effects. From their respective standpoints, both are right; for certainly the endless interweaving of these three dominant threads, glinted here and there by the gossamer strand of compromise, would bring from the loom of life a fabric that, in its finished form, would seem to the ordinary observer to be complex.

Perhaps, then, we can best sum up this remarkable man by repeating what Antony said of Brutus:

> . . . . the elements
> So mix'd in him that Nature might
>   stand up
> And say to all the world, "This was a
>   man!

PRACTICAL APPLICATIONS OF THE TYPING PROCESS

How can we practically apply what we learned from the foregoing study and resultant typing of Franklin D. Roosevelt?

From that analysis, we get a rare glimpse into the pattern of qualities that make up great genius in political leadership. However, more important to our daily practice of management, we discover that these are the same qualities that trend the lives of lesser men, except that the intensity of the drive is slowed down; for certainly, the average person cannot marshal within himself and successfully harness and control such a multiplicity of life urges.

And while it is true that each of Roosevelt's many drives were, to a degree, conditioned by all the rest, when we observe how each type was manifested in him, we gain a picture of how it operates in most men. Learning how to recognize the characteristics of each type of life trend teaches us how better to understand those with whom we must deal.

The Roosevelt analysis brings home, in an emphatic way, the truth that no man is a pure, unmixed type; and by inference, it indicates that a single-type individual would be unbalanced and therefore, ineffective in the world.

That the average man is easily typed and described and his actions found predictable on the basis of only two dimensions in no way negates what is to be learned from the multi-dimensional individual. Each of the four types (three basic and one modifying) of the four-pointed Roosevelt are as true to pattern as the two types (one basic and one modifying) of the two-pointed person.

Thus, this seven types classification is not limited, but capable of accurately typing the most outstanding and many-sided figure among our examples. It is obvious that if Tugwell's descriptions of F.D.R. fit snugly into our types—and we have observed that they do—it is initially because the type delineations are accurate and inclusive, and secondly, because Mr. Roosevelt exhibited such typical characteristics for us to discover and classify.

In choosing individuals whose life trends exemplify the various types of men, we have cited, in addition to Franklin Roosevelt, others whose names and lives are well-known. This means that the press has told us much of the lives and accomplishments of these people. To the extent that the reader is familiar with them, we were able to omit much detailed description of incidents in their lives, happenings that revealed those characteristic and intrinsic traits which we wished to demonstrate. We chose men the reader knows in order to make clear a process of evaluation which the reader did not know.

But there is one drawback—the examples are not the everyday run-of-the-mill individuals, and there may be a tendency for the reader to say that the ordinary men and women whom the sales manager deals with do not fall so distinctly into type patterns. As we have previously mentioned, that is not necessarily true. The accuracy of the typing procedure is in no sense dependent upon the fame of the person typed nor upon the lack of it; rather it grows out of *adequate information* about the individual's traits, whether he be famous, infamous, or unknown to anyone other than the person who does the classifying. If the rater has a good cross-section "picture" of the individual's traits and characteristics as exhibited in his thinking and his actions, it is quite probable that the hiring executive can do a more accurate typing job than we have done here on public figures where the information is of a more general and less intimate nature.

In order to apply the typing process successfully, it is necessary to study the trends and directions as revealed by the types. Wherever the evaluator finds the type, he will find the trend; contrariwise, wherever he finds the trend, he will find the type. That is the clue to the usefulness of this appraisal method. Its stability and usability is predicated on this permanence of action and reaction, of cause and effect.

Indicator of Future Direction

This method of evaluation is a valuable tool for indicating the *future direction* in which a man is most likely to go. The exact scope of its usefulness is indicated by the two words *future* and *direction*. In other words, this scheme will not necessarily tell a sales manager unequivocally whether an applicant will or will not make a success of his sales job within six months; but it *will show*, often with astonishing accuracy, the *direction* in which the man will go. Believe it or not, over the long pull, he will tend to move in the direction indicated by his type despite all temporary, external evidences to the contrary. This method adheres blindly and unimaginatively to that view—that a man's type will inevitably manifest itself in his life trend. It ignores what a fellow *says* he is going to do or, what his momentary acts *seem* to foretell. These acts are judged as transitory manifestations and are but epicycles, those little wheels of small events which are merely turning within the larger wheel of the individual's basic trend, and inexorably geared to it.

Even if man possessed some magic Archimedean lever by means of which he might change his life trend from one type to another, he would still find himself in the ancient dilemma—that of having no place to stand. In other words, his life drives have no foundations, no standpoints from which to operate other than those of the types to which he belongs.

It will be seen, therefore, that this typing scheme is not a means of foretelling what a man will do *tomorrow*, for example, but a procedure, let us say, for pre-plotting the points on the chart of his *future* life, those points which, when a sufficient number have been located and linked together, will turn into his life trend line.

For example, let us take an applicant for a sales job with a drug specialty house, selling to retail druggists. This chap is a registered pharmacist; he has had a stint in business for himself as a retail druggist. The record shows that as his own boss, he did not succeed too well, with the result that he now seeks a job where the salary and expense checks will come in regularly.

During the interview, the hiring executive decides that he types as a Number One Dynamic Driver, physically energetic, ambitious, motivated at this time by a need for income. His modifying trend is Type Five, the abstract thinker, or scientist.

The continued use of the seven types method of classification has made the appraiser instinctively cautious about hiring as a salesman, a Type One with a modifying Type Five trend. Why? Because in the job now open, there is no outlet for his Type Five drive. The available position is a merchandising job, selling to retail druggists, and helping them with ideas to move the merchandise off the shelves into the hands of the consumer. In this job, the need for abstract or scientific thinking is practically *nil*.

But, as is so often true at the time of interviewing, the company needs a man. This applicant is thirty-six years old, commanding in appearance, exhibits a good measure of dominance, is well educated; and especially in his favor, he is a registered pharmacist and can talk the language of the druggist-customer. His obvious and visible plus values override the instinctive doubts and fears of the interviewer, who *hires him*.

The former druggist takes hold quickly; his volume is satisfactory; the customers like him. In the immediate, near-term view, it looks as if the hiring decision rang the bell! Of course, our sales manager had a couple of irritating brushes with him, in the first three months; he wanted the company to change certain policies and to modify an important merchandising plan, but these were trivial matters, quickly disposed of.

Then—bang! !

Eleven months and one week after he was hired, he walked into the president's office (Observe, *not the sales manager's office!*) and resigned. He had bought a half-interest in one of the drug stores on which he had been calling as salesman!

The combination of Type One and Type Five drives, which he had largely held in check during the eleven months he was getting his back bills paid, suddenly burst forth. We use the word "burst" advisedly—emotionally, he had literally "busted his britches!" His compulsive drives were so powerful that they had to break loose like a spring freshet after a snowy winter in the hills. These drives inevitably must expend and exhaust themselves; they can neither be transmuted nor absorbed. (Just to complete the account, the ex-salesman is making good as a partner where he failed as the sole proprietor!)

That is not only a true story, it is the *type* of story that is repeated time after time in the drug business. The lure of the prescription counter is almost irresistible to the Type Five individual with both a degree in pharmacy and a powerful interest in that profession.

This applicant's Type "Five-ness" revealed itself in his analytical approach to the change in company policies and in the suggested modification of the merchandising plan. For the "One-Five" man is not likely to be happy carrying out the plans of others, particularly where his Type Five drive toward pharmacy, as in the foregoing example, had no substitute outlet. His Type "One-ness" was exhibited in his going to the president, not the sales manager, to resign.

The French have a seemingly contradictory proverb—*Plus ça change, plus c'est la même chose*. When translated, it reads: The more it changes, *the more it is the same thing.*

The experienced sales manager, proficient in the use of this typing procedure, will eventually evolve for himself a similar proverb to help him avoid being misled by the transient and superficial symptoms of human behavior which seem, at the moment, to manifest contrary to basic type: The more a man seems to change, the more you may be sure that, in the long run, the sum-total of his thoughts and actions will be consistent with his type.

The manager will recall what the little girl replied, when asked the difference between *weather* and *climate*: "Weather lasts only a little while, but climate lasts all the time!" Weather is equivalent to an individual's day-to-day acts; climate is the long-pull response to the pressures of his basic type. Weather gets a lot of attention in the headlines; but all the vagaries of weather take place within the larger framework of the basic climate of the area.

An Indicator of Trend, Not a Caliper of Virtue

History records endless instances of small groups forcibly separating themselves from their fellows and ascribing to themselves virtues and superiorities which the "others" are not permitted to possess. The racial supremacy theory of the so-called Aryan Nazis and the Elite Corps of Adolph Hitler is one of the more despicable examples.

Similarly, those using this "typing" scheme may fall prey to the temptation to create around one or more of the seven types an aura of special superiority. This is an error, and a symptom of over-subjectivity. The seven types are not in any way the levels of some kind of caste system; they are the designations of seven different basic life trends.

It is somewhat as if the Creator had said: "No one individual in my Creation can be all things in the world, for no one individual can contain the whole. Therefore, I must specialize somewhat." And so, men came into life on one or another of seven paths, each trended to do one of the seven great Labors of the World better than the man of another type. The sharp edges of this theoretical specialization are vignetted into many shadings by the second dimension, the modifying trend; and the variegations are further multiplied by the differing "amounts" of each "quality" contained in one individual.

It is easy to see that to ascribe some degree of general superiority to any one of the seven types is not only incorrect, but unjust. There are great men in all types; but their greatness, their genius is allied to, and in fact, grows out of the mixture of intrinsic qualities which are common to their trends. And just as it is true that certain outstanding individualities do manifest superiority within their respective types, so also, as Elbert Hubbard often repeated, "do they manifest the defects of their qualities!" The most nearly-balanced man is the most nearly-perfect man; but no such proximity to perfection is found in human form.

Think of the seven types not as ascending or descending rungs upon a ladder, but as equally-spaced aggregations of attributes and qualities resting upon the outer rim of the great circle of life, none elevated, none dipped, but all level and equal upon the horizon of heavenly esteem. As the great circle spins upon its vertical axis like a top, travelling its never-ending journey, one type merges into another until the separation into types disappears. To the average non-analytical man who views this spinning wheel of life, only the blended composite result is seen; and not once does he suspect that it requires him, and his neighbors, and countless others of varying "mixtures" to make that resultant human civilization what it appears to him to be.

Use of Simple Scoring Sheet

To start the appraisal experiment with a small group is an easy and entertaining way to get acquainted with the process, particularly if the members of the group are well-known to each other.

Why is this last point important? Because this seven-types exploration seeks to identify *life trends,* not the ephemeral mood of the moment. Any economist will tell you that a trend is not discernible until the data is plotted over a sufficient number of time periods to reveal a general direction of movement when the points are connected. This trend line may be thought of as the footprints of an individual as he travels through life.

Consequently, it would appear that the longer the appraiser has observed a person, the more accurately should he be able to type him. In actual practice, of course, this is not strictly true. For one thing, there is a wide difference in the powers of observation of the observers; for another thing, in typing a friend there is bound to be bias, either favorable or prejudiced. Finally, there is what psychologists call the halo effect—the tendency, in making an estimate or rating of one characteristic of a person, to be influenced by another characteristic or by one's general impression of that person.

But these difficulties are intrinsic in all situations where one human being evaluates, appraises, or passes judgment upon another. They are not peculiar to our present seven-types procedure and affect its results no more than they affect any other evaluation method.

On the opposite page is a sample of a simple scoring sheet for use in doing the typing. You will observe that down the center are listed the seven basic types from one to seven. On the left is a column in which the rater indicates, with a check mark, his decision as to the basic type of the person whom he is appraising. On the right-hand side of the sheet is a column in which the rater indicates the modifying trend.

To use this Scoring Sheet for a group, copies will need to be made, several for each individual who is to participate in the rating process.

In launching the group experiment, the first step is to explain the idea, using the large Key Chart for this purpose. Read the descriptions of the qualities which characterize each of the seven types; indicate the major occupations normally

SCORING SHEET

Life-Trend Analysis

For Recording the Basic Type and Modifying Trend of an Individual

BASIC TYPE (Check One)	NAME:	MODIFYING TREND (Check One)
	1. THE DYNAMIC DRIVER	
	2. THE HUMAN SERVER	
	3. THE ACTIVE ADAPTER	
	4. THE "BRIDGE-BUILDER" — HARMONIZER	
	5. THE ABSTRACT THINKER — PURE SCIENTIST	
	6. THE ENTHUSIAST — THE DEVOTEE	
	7. THE MAN OF "LAW AND ORDER" — THE RITUALIST	

In the column to the left headed "Basic Type" place a check mark in the box opposite that one of the seven types which most nearly describes the person's MAJOR life-trend. In the column to the right headed "Modifying Trend" place a check mark in the box opposite the type that includes those characteristics which, in your opinion, are SECOND in importance when describing that person's life-trend.

NAME OR INITIALS OF ANALYST

If this is a SELF-ANALYSIS, put a check mark in the square at the left.

Burton Bigelow Organization
MANAGEMENT CONSULTANTS

associated with each life trend; and then mention the typical individuals whose names will be found in the last column.

Let the members of the group hold the small Scoring Sheet before them, so that they may associate the brief names of the seven types with the more detailed descriptions which are read from the Key Chart.

Before proceeding, ask for questions; answer them; clear up any confusion. Then the leader asks: "Whom shall we type first?"

Usually the group will suggest that the leader be typed first. Defer this step until later, however, and suggest one of the group who is "different enough" to be interesting. Get the group to agree on this individual; then let each one take a copy of the Scoring Sheet and with check marks record the basic type, in the left-hand column and the modifying trend, in the column to the right.

Let each member write his own name at the bottom of the small Scoring Sheet before he hands it in. If the member being rated, wishes to type himself—and he should be encouraged to do so—let him check the square at the left of the bottom line, for self-analysis. The Scoring Sheets may now be collected and the results totaled.

Unexpectedly enough, even the first results will be amazing in their relative unanimity. If there is not considerable agreement and the scoring is evenly divided, the leader must decide the cause. Perhaps the individual is difficult to type; it may be that the group is not sufficiently well acquainted with him to possess the necessary facts; or, it is always possible that the whole typing scheme and method of procedure is not understood.

No matter what the results, the tally should be announced and visibly posted, if possible. If there are murmurs of surprise or disagreement, these differences of opinion should be discussed, and several members of the group called upon to give their respective viewpoints. Friendly argument and discussion at this stage is a healthy activity and contributes much to the better understanding of the whole idea.

As the score is announced on each individual, interview the person who has just been rated. Does he agree with the result? If not, how did he rate himself? Ask him to explain his reasons for his own rating, and also, the basis of his disagreement with the majority group result.

Courteously terminate the discussion before it begins to lag, taking up the second individual, and so on throughout the entire group, if there is time available for all.

By the time three or four members of the group have been rated, this "game" should begin to progress more rapidly. Less preliminary explanation is needed; the actual rating and scoring is completed more quickly; and finally, there is a larger area of agreement and consequently, less discussion and argument. If the game does not accelerate its pace as it proceeds, the leader should look for the reason and take steps to correct it.

Should one of our sales manager-readers experiment with several groups, he may discover a marked difference in their capacity to understand and successfully operate this procedure of analysis. One group will take to it like a duck takes to water; the next group may seem slow and stolid by comparison. Such a discrepant situation provides an excellent opportunity for the sales manager to test his powers of observation and analysis in determining the cause of the difficulty, and later, his skill as a teacher and leader in correcting it.

Accurate Appraisal Based Upon Facts

The accuracy of the "predictions" which this method makes feasible is obviously dependent upon the correct "typing" of the individual by the appraiser. And this typing, in turn, must be based upon facts. That is equally obvious.

What facts? What *kind* of facts? Facts which aid the sales manager in identifying the basic and modifying trends of the individual; facts which help answer questions that can be asked through the usual hiring aids, such as the personal history record or application blank, interviews, independent outside history and character reports, and contact with previous employers. For example:

Do his activities at college and in previous jobs suggest that the applicant is a self-centered, single-pointed Type One, aware chiefly of himself and his own aims? Or do they suggest that he is a born human server, who thinks of others first and himself last, as is true of the Type Two humanitarian.

While the executive is interviewing the applicant, he responds by talking about himself. Is there evidence of Type Three adaptability and action? Or, does the applicant exhibit a tendency to see both sides of the question, manifesting a judicial mood, typical of Type Four? Is there any indication that his Type "Fourness" is so strong that it inhibits action, often leaving him immobilized in pure contemplative thought?

Do his education, experience, ambitions and future objectives, as he talks about them, seem to reflect a capacity for abstract thought and an interest in pure research, or the leanings of the scientist, the mathematician, or the physicist? If so, should he be labeled as a *basic* Type Five or, does this trend appear only as a modifying drive?

Should his personal history and his conversation record a sustained interest in "causes" (not necessarily the same one throughout his life experience), if he seems frequently to have become attached to "movements" which have engaged his attention and effort, not because of the possible financial reward which might come to him, but because of an inner personal *simpatico* with the aims of the movement—then the hiring executive may say: "Here is a distinct Type Six, the devotee, the enthusiast for causes. Perhaps I can make him an enthusiast for our job, our company, and our products."

Or, there may be an applicant who sends along an extraordinarily neat and well-organized personal resumé as part of his application for a position. Further, he sets out certain related facts in a clear, concise crossline chart, or table. His paragraphs are numbered; like subjects are discussed together; changes in subject matter are indicated by paragraphs, each beginning with an appropriate lead sentence. During the interviews, it is discovered that the applicant studied architecture; he speaks appreciatively of a recent exhibition of Italian mosaics in the local art museum. In short, everything about him—his manner of speaking, his choice of subjects, his education—suggests order, rhythm, precision, symmetry. Without difficulty, this applicant would be labeled Type Seven.

When the sales manager has experimented with the typing method until he not only *understands* it, but also has an easy familiarity with it, he will suddenly discover that subconsciously, if not consciously, he has made certain changes in his whole approach to hiring men. For example, he may find that:

1. He is studying each applicant's application blank and personal history record with a new focus and purpose, in order to squeeze out of these documents the facts needed for a more accurate typing of the man.

2. He changes the slant and content of his interviews, including the questions he asks, and the comments he makes—all with the purpose of evoking from the applicant the explicit information he needs to type the man more effectively.

3. He is asking for a different pattern of information from former employers, *symptomatic* information which formerly, perhaps, he would have considered trivial, even useless.

4. He is requiring of the outside rating service a new set of details about the applicant's past, areas heretofore little touched upon because their usefulness in evaluating the individual were not realized.

5. He changes even his manpower specifications, in an endeavor to secure applicants conforming more closely to the type of man who seems to prove most successful.

In other words, the sales manager doesn't read this chapter on Monday, and on Tuesday, start using this "typing" procedure like an expert. He grows into the method, pretty much in the same way and at the same rate with which it grows into him. And as the mutual process of getting acquainted proceeds and matures, the manager gradually equips himself to make better and better use of this seven-types classification.

But, unless he is a thorough-going Type Six devotee (!), he won't throw out his psychological tests, nor his established devices for evaluating men's work on the job. He will add this new typing procedure to those which he now uses. Each method has its proper place; each has its area of usefulness. None is a complete substitute for any other; and each reveals some facets of the man that the others do not expose.

If the sales executive has the patience fully to master this process, he discovers that he understands himself and his men (yes, even his own family) much better than before. Some of the formerly mysterious contradictions of human behavior now seem to be comprehensible; the habit of a man to return again and again to the same path of life begins to make sense; and he is able to trace the external actions of an individual to their inner and heretofore hidden sources.

RESULT: He selects better salesmen. And once he has secured them, he manages with greater understanding, greater effectiveness, greater success! In fact, he knows, almost always better than they know themselves, the direction in which life will take each member of his sales force.

CHAPTER IV

Eight Common Weaknesses
of Salesmen

When a sales manager takes over the leadership and direction of a group of salesmen, be that group large or small, he is taking over the virtues and faults, the strengths and weaknesses of a group of human beings who, like himself, are far from perfect.

Since much of his time must be devoted, willy-nilly, to the task of eliminating, modifying, counteracting, or living with, these weaknesses, it seems likely that it would prove helpful for us to discuss together the most-often recurring of these failings, and to examine how they have been and are being handled by sales managers.

1. Few Salesmen Are Self-Starters.

Older sales managers, able to compare the men comprising the smaller sales forces of earlier days with the larger groups of today, often complain: "There are very few self-starters left in today's groups. They just don't have the initiative they used to have!"

There is a deal of truth in that contention. For one thing, salesmen generally are not good planners; not having been born with a large helping of creative imagination, they do not easily visualize the future situations in which they are likely to find themselves, and plan accordingly. They are inclined to meet the problems as they arise, not to prepare for them in advance.

The social revolution of the 1930's erased the old feeling that the individual must be responsible for his own security and substituted a new and more easy-going concept—that it is the duty of "the state", or of "society", or more definitively, of "my employer", to look out for the individual. This shifting of the responsibility, from the individual to some amorphous "father" who will look after his own regardless of their efforts, has caused a decline in initiative and self-generated responsibility. Some men, of course, are self-starters from birth; they have the urge, the drive to get going and accomplish worthwhile things; but in others, what seems like initiative is the hidden drive of necessity, a sort of civilized "work-or-starve" concept which no longer has the same compulsive force.

Out of this evolution of thinking and attitude, management has found need to take two steps: *first,* to provide more security; and *second,* to apply greater skill to the motivation of the individual salesman; in other words, to supply from the outside the kind of motivation that used to be derived from within the man himself. Let's face it—this has greatly increased management's burden.

As sales managers, we are interested in these broad social changes, or changes in attitudes, only because we know that we cannot ignore them; we must adapt our managerial techniques to the widespread realities of life as it is.

In brief, managers must now supply the drive that, of necessity, used to be intrinsic in the men they hired. We must paint the "vision splendid", dangle a somewhat more enticing plum of success before them, plan for them, schedule their work, supervise more closely, train more thoroughly, correct more promptly, and thus try to instill in today's manpower the habit of initiative that once seemed to be a part of what the man brought to his job.

And in our thinking, we must not charge all of the change to the men themselves. Compare the freedom of action of the men on the old-day sales force of twenty men with the carefully-planned assignments of the present-day sales force of two or three hundred men!

Ask yourself: "Would the individualistic operator of twenty years ago be welcome in today's modern sales force? Would he not soon be frustrated by the confining fences of policy and find himself tied down by the chains of standard procedure?" Fixed territory boundaries; the need for standardization of methods; the physical, mental and emotional impossibility of having two hundred "prima donnas", each doing the sales job in his own way—these developments on the management side of the fence have contributed to making the individualistic salesmen—and the self-starters were almost always individualistic—no longer fitted to the sales force of today. In other words, the remedies we applied to ameliorate the effect of social change have made the old-type individual less fitted for our work and, in his place, has come the "teamwork" man. We are not sure that the change has made us poorer; it has only put a little more responsibility upon management's shoulders and taken a little off the shoulders of the field salesman.

2. Salesmen Are Seldom Abstract Thinkers.

It was stated long ago, that from the standpoint of their major interests, all human beings can be divided into three types:

1. Those who are interested in THINGS
2. Those who are interested in PEOPLE
3. Those who are interested in IDEAS

The two groups who are interested in things and people are likely to be predominantly *concrete* thinkers, those who reflect mostly upon what is comprehensible to the five physical senses. Those manifesting an interest in ideas, of necessity, must lean toward *abstract* thought.

Salesmen, as a class, are more frequently to be found among the CONCRETE thinkers, less often among the ABSTRACT thinkers. Broadly interpreted, this means that salesmen do not think in terms of laws, principles, or basic concepts. Only when abstract ideas have been concreted into form, do they interest the typical salesman who does not tend to be philosophical in his approach to life or work. Salesmen ordinarily do not search for the underlying pattern, that lowest common denominator which both the philosopher and the scientist are seeking constantly.

Further, we find that salesmen are not generally attracted to symbolic or poetic concepts. However, when these abstract approaches are turned into sculpture, or a beautiful painting, or transformed into the grandeur of a great building, or even a moving poem—such well-materialized, well-clothed ideas do appeal to them; but as observers, as "enjoyers", not as *creators*.

These thinkers seldom generalize; they rarely see the similarities in like things, except when found in highly concrete objects such as blue eyes or Roman noses in people, or the amazing uniformity of the new headlights on the season's automobiles.

What does this mean to the sales manager? How does this understanding of his sales group make him more competent to manage and deal with them?

For one thing, it gives the sales manager a clue as to why salesmen, generally, are better sellers of physical things—the see-able, touch-able, taste-able, or hearable items of merchandise—than they are of intangibles.

Also, it explains why the astute sales manager, who has intangible services to sell, insists upon visualizing, tangible-izing, physical-izing, and concrete-izing the results of the use of such intangible services, in order to make them saleable by the ordinary salesman (and incidentally, understandable to the average prospect who is also likely to be a "thing-thinker").

Knowing these truths about salesmen's interests also warns the sales manager to watch his own presentations to his sales force. It suggests the use of concrete words and phrases; it emphasizes the need for visual aids in presentation. It points up the necessity of "exterior-izing" all mental pictures which are to be conveyed to salesmen. It spotlights the superiority of an appeal to the physical senses as against an appeal to the intellect. In other words, if you fail to make your sales force SEE it, HEAR it, TASTE it, or FEEL it—you may lose their interest.

Should it be, of necessity, that the sales presentations of your products must be made partially in abstract terms, drill your salesmen repeatedly in that part of the presentations. Where their natural leanings might cause them to fail, let habit, derived from repetitious practice, take over.

Two final points: To be a concrete thinker does not imply ignorance, stupidity, or lack of education or intelligence. It relates only to the direction of the person's interests. If the reverse situation were true, and most of your representatives tended to think chiefly in the realms of the abstract, then you would face another problem, but a different one. It would be necessary for you to bring such men down from the higher clouds of logic and reason, perhaps even from the highest range which is intuition, onto the more comprehensible and more communicable levels of concrete thought. The latter task is more difficult than the one most sales managers now face.

These observations about the salesman's interest in the concrete levels cannot be universally applied to *all* salesmen; a few of them will be abstract thinkers, interested in ideas; others will be a fortunate combination of the three types and thus will be interested in people, things, and ideas, indicating that they have reached an unusual state of balanced interests which gives them a wide range of usefulness on both abstract and concrete levels. (Study such men for managerial leanings; they may prove to be excellent material for field and even home-office managers of salesmen.)

3. Salesmen Have Little Faith in Their Own Destiny.

A third widely-found weakness in the average man who makes up the typical sales force is this: *He has little faith in his own destiny!*

None of us know for a certainty where life will eventually lead us; nor do we have in hand a road map showing exactly how we are going to get there—wherever "there" is! But this lack does not entitle us to harbor a self-conscious fear that we are the victims of some unknown divine trickery; we can still have a deep and abiding faith in the rightness and the worthwhileness of our lives.

How does this weakness concern the sales manager?

It puts on his shoulders the necessity of constantly reselling his men on their own abilities; it requires him to emphasize the certainties of life; it offers him the opportunity to quench fears and quell doubts by calling a man's attention to each step of his progress, each gain in income, each improvement in his security, each advancement in the esteem of his fellows and his leader.

The old negro preacher was making his Sunday morning prayer; it was short, but it bodied forth a faith that knew no limit. He prayed: "Oh, Lord, I know that you ain't gonna send me no trouble that You and me together cain't handle!"

A manager must feel like that preacher, and he should be able to communicate to his men that same glow of joint confidence. He must literally inject into them, mentally and emotionally, the sovereign antidote for their own lack of faith, the "neutralizer-booster" for their endless series of fears. To make his men believe in themselves, to aid them to have faith in their individual destinies—this is a tremendous and often overlooked part of the manager's job.

4. Salesmen Don't Like to Make Decisions.

More often than not, the typical salesman is reluctant to make a decision; he may be able to add up the pro's on one side and the con's on the other, but at that point, a sort of kinetic paralysis sets in and he finds himself stymied on dead center, unable to take action.

To the average man, decisions are difficult. Victor Hugo recognized this when he wrote: "Destiny is made up of crossroads. An option of paths is dangerous."

Why is the average man afraid to make a decision? We believe it is partly because he is mistakenly impressed with the fatal irrevocability of decisions; partly because he hasn't the facts to act on and the experience to reassure him on the probable results of his decisions. To encourage workers to make more of their own lesser decisions, managers should give them small assignments which are bound to turn out well, so as to build a habit of self-confidence.

A great Oriental potentate once asked the wise men of his kingdom to bring him one axiom, one proverb, which would be true under all conditions and at all times. Hundreds of proverbs were submitted, but there was only one which filled the bill. What was that? One wise man of the East brought him this simple sentence: *"This, too, shall pass away."*

Not all the stories in the Arabian Nights, nor all the small undertakings you can beguile men to attempt, will completely cure the fear of making decisions. But, these steps help a bit.

5. *Most Salesmen Are Poor Planners.*

In the past twenty-five years, we do not believe our organization has prepared even one sales training course that did not devote a substantial amount of space and time to coaching the men in the need for, and the how-to-do-it of, the type of planning which individual salesmen should do for themselves. For, they are *notoriously poor planners!*

The salesman *dislikes* planning, and his perennial remark is: "If I were to invest in selling the same amount of time you wish me to devote to planning, I would make a lot more money!" You can rebut this argument, of course, by pointing out that he has been selling all his life and doing no planning; so with all that extra time to invest in field work, where is his big surplus?

The second universal brush-off when you start to sell a salesman on planning is this: "Oh, I have to change my plans so often, it doesn't do any good for me to plan." Of course, he hasn't learned the obvious truth—that because he is compelled to make the most detours, he is the fellow who most needs a road map!

Other than the chore of making out reports, there is no task in the salesman's whole duty-outline that he resists as much as the task of planning ahead.

Sometime ago, we attempted to define planning from the salesman's point of view:

> PLANNING is the process of projecting yourself into the future, visualizing the places you will be, the people you will contact, the circumstances in which you may reasonably expect to find yourself, the problems which are likely to present themselves, and the tools and course of action which you will probably use to mould the entire situation to your objectives. That sounds like a big undertaking! It *is!*

> Planning is not easy, because it demands so many contributions to make it effective. You must have experience on which to draw in order to foresee what circumstances and situations are likely to present themselves. You must have a good memory to recall all the details of significant and similar prior experiences. You must have imagination to translate

the experiences of the past into the pictured probabilities of the future.

Planning must correlate TIME, PLACE, PEOPLE, and PURPOSE. That is, you must be at a certain *place*, at a certain *time*, to see certain *people*, for a certain well-defined *purpose*.

Since planning involves *time* and *place*, it must inevitably involve SCHEDULING, which means deciding upon the date and time at which certain steps are to be taken, or certain purposes realized.

Observe the varied talents which the salesman must possess, if proper planning is to be done: creative imagination, the power to visualize, experience to draw upon, a good memory, the ability to correlate and coordinate, and a gift for scheduling. Perhaps that explains why salesmen don't plan well and why they dislike planning. Is it hard work? Yes, if you lack the faculty of projective imagination that enables you to look ahead and visualize the varied assortment of situations in which you are likely to find yourself; yes, again, if you can't translate your past experience into a yardstick that will equip you to plan for the future.

If a fellow is a member of that group of salesmen who sell by instinct and not by conscious technique, and that includes the largest percentage of salesmen, then the successively progressive steps by which he completes his sale are unknown to him. Further, since he probably lacks analytical ability, he is unlikely to reduce his own process of selling to a step-by-step method. That lack also handicaps him in his efforts to make an orderly plan for next week, or next month.

Yet, the sales manager must never give up his attempt to make planners out of his salesmen. The difficulties are many, but the accomplishment is so rewarding that it is worth the effort. In most lines, salesmen need a monthly plan, revised down to a weekly plan, as the month progresses. The weekly plan should later be converted into a daily plan, made the night before; and often, the daily plan needs to be translated into an individual call-plan for situations where the potential is large, or the prospect important. When we use the word "plan", we don't mean merely a route-list, a "where-to-send-my-mail-and-my-expense-check" sort of plan, but a schedule that decides what company to see, which men in that company, what to talk about, what "tools" (literature or samples) to have available, and what facts to get together before the salesman starts talking.

The men older in service can be sold on doing a better job of planning than they now do; although you may never be able to sell them on doing a full-fledged job of scheduling the way it should be done. But the new men, those who are not spoiled by NOT planning, can be trained to do planning just the way you want it done. In them, you have no habit-patterns to overcome. Start them right, fully equipped with the tools of planning, completely sold on its value and necessity; and you will see the difference between the salesman who really plans and the one who doesn't.

Victor Hugo has described this difference in clear and vigorous language. Let him speak:

> He who every morning plans the transactions of the day and follows out that plan, carries a thread that will guide him through the labyrinth of the most busy life. The orderly arrangement of his time is like a ray of light which darts itself through all his occupations. But where no plan is laid, where the disposal of time is surrendered merely to the chance of incidents, chaos will soon reign.

6. Salesmen Have a Tendency to "Take Things Easy."

Frederick Taylor, the father of scientific plant management in this country, voiced a basic axiom in his first book. He wrote:

> There is no question that the tendency of the average man in all walks of life is toward working at a slow, easy gait, and that it is only after a good deal of thought and observation on his part, or as a result of example, conscience, or external pressure, that he takes a more rapid pace.

This axiom applies to salesmen generally with the same force with which Taylor applied it to plant workers. This does not mean that salesmen are LAZY. We have little patience with the manager who uses laziness as an alibi for a salesman's failure. We have encountered but few lazy salesmen over a period of many years during which we have worked with them continuously. Even those who were called "lazy" really were not. To call a man "lazy" is to use a vague, foggy word which obscures the real trouble; and, with the wrong diagnosis, how can you expect to remedy the disturbance?

We have found that some men called "lazy" were ill in one way or another; some were low in energy. A few of them were afflicted with low blood pressure; others had stomach ulcers. One or two were gland cases whose endocrine glands, which seem to supply that super-drive possessed by the "go-getter" salesmen, were not functioning properly.

One overweight fellow who had bad feet couldnt take the continuous punishment of the pavement-pounding that had to be done if he was to succeed in his job. Another overweight salesman, for a further example, was physically unfit to climb up the narrow ladder, or stairway, leading to the head of a grain elevator. Yet, he had to go up there to make a brief survey before he could recommend the capacity of automatic grain-weigher which properly fitted the prospect's needs.

When saying that men tend to "take things easy," we do not refer to such cases as the foregoing where, in each situation, there were hidden physical weaknesses which explained the man's difficulty. We refer, for example, to the pharmaceutical detail man whose company has established a yardstick of eight physician calls per day; after he accomplishes that much, even though it be but 2 p.m., he goes home! Or, in the same class, we place the vitamin salesman for a drug house who leaves his display material with the druggist, expecting someone at the store to do the installing that is definitely his responsibility. Both of these men are "taking things easy."

Or again, there is the farm feed salesman, who passes within three miles of Aunt Jennie's house every time he makes his number two route. He stops by, chats a while with the dear old lady, consumes a couple of pieces of her unexcelled apple pie; and then, stomach overloaded and only half-awake, he tries to make the rest of his calls effectively. He is "taking things easy."

One of the great unsettled questions in almost any line of business is: "What is a full day's work?" When one brewery, in a metropolitan area, demands 40 stops per day and one of its competitors, calling on the same taverns and package stores, demands only 16 stops a day; one of them is wrong. Either one sales force is grossly overworked, or the other is greatly "underworked."

Work demands should be standardized at the level of the average man's capacity. If the standard is set at half of what a man can can do, then, the company is openly inviting its salesmen to "take things easy."

There are situations where many men *seem* to be "taking it easy" when, from their point of view, they are doing a normal day's work. If management can't agree upon a standard workload, why should we criticize a salesman who has honestly set up his own yardsticks? Such a fellow can become a triumph of managerial insight and skill if he is awakened from his mistaken concept of a full day's work. After he is trained and patiently drilled to work more efficiently, he will accomplish more each day. This kind of high-level human-salvage operation benefits both man and manager.

The wise sales manager, digging deeply, will find the source of seemingly lazy work habits. He needs to keep in mind that a salesman may "take things easy" because:

1. He is in bad health.
2. He is worried about money or home affairs.
3. He is afraid of his job; he doesn't know it well enough to have that sense of mastery which would lead to joy in his work and a driving desire to keep at it.
4. He is already convinced of his failure and is only waiting to be fired.
5. The whole sales staff is "soldiering on the job" and one fellow who would like to work, decides not to "stick his neck out."
6. His superior is "taking it easy," so the salesman imitates him, not wishing to "show him up."

May we, for once, be completely dogmatic and offer one bit of unqualified advice to the sales manager? It is this: When you are tempted to explain a salesman's failure by calling him "lazy", hold it, will you? Stop and realize that it may be YOUR failure to get out of him what you thought he had when you hired him! *Analyze* the *situation;* analyze the *man;* look beneath the surface. Dig deeply for the real reason; and don't be too lazy yourself to hunt for that important inner truth. Success in finding it may help you to save the next man who *looks* "lazy".

In most cases, that great body of salesmen who "take things easy" can be "saved", when management understands that they do not deserve the unhappy tag labeled "lazy". The process calls for good training, intensive and frequent supervision, careful inspection, and prompt correction of wrong habits and wrong thinking. It also calls for incentives, not only in the form of basic compensation, but also in praise, recognition, place. If the go-getter and he who "takes it easy" come out at the same place in respect to those rewards which men seek from their work, then management must remove the beam from its own eye, before it seeks to pluck the mote from out of the salesman's eye.

7. *Fiery Zeal and Confident Certainty Are Not Traits Common to Salesmen.*

Despite the widely-held stereotype of salesmen as merchants of pep and evangelists of business, the truth is, that among themselves and within the framework of their business life, they are not the bold, blustering, independent, irrepressible enthusiasts that they have been pictured by playwrights and novelists.

Generally, they are not quite certain as to which things they ought to be enthusiastic about. Some of them are mildly of the opinion that to exhibit enthusiasm about anything connected with their jobs is to tempt the boss to raise their quotas, or demand more from them than they may be ready to give. In other words, they fear that a show of enthusiasm may result in their being imposed upon. And, some believe that too much zeal is the earmark of the very young, or the wholly unsophisticated. Admittedly, these are the beliefs of the emotionally immature individual. But salesmen, like most other humans, are emotionally immature, and must be dealt with as they ARE, not as we would wish them to be.

To consider himself an expert judge of merchandise and markets, of selling policies and selling methods, is necessary to the satisfaction of the salesman's ego. It is a partial compensation for his feelings of unsureness in other directions.

His experience with professional buyers indicates that they avoid enthusing over any product which the salesman offers. If that's a good policy for the buyer, why isn't it a good policy for the salesman? In relationship to his employer, the *salesman* is a buyer, too; a buyer of a job, of better pay, of more liberal work arrangements, etc. Therefore, without exactly knowing why he does it, he restrains his enthusiasms. He assumes a stoic attitude, which he hopes will make him appear to be a cool, detached, and impartial judge of his firm, his manager, their products, terms, deals, selling techniques, and policies. If he carries his play-acting too far, he may rob himself of a priceless habit-of-enthusiasm which often sets the buyer on fire and gets bigger orders for a larger portion of the line.

Once again, as we have frequently pointed out, what appears on the surface— the mask, as it were, that the salesman wears—is not quite representative of what goes on inside, hidden from the eyes of other men. But much of his seeming lack of enthusiasm traces to this partly conscious, partly subconscious, bit of pretense. Once the sales manager gets behind the mask, as he must try to do, he will find not one type of salesman, but four. One type will enthuse himself; get up his own head of steam, and ready himself to transfer it to prospects and buyers. We call him the Self-Starter.

The second type will respond to the sales manager's efforts to instill enthusiasm, and without too much managerial pepping-up, he will grow enthusiastic. We call him the Easy Starter.

The third type is the Dead-Center boy, the salesman who is neither hot nor cold, but tepid, lukewarm, a half-way man who lives in a sort of indeterminate dead vacuum of his own creating.

And finally, the Reverse-Gear men, those who seem to be negative, who find fault with products, policies, terms, deals—everything. But, this is a pose, too, or they wouldn't be long on the payroll; in the end, these seemingly professional fault-finders are likely to be much more easily enthused than those perpetually undecided Dead-Center boys. (All of this is set out in much more detail in Chapter XI.)

The subject is introduced in this chapter for another reason: to show sales managers that enthusiasm is not a natural attribute of a man just because he is a salesman. In other words, to warn sales managers not to accept the popular conception of a salesman as a second John Wesley, or Billy Sunday, or Billy Graham, full of fervor for everything the manager and the firm may wish to do. Salesmen, like buyers, must be *sold*. Being professionals, they are harder to sell than the typical customer. And, posing as more judicial and objective than they really are, they often seem, from outward appearances to be very difficult to enthuse. But, this is not wholly so; after all, their bread and butter is on the same plate with that of the company. It also costs them money, if they carry their resistances to enthusiasm too far.

8. *Salesmen, Generally, Can't Find Their Own Problems.*

One of the least understood weaknesses of salesmen is their inability to find their own problems. As a class, salesmen are not analytical; nor are they adept in interpreting observed conditions in terms of the meaning behind them.

This lack in salesmen is of great significance to the sales manager; for as a rule, he thinks of himself as Mr. Problem Solver, in person. To his salesmen, he grandiosely announces: "Bring your problems to me, men! I'll help you solve them!" But the truth is, the salesmen do not want the sales manager to SOLVE their problems; they want him to FIND them.

Salesmen are in much the same situation as the citizens of the little country village whose selectmen had engaged a professional rat-killer to rid the town of its pesky rodents. His deal was so reasonable; he would kill all the rats in town for a penny each. So they signed his innocent-looking, printed contract and sighed with relief: "Now, we'll get rid of our rats."

The rat-killer got himself a new hatchet at the local hardware emporium; sharpened it to a lethal edge; and found in the village dump an ancient butcher's block, which he smoothed up and brought to the village square. Sitting on a stool in front of the chopping block, he admonished the villagers, with a great air of confidence: "Now, bring on your rats!"

Like the disappointed villagers, salesmen yearn for someone wiser than they to *find and catch* the rats; they themselves are quite expert in *killing* them. In other words, they seek a problem-*finder*, *not* a problem-*solver*. Try this experiment at a meeting some day. Present to your salesmen a clearly-defined problem; pretend to be stumped by it. Ask for suggestions—and observe how rapidly the solutions come tumbling over one another. Salesmen are fertile in solving problems, barren in finding them.

A sales manager, therefore, who sits on the throne of power in his regal robes and proclaims—"Now, boys, bring on your problems. Here, at the Fount of Wisdom, I will solve them all!"—is not helping his men. He is only duplicating talents they already possess.

Instead, let him undertake a more arduous task. Let him travel with his men, observe them in action; or, let him have a field survey made by an experienced group of problem-finders, and then, present their findings and interpretations to the men. Thus, he will aid them greatly. Once the salesmen get their teeth into a clearly-defined problem, they will propose numerous, valid courses of remedial action.

This unusual procedure admittedly will not give the sales manager the same degree of ego-satisfaction as playing the big shot; but it will get results. Not only will the salesmen solve their problems; but, because they participated in the process of arriving at the solutions, they are more likely to accept them and put them into effect with enthusiasm.

In conclusion, let it be said that no one man in a sales force is likely to reveal all of these weaknesses; but he may exhibit others which have not been listed here.

There will be a few men, in almost any sales group, who will successfully conceal their weaknesses. That type of salesman has learned to control himself, to master those negative leanings which might interfere with his work. To Him That Overcometh, the Good Book promises great rewards; and it should be equally true of that man in a selling job. He should be well-rewarded. By conquering his common failings, he has saved the sales manager a good deal of extra work and worry.

For, the eight common weaknesses discussed in this chapter, are not common to salesmen alone; they are the everyday failings of ordinary human beings. They have been isolated and emphasized here because they especially inhibit success in the man whose job is to sell. The sales manager who spots and properly diagnoses these weaknesses early in a salesman's experience can do much to eradicate the trouble and, thereby, help the man to a bigger and a quicker success. "A disease exposed is half cured"—so runs an old adage. The purpose of this discussion is to further the early "exposure" of these common weaknesses and their prompt amelioration, before such men drag themselves, and perhaps the whole sales staff, down to the "dead level of mediocrity"!

SALESMEN'S "PERSONAL ASSETS" INVENTORY

List Salesmen by name, indicate appraisal opinion by
check marks in proper columns, and enter total score in last column.

SALESMEN	SELF-STARTER	ABSTRACT THINKER	SELF-CONFIDENT	DECISIVE	GOOD PLANNER	MAXIMUM DRIVE	ENTHUSIASTIC	FINDS OWN PROBLEMS	TOTAL SCORE
POINTS→	15	5	5	10	15	20	10	20	100
1. Johnson		✓		✓	✓			✓	50
2. Brown	✓		✓	✓		✓	✓	✓	80
3. Elion	✓		✓	✓		✓	✓		60
4. Marks		✓		✓	✓			✓	50
5. Williams	✓		✓	✓		✓	✓		60
6. Haynes		✓		✓	✓		✓	✓	40
7. Smithson	✓	✓	✓	✓		✓	✓	✓	85
8. James	✓		✓	✓		✓	✓	✓	80
9.									
10.									
11.									
12.									

NOTE: If you wish to give different weights for the various "Personal Assets" you can change the point value
under each asset to suit your own situation and score each man accordingly.

CHAPTER V

The Salesman in Trouble:
Woman Problems

Salesmen are people; and they find themselves in the same familiar kinds of trouble which beset other human beings, plus a few special difficulties which arise from the occupational situations associated with a salesman's life. A salesman, usually, is far from home, away from the eyes of his family, and out from under the close observation of his supervisor. In brief, he is largely "on his own", both in a business way, and personally; in the nature of things, temptations—to waste time, to neglect his duties, and even to "have a little fun"—constantly assail him.

Let us consider first that group of problems which threatens to cause a great deal of trouble for the man "on the road". These are "woman problems", derived not only from the familiar "other woman" relationship, but originating from the continual influence of the salesman's mother, his wife, and her mother.

TIED TO "MOTHER'S APRON-STRINGS"

One of the most elusive and probably one of the most frequently encountered troubles of the sales manager in the management of a large sales force is what Philip Wylie calls *"momism"*.

What "Momism" Really Means

Momism is Wylie's name for the cause of that particular type of emotional immaturity which is fostered and developed by the over-solicitous mother. She hovers over her male child like a hen over a fresh-brooded flock of chicks, herding him constantly in the direction in which she thinks he should go, all the while *over*-protecting him, *over*-educating him, *over*-loving him, and *over*-directing him. Sometimes this is called being tied to "mother's apron-strings". It is a misdirected form of the protective maternal instinct which often ends up as a narrow, selfish, and limiting kind of protection. This mother would shield her offspring from life-experience; in fact, she often attempts to do his *thinking*, his *feeling*, even his *deciding* for him.

Like some sales managers, this mother wishes always to do *for* her son what a strong man insists upon doing for himself. She keeps him closely under her wing; she prevents him from gaining experience in the world of reality for fear he might be tainted, injured, or destroyed.

Weakening Influence of Not Being Reared as a Man

In a conversation we had with General S.L.A. Marshall, who was one of the chief researchers of World War II and of the Korean conflict, he expressed the opinion that, unless there is a new breed of mothers before the next world war, we might not have any foot soldiers fit to be put into the field.

In the concluding chapter of his book *Men Against Fire,* he says:

> . . . The final and greatest reality (is) that national strength lies only in the hearts and spirits of men. The Army, Navy and Air Force are not the guardians of the national security. The tremendous problem of the future is beyond their capacity to solve. The search begins at the cradle *where the mother makes the decision, either to tie her child to her apron-strings or to rear him as a man.* (Italics ours.)

Momism is not something which the salesman himself can be blamed for. It was imposed upon him during his formative years by an over-anxious and solicitous mother and is as much of a disaster for him as it is for the sales manager who hires him, and who thereafter must manage and deal with him. Broadly, momism results in the man not growing up emotionally. He grows up physically and intellectually; but emotionally, he remains a child.

Surprisingly enough, it is possible to witness the effects of momism even in the older executives of sizeable companies. You will find many men in executive posts who are intellectually very keen; but when it comes to judgments which are charged with a high emotional content, they are still children. Such men often indulge in temper tantrums, judge an individual by his personal response to their personalities, and are almost completely subjective in their decisions. They remember unintended personal slights for years; and every judgment they make of a man who once incurred their disfavor is tinctured and colored by that single incident which happened, perhaps, years ago.

Symptoms That Signal Trouble

The sales manager who is on the lookout for the influence of momism in his salesmen, will find several symptoms that show up very frequently. These will include:

1. The man blames others for his failures.
2. He runs away from his problems instead of facing them.
3. He avoids and evades responsibility.
4. He manifests a low level of initiative in unfamiliar matters.
5. He is generally an escapist—he endeavors to escape *work, thought, burdens,* and more particularly, *the results of his own mistakes!*

In fact, it can be said that the foremost symptom of this man's immaturity is the *tendency to blame others for his failures.*

Unadjusted to WIFE-Difficulties

The second most frequent woman problem which the sales manager will meet in handling the personal difficulties of his salesmen is likely to be "wife trouble". In our management training groups, where division and district managers of companies in many lines of business are trained better to perform their own jobs, the investigative surveys made prior to the training almost invariably show that "wife trouble" is one of the problems about which the managers are most disturbed. Yet, it is a problem about which they possess only a modicum of knowledge on the handling side.

The Overly-Dominant Personality

Let's look at some of the aspects of "wife trouble". The first exhibit is the *"bossy"* wife. This is a woman who insists upon wearing the pants in all departments of family life. She is that female who constantly reiterates the idea, whether in words or actions—"Mother knows best!" Sometimes, unfortunately for the man of the house, "mother" *does* know best. At times, the wife *is* the better *planner,* the more competent manager of the family finances, the more capable purchasing agent, the more knowledgeable psychologist; in short, a more well-rounded human being than her husband.

However, if she is superior in all these aspects of living, she should be wise enough to know that it is impossible for the woman of the household to dominate every phase of the family life without further complicating and multiplying the weaknesses and fears of the salesman-husband. It might be said that the overly-dominant wife, the "mother-knows-best" type, is but a wifely prototype of the overly-anxious mother. She perpetuates into her husband's adult life her own brand of momism, differing only a little from that inaugurated in childhood by his mother.

In fact, if a man has had a dominant mother, overly-solicitous, overly-protective, and overly-possessive; and if—to escape his mother—he marries early in life and has the misfortune to get one of these "mother-knows-best" women for a wife, his fate is sealed. He has small chance ever to escape the domination of the aggressive female. Yet, this escape is obviously one of his most crying needs if he is ever to grow up!

If his wife really *does* know best, she will recognize that she must suppress the exterior evidences and outward manifestations of her superiority and must play her part of the game softly. She must work out a division of responsibility which will save the face of the husband and which will assign to him those tasks in the family set-up which he is best qualified to do. Thus, she will strengthen the man who is weak; she will educate the man who is unknowing; she will train the emotions of the husband who tends to be subjective and unstable.

If she is unable to accomplish this, then you had better hire *her*—and let the husband do the dishes!

The Habitual "Nagger"

Another type of troublesome wife is the "nagger"—a term which is most frequently applied to wives and one which is much too freely tossed about and not always deserved. Sometimes, the "mother-knows-best" type of wife will express her vaunted superiority of judgment by nagging. Her persistent faultfinding is made more poisonous by the fact that it is usually done *after* the event it pertains to, when very little can be done to correct the situation. Why is it that the woman who has the instinct to nag will not talk to her husband *before* the incident, in other words, in the planning stages?

Nagging is often the result of an extreme nervous condition. It may be caused by an insecurity complex on the part of the wife, or by glandular changes, or other illnesses from which she is suffering and over which she has very little control. In other words, solving the nagging problem is seldom a matter of simply inducing the wife to take a compassionate attitude toward her husband, to treat him with respect and consideration. If her nagging has its roots in illness and disease, the woman is as little able to control it as the man is to contain, digest, and transmute it.

MALADJUSTMENTS IN SEX LIFE

There is another kind of husband-and-wife trouble which has to be talked about, although a few years back, it might not have been considered good taste to discuss this subject openly and frankly. We refer to the sex problems of the salesman and his wife. This type of difficulty has a concealed and insidious aspect, like halitosis, in that the two marriage-partners seldom recognize the source of their trouble. They aren't likely to talk it over, and the very nature of the problem inhibits discussion during family conferences.

Sex maladjustment most frequently springs from three sources—fear, physical and psychological incompatibility, and the changes of middle life.

1. Fear

One or the other of the partners may have an undue fear of sex. Along with this is often a feeling of shame, a sort of guilt complex, which has usually been rooted in the consciousness by the training of an overly-prudish mother or father, or by the religious climate in the home; in some cases, by the influence of a religious leader during the formative years of childhood and adolescence. An actual physical malformation would cause less difficulty.

In fact, most of the vague stories about frigid women (or reluctant men) stem from psychological and psychosomatic factors such as these, rather than from any organic situation.

2. Physical and Psychological Incompatibility

Closely allied to the guilty or fearful approach to sex, there is the problem of the man or woman whose sexual desires occur with a greater or lesser frequency, or with more or less intensity than those of their mate. The partner with the more frequent or more intense need must make some sacrifice in favor of the one with the less frequent or less intense drive; or the latter must be made medically or emotionally to reach a higher level of activity. Which method is most likely to succeed is a matter to be decided jointly by the physician and the two people involved. We wish only to call the sales manager's attention to the problem—not to usurp the physician's function in remedying it.

At this point, many sales managers will say: "I am neither a psychiatrist nor a marital counselor, and I do not intend to get into these intimate matters which are private to the inner lives of my salesmen!"

Such an attitude on the part of the sales manager is understandable. As long as his decision to act, or *not* to act, is based upon calm judgment, rather than upon the *fear* of intervening, his position is likely to be a wise one.

But, even a decision *not* to intervene does not excuse the sales manager from at least KNOWING what is at the bottom of these problems. These "undiscussable" matters constitute a very large portion of the troubles of salesmen who fail, even temporarily, to carry on their jobs properly.

3. *Changes of Middle Life*

Another woman problem associated with sex—one which upsets the older salesman both at home and on the road—is the problem of the wife's change of life, or the menopause as it is technically called.

Men, not having suffered in this inevitable Gethsemane, have little or no conception of the peculiar brand of emotional and psychological "hell" which a wife imposes upon her husband at such times. And the average man, never having really understood women anyway—and this is true of most men—is, at this time, confused and discouraged and in the deepest of personal fogs.

For example, his distraught wife will invariably accuse him of infidelity. One of her favorite phrases is sure to be: "You don't love me any more." Further, she will charge him with being inconsiderate, unaware of her physical illnesses, and indifferent to all her special problems.

In many cases, the wife will threaten to leave home and husband (which, of course, is actually the last thing she will do). So, Mr. Salesman goes privately out to the dog house where, in confused and undocumented puzzlement, he meditates upon his neglects, tries to recall his brutalities, his cruelties, and his indifferences. Out of such a self-searching session, every man can emerge with an inventory of small crimes. Therefore, not only for the benefit of his ailing wife, but also as a step toward the preservation of his own peace of mind, he pledges to himself—and perhaps even to his wife—that he will reform and do better.

He attempts to be gentle and solicitous; he makes his sexual advances more frequent and more endearing; he tries to reverse his whole pattern of behavior toward his wife and does the opposite to that which she complained of. Once he sets out upon this course, he enters a still deeper fog. For his attempted ministrations are again rebuffed; sometimes it seems with even greater fury than before.

At that point, masculine confusion and frustration have reached their limits; figuratively and perhaps, even literally, the man begins to wring his hands in desperation. He is mentally and emotionally without recourse. He is lucky if he has a friend to whom he can appeal, or a physician with whom he can talk things over. And he is especially lucky if he has a sales manager who understands this acute problem of middle life.

This stage of marriage, judging from our observations in the field, throws more older salesmen off the track, puts more men into a state of nervous and emotional shock, and interferes with their work to a greater extent than probably any other man-and-wife situation which transpires during the first twenty-five or thirty years of married life.

No one can criticize the sales manager who prefers to ignore these problems. They are inevitable; they are intimate and private; and it is indeed a courageous sales manager who steps in where even angels would properly fear to tread. Yet, the sales manager's interests and his own progress are inevitably tied up in these personal difficulties which may depress one of his salesmen to the point of failure in his selling job. Who, if not the sales manager, has a greater dollars-and-cents interest in organizing and carrying through a "rescue" operation? Usually, this will save a *man,* often it saves a *marriage,* and certainly there is a very good chance that it will save a *salesman*—the latter result, from the sales manager's point of view, being, of course, the *main* objective!

Two facts, not directly concerned with the sales manager's interest in this problem, should be set down here, in order to leave the reader with a fair and balanced view of the situation.

First, to be just, we must consider that the wife involved also goes through her own kind of "hell" at the time of menopause. Her glandular system is giving up, reluctantly and with difficulty, its reproductive function which it gained, also with some difficulty, at the time of puberty or adolescence. Those cruelties she inflicts upon her spouse are not craftily premeditated; they are products of her own suffering and imbalance. In short, she is as much in need of sympathy as is her husband; but she has the advantage of understanding her own dilemma better than he comprehends his bitter sharing of it.

Secondly, we must recognize the fact that a man has his "time of change", too —"climacteric" is the usual technical name for it. It is not much talked about, nor does it seem to affect a man so deeply. But when he feels his vital power declining, the unstable male often reacts more childishly than usual; he has his cranky spells too; and he is often difficult to live with during that period.

Facts That Help the Sales Manager to Manage Better

But there is a plus side to the woman problem, too. If the sales manager can convert the wife to his cause, he has an assistant in the home who occupies a position of even greater power and influence than his own, and who can accomplish more to direct the husband-salesman into the proper channels of activity. Therefore, the sales manager must try to make the best use of this situation, all the while understanding the peculiarities of the woman's behavior and the emotional motivations which guide her life. To paraphrase Byron: "Emotion is of man's life a thing apart; 'tis woman's whole existence."

Man does not necessarily encounter fewer emotional situations than the woman; and judging man's outward reactions, he might appear to be the *more* emotional of the two sexes. Unless he is a very unusual male, however, he outwardly disclaims any interest in emotional situations, or in problems arising from the emotions. Consequently, he has not developed a conscious technique for dealing with emotional problems, and when he meets one, he is likely to become a child under its impact.

The woman's attitude, on the other hand, is quite different. She has been prepared by her parents and by her experiences throughout her entire life, to recognize and accept her emotions. She has been trained, almost from birth, to deal with them effectively. In the long run, therefore, the man is likely to come out of the emotional crisis looking much less capable and suffering much greater damage to his inner nature than the woman, in an equivalent situation.

Here are some basic trends of the feminine personality which need to be well understood by the sales manager:

1. A woman will reveal a weakness—such as pain, fear, discomfort—much more readily to a man than to another woman; and, in equivalent circumstances, she will lean upon the man more heavily than she would upon another woman.

2. A woman has a tendency to experiment with a man—to determine "how far she can go" in influencing him through female enticements, criticism, threatened withdrawal of herself or her favors. She enjoys manipulating and maneuvering the male, almost as a sort of cat-and-mouse, "Bunty-pulls-the-strings", sort of *game*.

3. A woman is very sensitive to masculine strengths and weaknesses. She emphatically enjoys subjecting herself to the strong man who is, at the same time, wise enough to be gentle and tender in administering his power. As Cleopatra said: "O happy horse, to bear the weight of Caesar!" But, at times unpredictable, she will nevertheless exploit his *weaknesses,* sometimes openly, sometimes covertly; sometimes consciously, sometimes unconsciously.

4. A woman, generally, is possessive. What she touches, she would own completely. She will trade protection, intense loyalty, devoted service—

for that right solely to possess. She never ceases to reach for that document bestowing sole rights and exclusive ownership.

The sales manager who wishes to employ an assistant in the home, without pay, needs to know these things. He needs to know them too, in order to locate and explain hidden resistance to certain plans—resistance which seem illogical. He needs to understand these feminine traits in order to understand why a change in territory and a raise in pay is frequently refused; to sense why a good salesman, seemingly satisfied with his job, suddenly blossoms out with a stubborn demand for an unreasonable raise.

And finally, to complete the picture of this male x-raying of the mysterious female, let it be said: No wise salesman nor sales manager will negate the wife's abilities, nor will he exclude her from active participation in the partnership of life. He will joyously accept her help in those many ways where she can help better than any other person.

The salesman will divide the responsibility of the household, always having due regard for his wife's feelings and her capacity. He himself will avoid being a nagger; he will treat his wife like an adult, as a woman of mature judgment and intelligence. He will remember those important dates in their joint lives which are dear to a woman's heart; and he will not forget that the most delightful personal relationship of marriage is easily bedecked with garlands of thoughtfulness upon those days when anniversaries are to be observed—and once in a while when there is no specific reason whatsoever. These last occasions, the surprise remembrances, are very dear to the heart of a woman, and they compensate her in a great measure for her problems, difficulties, and disappointments.

The "Anonymous Letter" Bombshell

The married couple's book of troubles can never be said to be complete, until they have suffered through one or more experiences with that poison-pen artist, the writer of the anonymous letter.

Scarcely any family escapes this scourge. It may strike at the husband; it may strike at the wife. And it may strike more than once.

The unsigned letter, vicious in intent, and usually the product of a disordered mind, attempts to destroy character, and drives invisible barriers between husbands and wives. One letter may hint, infer, question; another may indict its victim openly and violently and supply the most lurid details of dates and places and persons—all false!

Many a home has been split by such a letter because, in preference to holding fast to confidence in his mate, the recipient believed a writer who was unwilling to sign his indictment or appear for cross-examination.

Neither husband nor wife would admit a known character-assassin into their home, but they accept his cowardly unsigned missive as proof that the one anonymously indicted is guilty! How silly! How unobjective! How unfair! Yet experience shows this frequently to be the result.

Let the sales manager whose salesman is confronted with this problem step into the situation boldly. Let him recommend that the anonymous letter be destroyed, if possible, without ever mentioning the matter to the indicted party. Never consent to the letter being kept—insist upon its being destroyed—as would be the dangerous egg of a poisonous snake! Such a letter, admittedly, is difficult to forget, for suspicion ever gnaws at the hearts of all except the staunchest souls. But if the document is preserved, every future hurt and suspicion will cause the box to be re-opened and the mind to ask: "Maybe it was true after all?" Insist that the paper be burned, if need be,—and FORGOTTEN!

Entangled With The "OTHER WOMAN"

There is another type of woman trouble which, oddly enough, does not often present as much of a problem to the sales manager as does wife trouble. This is the "other woman".

Some men (and a few women) are born philanderers. Such men lack a sense of responsibility to their families. Once they have left their own dooryards, family obligations fade from their minds.

There is not much a sales manager can do about these fellows—there is small chance that he can change their trend of character. He is not likely to transform the philanderer into a loyal father and husband, no matter what he says or does.

To complicate the sales manager's position, these typical philanderers are often excellent salesmen. The salesmanship they use in their personal affairs is not lost to them when they get into business-selling. The sales manager may be reluctant to part with one of his best salesmen solely because he does not stay "on the reservation".

Rules of the Ancient Guild of Don Juans

What can the sales manager do? He can at least point out to the errant salesman that the Ancient Guild of Don Juans has very strict rules governing the conduct of its members. Let these ancient regulations be made known to the philandering culprit, in the hope that he will observe the rules of the Order, as follows:

1. A loyal member of the A.G.D.J. keeps all aspects of philandering outside of business. No involvements are permitted with lady-prospects, or with the wives of gentleman-customers; and entanglements with their sisters, cousins, aunts, and female employees are also prohibited.

2. No member in good standing ever brings his pleasure-partners to the home office city and absolutely never to the office.

3. A member keeps all conquests confidential; he does not brag about them to others, especially not to his associates in the company sales force.

4. A member does not permit flattery, praise, "understanding", "sympathy", or the other party's "*need*" to result in building up permanent attachments.

5. Every member must conduct himself like a gentleman at all times.

6. A member who makes a "damn fool" of himself is promptly expelled.

The sales manager won't reform this chap—but he may be able to minimize the damage he does by inducing him to play the game according to the book.

Disturbed by the MOTHER-IN-LAW

The mother-in-law, whether she be the mother of the wife or of the husband, has long been the butt and target of endless jokes and slurs, many of them unfair and inconsiderate.

But no amount of glossing over can conceal the fact that in the typical household, the mother-in-law is likely to be a complicating factor in family life. A man and woman brought together by marriage find themselves in one of the most intimate relationships that can exist between two human beings. They may have to undergo a process of education which involves modifying and adjusting the physical, emotional, mental, and spiritual aspects of two separate individuals of different stock, background, and life experience. To accomplish a tenable adjustment between themselves is no small task; to have that job complicated— especially in the early days—with another personality, not only triples the number of relationships to be established, but actually cubes them, if the personnel statisticians are correct. In short, the ensuing difficulties are not to be charged to the shortcomings of any of the individuals involved, but rather to the complications implicit in the situation.

The problem takes a different shape depending upon whether the "extra" member of the family is the mother of the wife, or the mother of the husband.

The Wife's Mother

If she is the *wife's* mother, it is often the *daughter*, not the son-in-law, who is most deeply affected. Even though the daughter in her role of wife has proved to be decisive, independent, even dominant, it is nevertheless true that once she begins to live daily in the aura of her mother, the independence, the decisiveness, the dominance suddenly vanishes, and often most of the daughter's individuality disappears at the same time.

The wife's own plans, her ideas of *what* to cook and *how*, her methods of ordering the household—all of the familiar routines are suddenly modified under the influence of a mother who, either consciously or subconsciously, refuses to accept the daughter's adult, wifely status in the home.

As a result, the wife's attitude toward her husband is remoulded; she handles the children with a lack of confidence that she never exhibited when managing the household on her own. Life in the home takes a turn toward turmoil. This occurs even where the wife's mother is a superior cook, housekeeper, and manager. It happens partly because the woman of the house is unwilling to yield up her prerogatives to her mother, while the mother, on her part, takes over certain activities as her motherly privilege. Thus is the battle automatically set in motion—and it will not cease until one or the other of the women are eliminated. Meanwhile, some of the innocent by-standers are injured.

Not infrequently, the husband is very well looked after by his mother-in-law. She often makes a special point of gaining and holding the favor of the man-of-the-house: she cooks what he likes to eat, pets and pampers him, and takes special pains to avoid his disfavor. In thus taking over many of the duties and privileges of the wife, the mother-in-law only makes her daughter's life more difficult.

If the mother-in-law wishes to manipulate the husband to her own ends, she is usually shrewd enough to do it through her daughter. Mamma comes triumphantly out of it all as the sweet cookie, always with the icing side up. It often turns out that she is secretly in love with the personable and vital young man who is her son-in-law!

The man of the house must be mature and experienced, if he is not to fall into the habit of accepting the ministrations of two women instead of one. If he is short of compliments to go 'round, he is wise to save them for his wife. With her own mother in the house, the wife is likely to be in more difficulty than if it were her husband's mother whose presence created the intrinsically unhappy triangle. (Yes, this mother-in-law situation frequently forms as much of a "triangle" as does the wife-husband-"other woman" difficulty!)

The Husband's Mother

The husband's mother presents a different pattern of potential trouble, but still trouble!

She continues to practice her "momism" on the son who is now an adult. It is even more distasteful, because there is no excuse for this childlike treatment. She competes with the wife for the husband's attention and affection. And because she has the "inside track" with her son, just as the wife's mother had the blanketing effect upon her daughter, she is bound to disturb and even prevent the free exercise of a normal husband-and-wife relationship. (Under these circumstances, a man and wife cannot even have a quarrel in private!)

The man-of-the-house doesn't always come out as the petted male, however. In some cases, he finds himself bossed by two women instead of one; and those events which might prove disturbing to him with only one female in the house are now multiplied many times over.

Understanding the Inter-Relationships Involved

The basic difficulty, however, is not one of the goodness or badness of the people involved. *It is essentially a matter of polarity!* The mother-in-law is a female; her polarization is in the direction of the male, whether he is her son, or her son-in-law. The presence of another female in the house—especially one who has borne and brought up one of the marriage partners and feels, therefore, that she has special rights, as well as superior knowledge and wisdom—instantly and inevitably forces the wife out of her natural relationship to "her man". (Refer to Chapter XII, "Compounding the Successful Personality-Mix", and you will understand why this result is almost inescapable.)

This unfortunate result is only slightly tempered by the fact that the mother-in-law may be there because of family illness, or because of the salesman-husband's frequent business trips away from home. In short, there is no real solution until the *basic* "family triangle" is re-established.

What is the sales manager going to do about the mother-in-law problem? Certainly, he will not get "in-between". But he can talk to his salesman; he can help him to see the matter as a basic human predicament, rather than as a problem of "good" or "bad" human beings; and he can help him work out a plan for ameliorating its more glaring irritations. And, if the manager is patient and understanding and compassionate, he can take the man and his wife to dinner, and repeat his explanation; this will often remove the problem from the framework of a tangled human "wrangle" into the calmer framework of its intrinsic and inescapable basic dilemmas.

For the sales manager to *understand* the mother-in-law problem does not mean that in every case he will take some form of palliative action. His understanding will enable him better to recognize its symptoms when they begin to show up in a man's work, and it will better equip the manager to steer an impersonal course around the problem, both in behalf of the troubled salesman and himself.

In order not to leave this discussion without a word on the other side, let us admit that the role of mother-in-law is seldom an easy or a happy one. For she who plays it—more bravely, perhaps, than the onlookers can know—her home-nest is empty now; the fledglings whom she trained to fly have their own nests and they are absorbed, as once she was, in the same old task of launching the young safely into the world. Her once important niche is no more; the home and empire that once she ruled, quite happily perhaps, has slipped away to new allegiances and, with the passing of the years, has disappeared from all but memory.

And to her there comes, as to all whose days of high service have declined, the haunting beat of the night tom-toms which seem to say, over and over again, with frightening monotony: "Nobody needs me any more—nobody needs me any more." And what seems, even to her own, like unwanted intrusion is often but the last blind and tragic battle for the right to serve and be near those she loves the most. To her, whose graying locks are but a bundle of service stripes, the only hope of surviving is *more* service—service to the very end of serving.

> How shall the fresh, flooding tide
>   Fierce bent on its landward way,
> Know the grief of the ebbing waters
>   Whose ripples have had their day?

CHAPTER VI

The Salesman in Trouble: Health Problems

A salesman lives and works under conditions and amid circumstances which make it easy for him to postpone or ignore many of the everyday, common-sense precautions customarily taken by the average man to protect his health.

Both salesmen and sales managers know this—but they are so accustomed to careless living that they may accept it as the norm in their profession. Let's look at a few familiar situations.

OCCUPATIONAL HAZARDS

The salesman who, for example, travels long distances by car has a better-than-average chance of ending up in the proctologist's office.

Night driving, late arrival at his lodging place, the frustration of having his hotel reservation "sold out from under him", the unavailability of toilet facilities for long periods, the lack of proper sleep and relaxation—all contribute to increasing the number of potential threats to good health.

In order to make a train or plane, or to be on time for his next appointment, the salesman often eats at irregular hours, bolting down a hurried sandwich or a short-order lunch of fat-fried foods. This encourages ulcers and gall bladder trouble.

Lack of good food, still ridiculously prevalent in many sections of the country, and the haste and tension under which a salesman lives—such occupational hazards frequently lead to bad health.

100

These deviations from the ordinary man's normal pattern of existence are taken for granted as part of the salesman's life; and the sales manager can predict fairly well the results of these almost routine incidents.

In our present discussion, we are not chiefly concerned with these more predictable ailments due to tiredness, poor digestion, and the customary tensions of the job. However, we are concerned with the less predictable health hazards which are likely to come as surprises to the sales manager.

CONCEALED ILLNESS

Frequently, a sales manager unwittingly will hire a man who has a "built-in" poor health potential. Many applicants fail to disclose those health problems which they believe may not otherwise be discovered. When we hear of or see a "bull-of-a-man" succumbing to heart trouble, or paying the price for years of careless eating, with a gall bladder operation, most of us shut our eyes or close our ears and say: "It will never happen to me!" And likewise, the sales applicant who knows his own personal potentialities for trouble will say: "I can handle it", or "I can live with it!"—and thus excuse himself for not revealing the whole truth to the prospective employer.

Men with heart conditions, inactive or slightly active ulcers, diabetes, arthritis; or allergic individuals, particularly asthmatics—these applicants often "forget" about" their health liabilities when filling out an application blank or answering general health questions in an interview. Even in a routine medical examination, they often are able to conceal their ailments from the physician.

Five Ways to Uncover Hidden Ailments

Here are five preventive measures that the sales manager can take to uncover concealed health hazards:

1. Include specific health inquiries on the sales application blank.
2. Ask specific questions about health and "days absent from work", when interviewing an applicant.
3. Request the psychologist, who writes reports on the aptitude tests given to sales representatives, to call special attention to any signs of illness, potential illness, or excessive "time lost from work" that may incidentally come out in the answers to the queries which he scores and interprets. (While it is not the purpose of psychological tests to disclose medical symptoms, it is nevertheless true that, in the normal process of evaluation, a battery of adequate aptitude tests will often reveal hints of health problems. The report can call attention to these difficulties as signals for the sales

manager to make an especially careful investigation of the applicant's physical condition.)

4. Make specific inquiries of previous employers about the applicant's "time-lost-from-work" record, in addition to the usual generalized inquiries about his health.

5. Require a physical examination before hiring an applicant, being sure to alert the physician about specific conditions you wish him to examine in detail.

Many companies have liberal sick-leave allowances, provide fully- or partially-paid hospitalization and surgical care, and even home medical attention at company expense. Retirement with pay at an earlier age than normal because of health impairment, is also a part of the fringe-benefits which apply more and more to salesmen as well as to other employees.

These "extras" are a burden upon the company's earnings. And nowadays, the sales manager has a special obligation not to be careless in hiring men who are known or expected to be candidates for an excessively large share of these non-earned emoluments. In other words, the time to avoid the risks of hidden illness is *before* the salesman is hired.

However, this is not to lay down any invariable, dogmatic axiom that applicants with concealed ailments should not be hired; such a decision must come from the sales manager. He may have an applicant of outstanding ability who is overshadowed by possible health difficulties. Nevertheless, he may decide to hire this applicant, knowing that, in doing so, he is taking a "calculated risk". Sometimes, he will guess wrong; at other times, the gamble will pay off.

Sickness in the Family of the Young Salesman

Family illness presents a special problem for the young salesman—a problem which is likely to harass him and consequently his sales manager.

A younger man is in a new and unhappy situation when, for the first time, his child appears to be seriously ill. Lacking experience, he believes that no other man's child was ever quite as sick as *his*; that no one ever worried quite as much about his offspring as *he* is worrying; and that certainly his child's illness is one of the major catastrophes of the present age. This exaggerated anxiety-pattern is typical of the early stages in the life of a young man who has only recently become a father.

The young salesman, overly-concerned about sickness at home, is not likely to confide in his manager, unless a very cordial relationship has previously been built up between them. Thus, when torn between the responsibility of his family and that of his job, he gives priority to the family. He neglects his business duties and falsifies work reports—all of which may cause a general deterioration of job relationships.

His Exaggerated Sense of Family Responsibility

Often, the young husband and father will feel a sense of family responsibility totally out of proportion to the gravity of the situation, because he has not yet attained a mature sense of values and interprets his child's illness to be much more serious than it really is. As a consequence, he may stay home to take care of the child, or to help his wife whose responsibilities he believes to be particularly heavy. (Usually, the wife is more competent than her husband to handle the problem. Only time, however, will demonstrate this to the young father.)

The conflict through which the young salesman passes at this time is an old and familiar one; so familiar indeed that it has become one of the playmaker's most thoroughly standardized and stereotyped dramatic situations—the struggle between love and duty. On one horn of his new dilemma, the young man feels his tender family responsibility; on the other, his obligation to his employer and his job. Truly, to him, it is a difficult choice of paths!

Helping Him to Mature

However, the wise sales manager will not "bawl out" this youngster, even if he did fail to do his work for a day or two; or, still worse, omitted to record his absence from the job on his daily report.

The judicious boss will sit down with him in a friendly mood; outline the problem clearly so that the young man can see it objectively; and point out that life repeatedly presents such dilemmas where the conflict of responsibilities does not permit any wholly satisfactory solution. Then he will outline a simple pattern of conduct, a permanently usable dilemma-resolving technique which will guide the young father, not only in solving his recent problem, but also in handling later conflicts of a similar pattern.

To assist the young man in settling the recent crisis is, of course, helpful; but in order to make a permanent contribution which will enable him to deal more effectively with the next dilemma, it is necessary to provide a basic methodology. Thus do the young, led by those more mature, acquire a new proficiency and, even more important, they develop a stanch feeling of self-reliance, more strength to face life's problems courageously, and a knowledge that these moments of decision have confronted not them alone, but men throughout human history.

It is very important to rid the young salesman of his childish belief that Fate has dealt him, and him alone, the "Joker"—a belief widely held by the young and inexperienced. Remove this notion and you head off self-pity; you avoid his reaching a weak-kneed conviction that he is destined to be unfairly dealt with throughout life. When he learns that all men suffer thus; that he, like others, can learn to surmount these troubles; and that a mastery of untoward circumstance is a part of life's future lessons, the sales manager may find to his great satisfaction that the boy, so recently "green" and unknowing, has suddenly matured! This occurs so often that the sales manager can afford to gamble a little of his time and experience—in the hope that it will happen again in the current case.

The Plague of Alcoholism

The sales manager who is wary of alcohol in his sales force is not necessarily a "blue nose" or a professional member of the W.C.T.U. He is simply objective and realistic enough not to fly in the face of bad experience.

Overindulgence in alcoholic beverages has several, shall we say—"intensities"? It may be accidental, incidental, continuous, or periodic. A man may drink because he "likes the stuff", or because he "gets a kick out of it", or merely because "the rest of the boys do". Drinking may be a search for companionship, a method of escape from problems, a social gesture, a mistaken idea of "fellowship"—or a chronic bad habit.

But all of this knowing doesn't help the sales manager to deal effectively with the problem of alcoholism. Why not?

Because different men have widely differing capacities to handle alcohol from the standpoint of its ill effects upon their metabolism, their thinking, and their health. In fact, any one man will react differently from day to day, depending upon the "current chemistry" of his digestive processes. And the very individual who sails along imbibing freely without apparent ill effects for years, may suddenly end up in the hospital with cirrhosis of the liver or one of the other degenerative liver diseases. Two weeks later his name will be sadly decorating the obituary column. This bill is a long time in coming due, but the payment is demanded with frightening suddenness.

Even a colored textbook photograph of a "liquor liver" looks like a picture of the fiery entrance to Dante's Purgatory! In other words, too much liquor is an uncharted hazard for any of us.

Like the farmer who fitted a pair of green spectacles on his mule and fed him straw to save money—"Just about the time he got used to it, he up and died!"

The Dangerous "This-Round-Is-On-Me" Habit

In the salesman's life "on the road", hardly any habit is so dangerous as the "round-of-drinks" custom. A couple of cocktails with a friend at the end of the day, after work is done, are not likely to turn Mr. Salesman into an alcoholic. But if he has the bad luck to fall in with a half dozen or more thirsty pals—each of whom insists upon "vindicating his honor" by buying another and still another round of drinks—even the hardiest of the lot will be somewhat shaken before the elbow-bending is finished.

Often he participates because of the ridiculously foolish notion in the minds of many men that the fellow who can't down six or eight drinks without getting groggy is a sissy. This is a falsity and a negation perpetrated by the weak upon those who believe themselves strong, but it repeatedly motivates men to alcoholic excesses in which they themselves would prefer not to indulge and which frequently lead to serious health problems.

So what is the manager going to do to steer his salesmen away from *that* trouble?

Preventive Measures the Manager Can Take

First, he can check applicants for alcoholism by including in his battery of psychological aptitude tests an evaluation blank which will indicate alcoholic tendencies. This type of evaluation is regularly used by at least one of the psychological testing companies whose services are available to sales managers. The results of this test will at least serve to warn him in advance if a man is tending in the wrong direction or if he has already established a habit of alcoholism.

A second *protective* step which the sales manager can take is to sit down with the man who has a tendency to slip a little, and explain to him "How to be Sociable Without Being a Sap!"

Every wise man—compelled by his job, or his social position, to attend functions where large-scale drinking is to be expected—has learned how to "duck the drinks" without being caught at it. A clever juggler will "fondle" a single highball all evening; he will become so deeply engrossed in a friend's conversation that his cocktail glass will still be full when the refills start coming his way;

in more desperate situations, he will even water the artificial palms with his third martini.

If the host or hostess is completely boorish in his or her importuning, he may slip a fiver to the butler or bartender and get his glass repeatedly refilled with innocuous draughts of ginger ale! In other words, the man who is resolved *not* to "get liquored up" will find ways to avoid it!

What About the Chronic Case?

When alcohol gets a salesman down repeatedly, when he has become a confirmed *periodic,* or a full-blown *chronic,* experience does not provide any certain remedy. Medical science has tackled the problem with some success.

The organization known as Alcoholics Anonymous has a most commendable record of having battled with the problem psychologically and in a helpful human way. Many of those who have quietly and unobtrusively been restored to normal living through the A.A. express their thanks by making incredible sacrifices of time, money, and personal effort to lend assistance to the next man who falls to their lot. It is not too much to say that in the A.A. true brotherhood seems to have reached a high-water mark. This is not the place to give the details nor to grow sentimental, but every sales manager with a good salesman whose problem is alcohol, should find out about this group whose work is quiet, effective—and distinguished by a unique lack of self-praise.

8 Major Threats to Your Health and Working Efficiency

You cannot escape it: You live a high-pressure life. Your normal routines are upset by travel. You must entertain quite often. If you are typical, your concern for your health is spasmodic. Yet, without systematic medical check-up and a sane and consistent health program, you run a grave risk of being forced into early retirement or "conking out" while you're still on the sunny side of sixty.

Life Extension Examiners, New York, collaborated with Sales Management's editors to design this simple check sheet to remind you of common abuses to your health... to note the symptoms that go with each... to specify the diseases that arise out of them... and to suggest what you can do by way of correction.

THE CRIME	THE CLUE	THE SENTENCE	THE SOLUTION
OVER-EATING	"Indigestion" Sluggishness Abdominal "fullness" Burping	OVERWEIGHT—an open invitation to: 1. HEART DISEASE 2. HIGH BLOOD PRESSURE 3. DIABETES	Keep your eye on the scales and your weight within normal limits. If you can't control your weight, don't diet temporarily, change your eating habits permanently.
POORLY BALANCED DIET	Digestive Disturbances Constipation Overweight Underweight Lack of Pep	ANEMIA NUTRITIONAL DEFICIENCIES GALL BLADDER DISORDERS	Each day your menu should include: meat fish or eggs; milk or cheese; fresh fruit (citrus included); green and starchy vegetables; butter; bread; and whole-grained cereal.
INADEQUATE SLEEP	Fatigue— physical and mental Nervousness Irritability Headaches	NERVOUS DISORDERS DIGESTIVE UPSETS FUNCTIONAL DISTURBANCES PSYCHOSOMATIC EFFECTS	You should average 7-8 hrs. of sleep each night. A short walk, glass of warm milk or warm bath will induce sleep. Use sedatives only with medical supervision.
INSUFFICIENT RELAXATION	Nervousness Loss of Interest Fatigue Job Inefficiency	NERVOUS PHYSICAL CIRCULATORY DISTURBANCES	Get one full day of rest from business a week. Take an uninterrupted 2 week vacation every year. Change your routine for a while each day through hobbies, interests, exercise.
IMMODERATE SMOKING	Nose, Throat, Bronchial Irritations Nervousness Palpitation Chest Pains Leg Cramps	HEART IRREGULARITIES BLOOD VESSEL SPASMS INFLAMMATION OF NOSE and THROAT	Cut down or cut out your smoking!
IMMODERATE DRINKING	Digestive Disturbances Loss of Appetite Nervousness "D. T.'s"	STOMACH DISORDERS LIVER DISORDERS MALNUTRITION (Vitamin Deficiencies) MENTAL CHANGES	An average of two alcoholic drinks a day will not harm the normal person. If you average more, better start tapering down.
OVER EXERCISE	Chest Pains Shortness of Breath Palpitation Excessive Fatigue Acute Indigestion	HEART STRAIN	Exercise in moderation. Know your limitations! Avoid strenuous exercise immediately after eating. Never carry exercise past the point of fatigue.
INADEQUATE EXERCISE	Constipation Fatigue Sluggishness Loss of Interest	No particular disease, BUT, a run-down, flabby body is an easy target for any disease.	Try to walk 15 minutes 3 times a day -- more if you can. Maintain proper posture, sitting, standing, walking. Moderate sports will help. Golf and bowling are excellent.

CHAPTER VII

The Salesman in Trouble: Money Problems

Salesmen—because of the very temperament-patterns which make them effective and because of the conditions under which most of them work—frequently face money problems.

NEED FOR HOME MONEY PLANNING

Many of those whose jobs normally take them away from home for days or weeks at a time, often fail to plan ahead even for the more obvious household needs their wives will have to wrestle with during their absence. Often, a salesman does not realize that if his family is running close to its budget, in order to tide his wife over delays in receiving his pay checks, he must plan more carefully than does the head of a household with sufficient surplus funds to handle emergencies.

Send Checks Home When the Salesman Is Away

To avoid the effects of inadequate planning, some companies get the salesman's authorization to mail his checks home while he is away on a long trip. Companies whose disbursing office is distant from the salesman's home, will mail the checks two or three days ahead of pay day, so that the funds can arrive in the family mail-box before an emergency actually arises.

For the comfortably financed sales manager, it may be difficult to understand that the failure of a salesman's pay check to arrive on due date can throw the family into a panic. But this happens frequently; and some managers would be surprised at the great number of families who would be compelled to "kite" grocery checks or to borrow from their neighbors if the pay check were delayed even as much as from Friday to the following Monday! Not only is it important that the man get his pay check regularly, but equally essential to family well-being is the predictability of its arrival by a certain mail on a given day.

Handle—Don't Avoid—Emergency Calls for Money

Mr. Sales Manager may get a call from Jack's wife some Friday saying that her husband's check didn't arrive. "What do I do now?"—asks a plaintive and frightened voice.

The manager must be prepared to do something, something constructive and helpful, such as advancing the family some cash, if they are in the same city, or telegraphing emergency funds if they are far away. Above all, he doesn't get angry with Mrs. Jack, for he needs her assistance in too many ways. He may calmly discuss the problem and, with *her* aid, work out a plan that will help Mr. Jack to manage his finances in a more intelligent way.

But there is always the possibility that assistance easily secured in such emergencies may develop into constant calls for financial rescues. In such instances, the manager must have his "NO" ready. To avoid a refusal which might work a real hardship on the family, the foresighted manager talks the problem over with his money-careless salesman and helps him to budget his income and plan his outlays. Further, when it is physically possible, he brings the salesman's wife into money conferences so that she may know the truth about the family's financial condition (of which she is often tragically ignorant). It is also important for her to approve the "do-able-ness" of the plan which has been worked out.

In some cases, the manager must realize that false pride—a foolish, even childish desire of the man of the house to boast that he "wears the pants"—is often responsible for the salesman's unwillingness to turn the operation of finances over to his wife. However, many a man solved this problem early in his working career when he took his wife into partnership and permitted her to manage his earnings. Actually, the wife of the man on the road is the logical manager of the household budget. It is she who has the groceries to buy, the short-dated utility bills to meet, and the bill collectors to face. Such shiftings and improvisations as may be needed, are better made by her, right on the ground where the weekly financial battle takes place.

PLIGHT OF THE FINANCIALLY-INEXPERIENCED SALESMAN

When the salesman with little experience in handling money gets into his first real "fiscal" jam, he is likely to be panicked very quickly. His total indebtedness may be only a couple of hundred dollars, but to him it is as big as the national debt, and he can envision at the end of his financial road nothing but black ruin and disaster.

It usually requires repeated bitter experiences to teach the best of us the value of an hour or of a dollar; and when money problems pile up and overwhelm the money-novice for the first time, he is genuinely in need of his sales manager's help.

Understand the Problem

Pessimistic reformers would have us believe that such troubles arise from gambling, drinking, too much socializing and entertaining on the road or at home. But experience does not confirm that view. The salesman's financial problems—whether the man be young or old—stem from a lack of understanding of how little a dollar will buy, from failure to plan carefully, from an attempt to "keep up with the Joneses".

Also responsible for this plight in which young men find themselves is the natural idealism of youth. Many years ago, a story was told at a teacher's convention by John Robert Gregg, the originator of Gregg shorthand, about the champion shorthand writer Charlie Schwem, later private secretary to Woodrow Wilson. When Schwem was competing for the championship, he went into the national contest room fully equipped with notebook and writing material. A beautiful young blonde, who also made her appearance as a contestant, had not bothered with this paraphernalia. She had not even brought a notebook. Gallantly, Schwem tore his own book in half, gave one portion to the young lady, and kept the other for himself.

When the contest dictation ended, reported Gregg, the soon-to-be champion had only three empty lines left on the last page of his notebook.

So with younger salesmen—they enthusiastically buy their wives more than their incomes permit; they thoughtlessly undertake to help support dependent loved ones without measuring the cost of their generosity against their earnings.

On the road, salesmen—both youthful and mature—live in the best hotels because that is the company policy; they eat well; they entertain customers and prospects in better-than-average fashion. All this, of course, is paid for and authorized by the company. For the man following this policy daily, it is easy to get into the habit of living "at the top of the pot", forgetting the need for economy *when he is spending his own money!* It may take several months before this money-carelessness catches up with the salesman—but when it does, he often finds himself in a panic in a hurry!

Unfortunately, the sales manager can't write off these incidents by saying: "That's the salesman's problem!" Why not? Because the problem haunts the man day and night and throws a wet blanket over his thinking and his selling. The moment his sales volume is affected, it becomes very much the manager's problem. He might as well face it; the man on the road needs a lesson on how to handle his money.

Get All the Facts About Total Debt

The manager's first job is to get the facts—ALL the facts! Find out how much the salesman owes and to whom he owes it. That seemingly simple step is not as easy as it sounds. Strangely enough, when the man is faced with the promise of help, he is less than frank about his debts. Almost always, in a flurry he will hurriedly add up his indebtedness and give his manager a figure much smaller than the true total. The emotional content of the interview makes the truth very hard to discover.

Often, he must be put through a tempered "third degree" during which he must be compelled to list all his debts, including mortgage payments, amortization payments, and monthly installments to which he has obligated himself. To these must be added an estimate of the regular monthly budget of "maintenance" items which must be met so that the family can survive.

Once the manager has the total picture before him, the solution is not too difficult. The *easy* way out is to make a personal loan to the salesman. Usually, that is also the *worst* of all solutions.

The next-easiest way is for the company to advance the money. This may make the loan a little more official, a little less *personal* from the sales manager's point of view; but it has the disadvantage of seeming to give official "sanction" to the man's financial dilemma, and experience shows that the weaker-willed salesman may return again and again to this bottomless well, until borrowing to get out of trouble becomes a bad habit.

Considering the permanent good to be accomplished, the most satisfactory solution is for the salesman to sit down with the sales manager and work out his problem, not through a lump-sum loan, but by calling up his creditors one at a time and arranging for such deferred payment terms as he can realistically meet, keeping within his budget.

Give the Moral Support the Creditors Want

The creditor should know that the sales manager is sitting by, listening to the conversation; with this support, the salesman will discover that creditors, too, are human; and that only one, now and then, will refuse to cooperate. These tougher firms can be paid off together with those creditors to whom only petty amounts are due; while, with creditors claiming larger sums, budget payments should be arranged.

Such a program calls for some cash which, in most cases, the salesman will not have. However, the manager can arrange for him to go to one of the regular commercial banks where personal loans to steadily employed people are not difficult to obtain. (Never let him get in the hands of the loan sharks!) Usually, it is well for the sales manager to phone the bank in advance, to talk to a personal loan executive and tell him that the salesman is coming in. Furthermore, it is wise to ask the banker to report the result of the interview after the fellow leaves.

Keep Free from Personal Entanglements

The manager should not endorse the salesman's note, nor go on the obligation as a co-signer. This tends to weaken the victorious feeling which the debtor salesman will enjoy—the triumph of having ridden out the emergency on his own, which will make him more confident in the future. Instilling such confidence is the main purpose of what may seem to be a roundabout procedure for the financially-inexperienced man to get the money. However, in this way he achieves a new understanding of the management of his financial problems and a new self-reliance in doing so! This leaves the salesman better able to handle future crises on his own responsibility.

The manager may offer to sign a guaranty of payment if required by the bank, but the salesman should never be told about it. This saves his face, keeps him from "leaning" on his manager in money matters, secures the bank, and leaves the sales manager in the position where he can deduct from the man's pay check any payments which he eventually may have to make on account of this guaranty.

Personal Indebtedness

A serious aspect of the salesman's financial problem comes to light when management discovers that the representative has been borrowing from customers, from fellow-salesmen, or from office employees. If the man has been floating bad checks, or giving out I.O.U's, the sales manager should act promptly.

First, it is important to get from the salesman a list of all such creditors, showing the amount owed and in what form. Second, insist that the man write to each one, acknowledging his indebtedness and suggesting a date or plan of payment.

Third, these roving field debts must be included in the schedule of other indebtedness, so that the total obligation to be faced is in front of the debtor.

One point is worth re-emphasizing: Do not permit the debt-ridden salesman to escape with a *partial* disclosure of his total indebtedness! The very foundation-stone of a successful solution lies in getting every financial obligation out on top of the table. Otherwise the whole rehabilitation plan is repeatedly wrecked by surprise demands from creditors previously undisclosed.

Get Financial Progress Reports

And now one final suggestion: It is seldom wise to help the debt-ridden salesman make up his plan of debt-liquidation and then forget about it. Let him know that, like any parolee, he must report to you on his progress. If he makes headway and pays off according to plan, it will be a happy step for him to report his progress to you. If he is falling behind in carrying out the plan, then it is evident that he still needs help in staying on the financial track. This periodic report and check-up is the final assurance of success. It puts a brake on what may be a habitual slackness with creditors; it prevents the man from getting back into the same rut which created the original financial crisis; and if the representative simply can't follow a plan of financial rehabilitation, it gives the sales manager the cue to replace him with another salesman whose weaknesses do not require as much support from the manager.

Every sales executive must decide for himself how much time he will devote to the rehabilitation of the poor budgeter. If a modicum of help will save him, it is probably cheaper to rescue an otherwise good salesman than to invest the same or a greater amount of time in interviewing, hiring, and training a replacement.

CHAPTER VIII

The Salesman in Trouble: Outside Interests

A recent analysis, based on the sales performance figures of 150 commission salesmen of a livestock- and poultry-feed client-company, revealed that *23 of the 71 men in the low performance group had important outside interests—* interests which, in over half the cases, provided them with extra money income!

Other Sources of Income

Five of the men operated sizeable, income-producing farms, in addition to their selling jobs. One was a substantial owner of residential rental property in his home town; another was half-owner of a prosperous feed store, which sold not only the products of the company that employed him, but also the brands of three competitive companies. Still another of these salesmen had a one-third interest in a livestock commission firm. One devoted a good deal of time drumming up students for a local business college which his father had bequeathed to him and his brother.

The wife of one salesman ran a profitable gift-importing business which called for much assistance on the part of her husband.

One member of the sales force spent most of his working hours, his ears glued to the telephone, getting reports from his broker on price movements in the commodity market in which he had large speculative investments.

Still another of these low producers was married to a wealthy woman and her holdings claimed much of his time.

Briefly, there is the picture—salesmen earning so much from their outside interests that they lack the time or incentive to produce in their sales job the full measure of their intrinsic capacity!

In some companies, the problem of outside interests of salesmen is very important. In the company just cited, for example, the divisional sales managers should have put a stop to the diverting of time and activity from the company's business. They failed to do so largely because, under the company's policy, this loose practice was considered permissible. At one time, it is true, such a division of interests was tolerated; though not in recent years. However, no one had taken the trouble actually to "clean up" the sales force at the time the policy was revised.

These "part-time" men diluted the performance of the whole division. But when the word was passed along, the sales managers quickly put the "diversionists" to work or eliminated them from their divisional groups.

Pet Personal Projects

Yet not all of the "outside interest" problems are related to extra money income. Many cases fall into the class of "Pet Personal Projects".

This type is often more costly, because the diverting of time and effort is not easily discovered at the sales manager's level.

Most companies have no policy objections to salesmen who participate, within reason, in worthy civic activities, or local social life. But—and this is a *big* but— if the salesman is more interested in playing the bass horn than in getting an order, if he prefers to build hi-fi sets or fancy bird cages for his neighbors rather than study the sales manual, if being a member of the school board takes up more of his time than his sales job will permit, or if his recent election to the city council compels him to be home every second Friday when he should be attending a sales meeting—then, his personal, private life is definitely interfering with his success in his job.

How to Handle the Dabbler

Such cases should be handled by the sales manager promptly, frankly, and without kid gloves.

He should make clear that the company's sales job is a full-time occupation; that it calls for full-time effort, a full-time mind, and an undivided loyalty.

The dabbler should be given a blunt choice between investing full time in his job—or being replaced. If he refuses to give up his side-lines, a new man should promptly be put into the territory. The Good Book points out that no man can serve two masters—and we can add—the man who *thinks* he can is only kidding himself and his company.

How to Discover Outside Interests

How is the sales manager going to discover the existence of outside interests?

He must take preventive measures early—even before an applicant is hired. Above all, the manager must see to it that the application blank used for prospective salesmen has a few probing questions—both direct and concealed—on outside interests. Here are some samples:

1. Do you find you need to supplement your job activities with outside interests in order to obtain variety and to avoid boredom?
2. Are you a committee member, officer or leader in any civic or service organization, society, or association? Name such and indicate connection.
3. What obligations requiring your personal service do these memberships impose?
4. Do you have any outside interests or business participations which will augment your income from your sales job with our company? What are they?

The interviewing procedure should include a brief discussion of the question of outside interests. And field managers should be asked to be on the alert for any signs of over-shadowing outside interests. Whenever discovered, these should be reported to the home office, so that the problem can be discussed fully by the sales manager and the field manager at their next get-together.

Usually, the field manager can quickly spot these diversionary interests if he will keep his eyes and ears open. Blank days on salesmen's planning sheets, vague daily reports, indications from customers that they haven't seen the salesman for several weeks, unexplained failure to complete specific assignments promptly, delayed answers to home office memos, repeated daytime phone calls not related to the man's job, failure to follow route sheets and plans as submitted, unexplained absence from sales meetings or repeated tardiness in arriving—all such irregularities are symptoms which should be investigated. The field manager should not jump to conclusions. He should regard symptoms as symptoms only, and should not report them unless they have been confirmed by careful investigation.

Sales managers at the top, or those in field positions, should not regard these investigative steps as objectionable "policing operations". In the long run, they are as helpful to the salesman whose misdirected interest in outside matters is bound to lead him into trouble as they are to the company which seeks a full day's work for a full day's pay.

In summary, let the sales manager in his interviewing process try to avoid hiring the applicant who is perpetually lured away by side interests; let him and his field managers keep on the alert to spot those men headed in the wrong direction. Let him take prompt steps to steer them back on the road where the money is to be found—both for the salesman and for the company. And if the errant salesman won't be steered "that-a-way", the company should find men who will follow the safe course dictated by experience.

BASIC MOTIVATION CHECK SHEET

QUESTION: Does our "total sales job" offer the essential "built-in" motivations to meet the TEN BASIC NEEDS of salesmen?

HOW TO USE THIS CHECK SHEET: To the right of each numbered "need" place a check mark in whichever of the columns—A, B, or C—that most nearly represents the comparative attractiveness or need-satisfaction which your job offers in respect to this particular need. Then in column D, enter the total score for that item—60 if you have rated it "Below Average"; 80 if you have rated it "Average"; and 100 if you have rated it "Above Average." When you have checked and scored each of the items, add up the score in column D, and divide by 18 (or more, if you have added "needs" of your own in the blank spaces left for that purpose). The resulting figure will be your answer to the question at the head of this check sheet.

BASIC NEEDS OF SALESMEN	A BELOW AVERAGE	B AVERAGE	C ABOVE AVERAGE	D TOTAL SCORE
Scoring Values	60	80	100	
1. BASE PAY		✓		80
2. INCENTIVE PAY POSSIBILITIES			✓	100
3. PERSONAL RESPONSIBILITY		✓		80
4. IMPORTANT WORK TO DO		✓		80
5. JOB SECURITY (Stability, Permanence)	✓			60
6. COMPANY ASSISTANCE IN UNEXPECTED PERSONAL & FAMILY "DISASTER"	✓			60
7. ROOM TO GROW			✓	100
8. PERSONAL "PLACE"		✓		80
9. WORKING "PLACE"		✓		80
10. "PLACE" IN OTHERS' EYES		✓		80
11. INGREDIENTS FOR FAMILY "PLACE"	✓			60
12. OPPORTUNITY FOR SELF-EXPRESSION	✓			60
13. OPPORTUNITY FOR PERSONAL ACCOMPLISHMENT			✓	100
14. PERSONAL RECOGNITION			✓	100
15. PARTICIPATION IN GROUP SUCCESS		✓		80
16. A VISIBLE FUTURE GOAL		✓		80
17. A CHARTED ROAD TO FUTURE	✓			60
18. CONTINUOUS HEALTHY EXCITEMENT			✓	100
19.				
20.				
GROSS SCORE (Divide by 18 or more)				1440
TOTAL JOB RATING OR NET SCORE				80

CHAPTER IX

Motivating Salesmen to Action

*S*alesmen are people!

And because they come into the world as *human beings,* they need a manager who understands them, first, as *homo sapiens* and second, as practitioners of the art of selling.

Studying the success or failure of salesmen, we find that the total impact of their lives is as much influenced by the quality of leadership which they enjoy, as it is by those intrinsic personal qualities which they themselves contribute to the job.

Men, as a rule, do not succeed in life or business, certainly not to the peak of their capacities, if left to solve their own problems unaided and to fight their battles alone. Few indeed are they who, without assistance, are able to forge upon their own anvils, the tools of a successful life.

As a matter of fact, who among us can truthfully claim that we owe nothing of our success to those who aided and guided us along the way—to our parents or our teachers, for example, or to our coaches and athletic directors; and later, to our manager who so often combines, in one person, almost all of the skills of those who preceded him in the salesman's life experience.

If a manager is to build men—and is not this the chief objective of the dedicated leader?—he must constantly practice the arts of the skilled motivator, that "organist of the human heart" who knows how to finger the contradictory keyboard of human emotions and to evoke from that never-to-be-fully-understood instru-

119

ment, not only harmony, but the victorious strains of a rewarding personal life and a successful economic experience.

Three hundred years ago, Pascal, the famed French philosopher told us why the task is difficult:

> We think we are playing on ordinary organs when playing upon man. Men are organs, it is true, but odd, changeable, variable, with pipes not arranged in proper order. Those who only know how to play on ordinary organs will not produce harmonies on these. *We must know where the keys are!* (Italics ours.)

As we shall see when we begin to explore this matter of motivating human beings to action, Pascal's warnings as to its difficulties were fully warranted.

Motivation Defined

What is this managerial activity we call "motivation?" It is not something new, but a technique which every successful leader uses, and has been using, to move men to purposeful action.

Let us attempt to define it:

> Motivation is the science and art of releasing and utilizing the energies contained within the deep-seated emotional needs of the human being, and doing this in such a manner as to at least partially control the *direction, timing,* and *intensity* of the forces thus released.

Motivation, as the word implies, has to do with *motives,* and motives are the recognizable *channels* into which the emotional forces surge. As we all know, the emotions do *surge;* yes, and they *swirl* and *whirl,* and *push* and *pull!*

Let us trace the motivating power backward to its source, starting with its final stage, and following it in reverse order to its beginnings.

That final stage from which we start is, of course, ACTION, which is really the whole objective of motivational effort. That action has *its* roots in DESIRE. That desire, which we call by many names—craving, yearning, or hunger, for example—is in its turn the child of a basic human NEED. Or to restate the process in its natural cause-effect order: NEED is turned into DESIRE, and DESIRE into ACTION.

Each of these three steps represents differing stages or intensities of *emotional drive.* In fact, it is important to remember that motivation deals almost entirely with the emotions. The manager may employ his intellect, his reason, and his logical thinking in *planning* his motivational efforts. However, when it comes to *application,* he finds that not only the TOOLS he uses, but also the RESPONSES he procures, are EMOTIONAL IN NATURE!

Let us say that the NEED is a quiet pool of emotional energy. Once uncovered and aroused, this quiet pool of need becomes a more or less active, sometimes even *dynamic*, WHIRLPOOL of swirling force; and this whirlpool we call DESIRE. As desire is heightened, its eddying force whirls and swirls faster and faster, making a cone-like vortex, the pull of which results in ACTION!

The natural sequence of steps, NEED-DESIRE-ACTION, does not always operate smoothly and automatically. There are some counteracting forces which sometimes slow down the process and prevent need from turning promptly into desire, and desire into action.

FIRST DIFFICULTY: *Need* is often *latent* in the human being; it must be uncovered; and a keen awareness of its existence and implications must be established in the consciousness.

SECOND DIFFICULTY: In many situations, the conscious awareness of the existence of the need does not automatically arouse desire to anything more than a force of feeble intensity, insufficient to overcome the natural inertia of the human being and to result in action.

THIRD DIFFICULTY: External restraints—such as lack of time or opportunity or, internally generated inhibitions, such as timidity, fear, or doubt—interefere with the prompt translation of desire into *action*.

The remedies for these difficulties are comparatively simple. Latent need, of which the human being is not consciously aware, should be uncovered, identified, visualized, and dramatized in terms of its disadvantages. Then, the coin should be turned over and the positive implications and possibilities of the need should be similarly highlighted, thus stimulating the conscious awareness of the need, and the results of its continuance or satisfaction.

In connection with the second difficulty, low-powered, lukewarm desire should be heightened by a similar process, emphasizing on the negative side, the pain-loss aspects, and on the positive pole, its pleasure-gain possibilities.

The third type of difficulty—external restraints or internal inhibitions which restrict action—should be removed by a longer and more detailed dramatization of the situation and by a further intensification and comparison of the negatives and positives, interpreted as realistically as possible in terms of specific application to the individual.

However, in his initial efforts at motivating his men, the sales manager need not be too much concerned about these difficulties, particularly if he bases his motivation on the ten basic needs listed immediately below. For in that event, he will find the difficulties either substantially non-existent, or largely minimized.

Why so? Because, in these ten-basic-need situations, the manager can assume that the need has been uncovered, that the desire has been aroused to a "usable intensity", and that action depends only upon a further intensification of desire by the leader's reasonably skillful motivating efforts.

10 Basic Needs of Salesmen
1. Money
2. Responsibility and Work of Importance
3. Security
4. Room to Grow
5. Personal Place
6. Personal Accomplishment
7. Personal Recognition
8. Participation in Group Accomplishment
9. A Goal and a Road Map
10. Excitement

By skillfully intensifying the DESIRES growing out of these ten basic NEEDS, and by sometimes *partially*, sometimes *wholly,* (but never permanently) satisfying these urges, the manager can lead, direct, induce, persuade, and influence his salesmen to do pretty much what he wants them to do, without arousing even a small portion of the antagonism which would be built up by the direct, bossy approach.

It is helpful to remember that, in one form or another, this motivation process is involved in every human decision to take action. On some occasions, the motivation is self-generated; that is, the intrinsic elements in the total situation are of a type that reaches sufficient intensity to be self-propelling. In other cases, the action-generating suggestion comes from outside the individual, the latter being the case whenever the manager is consciously motivating his men. And since the average man is more easily and more rapidly moved to action by impulses which he believes to have originated within himself, the sales manager avoids any clumsy, obvious, or painful "injection" of the motivating idea. Instead, he plants the seed, and stands aside to let the "soil and sunshine" of the individual bring forth the strong, growing plant. And that plant, fortunately for the sales manager, cannot be distinguished, even by the person motivated, from the outgrowth of a similar seed *which he himself planted!*

Each of the ten needs previously listed provides its own special kind of opportunity. Let us examine these needs one by one and explore the specific motivational possibilities within each of them.

1. Money

"Money makes the mare go!"

Such was an earthy five-word proverb current among Midwest farmers almost a generation ago.

It's money, too, that makes the salesman "go!" For, money is one of the salesman's basic needs.

And his need for money is not the simple, single-cylinder necessity that, at first, it might seem to be. It is more than just having sufficient funds for his groceries and the prompt and honorable payment of the monthly rent bill or the installment on the mortgage. The salesman's need for money is many-faceted and has its emotional and social, as well as economic, implications.

Merely from the economic standpoint, a salesman needs enough money for himself and his family's current requirements, with a mite left over to give that comfortable feeling of comparative security which Charles Dickens' Mr. Micawber so succinctly described:

> Annual income twenty pounds; annual expenditure nineteen, nineteen, six —result HAPPINESS. Annual income twenty pounds; annual expenditure twenty pounds nought and six—result MISERY.

However, the salesman needs money enough not only to meet his current economic requirements and to give him a feeling of comparative security; but emotionally, he needs enough to enable him to hold up his head and face all the world with a feeling, if not of *pride*, then of sturdy *self-respect*. This feeling of self-respect is one thing, when considered solely from the standpoint of the man's own thinking; when it comes within the framework of the home situation, it is quite another matter.

For at home, the salesman's money earnings are tied up with the taut cords of family emotions which may make his financial status much more tensional. There, he needs enough money for an important psychological purpose—to command the respect of his wife, his children, perhaps even of his parents and in-laws. In this difficult arena of the home, the whole subject of Daddy's income may be almost continually charged with emotion. Not always does the tension break out into the open; often it exists as an always overhanging, smoldering threat to family peace, erupting only at moments of great economic or emotional stress.

True, there are few wives who seem to wear an almost permanent attitude of dissatisfaction with the pay check of the family breadwinner. It is not always fair to characterize this as nagging. It may reflect the wife's worry over genuine family needs; or it may be a farsighted "defensive offense" launched in advance to head off criticism of her own extravagance. It may be the wife's idea—sometimes naive and mistaken, sometimes correct—of keeping father under pressure to work harder and earn more.

When parents or in-laws meddle in the money affairs of their adult children, the situation, more often than not, is short on facts and long on irritants, often speeding up like an uncontrolled whirlwind of autumn leaves in the front yard, spinning blindly into respect-crumbling sarcasm and ending in angry and peace-destroying family conflict. Usually such parental prodding is based not upon a knowledge of prevailing salary levels, but rather upon a "father- or mother-knows-best" approach, or still worse, upon a demeaning comparison on the basis of: "At your age, I was earning so-and-so!"

But whatever the cause of the many money problems that may face the salesman, the sales manager is likely to inquire: "So what? Am I supposed to take upon my shoulders all the family money problems and tensions which may exist in each man's home?"

Emphatically not! However, let it be said with equal emphasis that, while it is not at all necessary for the sales manager either personally or vicariously to participate in the tensions arising from the home money problems of his many salesmen, every one of his men has a right to believe that his manager at least UNDERSTANDS these problems and makes allowance for them, not necessarily in his pay-check, but in his consideration of their total relationship.

Certainly, no employer is obligated to pay a man at the level of his own fanciful ideas about his worth, or to underwrite his own extravagances or those of his family, or to compensate him so that he and his family may "keep up with the Joneses" of their choice, or to recognize in any way what his wife or older members of the family believe to be the proper earnings for the hapless salesman in between. But the sales manager ought quietly to discover in which of his salesmen's situations such tensions persist. If he is wise, he will not ignore those negatives which are potentially so dangerous to the morale of his men.

To SUM UP: The salesman's need for money has many strange roots, most of them hidden in distant soil; certain of these problems can be traced to economic causes; but more of them will be found originating in the deep emotional subsoil, where the insensitive manager would not expect to find them. True, the wise and experienced leader knows how to be innocently blind to *unimportant* symptoms of money-based troubles. Similarly, he is shrewd enough to know that many times these roots are like fuses leading to destructive powder-mines of emotion which, if they blow up, may unexpectedly disrupt both individual and group morale. And this manager knows how to detect the early odor of the smoldering fuse, and how to "pinch it off" quietly and harmlessly before it reaches the explosive charge.

All of this indicates how many of the aspects of need for money tend to motivate the salesman, almost automatically, but largely in a negative direction.

In the main, these involved situations are more potential than actual; most salesmen and most of their families subsist in a more positive and constructive atmosphere. The fact that a man is on the payroll and regularly and reliably receives his semi-monthly check is, in itself, a major motivating force in the right direction.

But the sales manager's opportunity does not end with the manipulation of money motivations. For, as the Good Book says: "Man doth not live by bread alone."—and money is only one of the several basic human needs which provide the sales manager with his opportunities to motivate men.

The remaining nine motivational opportunities discussed in the pages which follow, have one common characteristic—they grow out of the less tangible, and more emotional needs of the salesmen, those needs which loom large in the total picture, but which can be satisfied only through the insight and imagination of the sales manager. Let us discuss each of these in turn.

2. RESPONSIBILITY AND WORK OF IMPORTANCE

It is a basic desire of the ambitious human being to do worthwhile work in the world. When a man looks forward, as each of us does from time to time, to the probable peak of his life and to the declining slope beyond (And young men, too, do this much more often than their elders give them credit for!)—he inevitably asks himself a half-formed, perhaps half-subconscious question: "Will my having been here make any difference when I am gone?" Whatever he says to others, whatever he may admit consciously to himself, he, nevertheless, fears the answer may turn out to be "No!" And he really never ceases striving to make sure that the answer will be at least a qualified "Yes!"

In the soil of this basic human yearning grows the second need of the salesman —the need for responsibility and important work to do.

Experienced managers know that salesmen wish to feel the weight of suitable responsibility upon their shoulders. Feeling it, they stop and straighten up, metaphorically speaking, take a deeper breath, and set out a little happier, a little more resolute upon the path before them.

A wise manager does indeed "temper the wind to the shorn lamb." He piles on the load according to the individual's capacity; but if he has the true insight of the real leader, he does not neglect to capitalize this much overlooked hunger of the human spirit to bear a fair share of the burden of the world's work!

In today's world, where many managers past fifty years of age are bemoaning the young man's flight from responsibility, his reliance upon the doctrine that "the world owes me a living!"—his concentration of attention upon the employee's fringe benefits, such as pension plans, retirement funds, and the like—our contention that the average man yearns for responsibility may sound like false doctrine, an idealistic, and unrealistic philosophy.

But it is not a false philosophy; it is a true picture of one of the deep running currents of the human being. That it is not evident and obvious to all merely emphasizes the need for managerial insight. As S. L. A. Marshall says: "What is needed primarily . . . are policies stemming from the top, which are based not upon slide rule calculations but upon knowledge of the human heart."

The sales manager will find it useful to audit the distribution of responsibility in his sales operation. Does he hug the major burden of the job to himself, or does he delegate and distribute it? Does he trust his field force to share the load and apply their united effort to the task, or does he permit them only to "peck" at the outer shell of the problem?

The roots of the basic hunger for responsibility go deep. A man likes to feel that the *important* work which his manager has assigned to him can be done, considering all the circumstances, by him alone, or at least *more effectively* by himself than by anyone else. He likes to feel that his success or failure will make a difference, not only to him, *but to the whole of which he is a part!*

To carry this need a step further, the salesman wants to believe that his company would notice his failure, if he were to fail, or his success, if it is above average. And he likes to hope that they would somehow lose by the one, and benefit—sufficiently for the fact to be noticed, at least—by the other.

The sales manager, who has his sensitive antenna properly installed and his receiver tuned to admit the powerful sendings of the human emotions, will understand the motivating power of this almost primitive hunger for responsibility and important work. And understanding this, he will never leave any man burdenless for long.

Thus he will instill in each of his salesmen a keener sense of an important purpose in his life. Instinctively, the recipient of this motivation will shift his efforts so that, in a hundred little ways, he may effectively carry out the purpose. He will start to work a few minutes earlier tomorrow; work a little later today; make another try for that close which eludes him; add an extra call to the former daily quota. His hours, his days, now fit into a purposeful, objective scheme of worthwhileness!

Do we promise too much as the result of this motivation? No, it is quite impossible to overestimate the subtle influence of these intangible, subjective forces working within a human being! These seeds, planted in the inner soil of a man's thinking, blossom forth into action at unexpected times and in unexpected spots where there is no recollection of such a seed having been sown.

"Burden me, burden me—and I will rise!"

3. SECURITY

"Security—that's all these youngsters talk about any more—security!" One need not travel far to hear similar scornful words from the mouth of a sales manager. For it is true that "security"—as a word, as an idea, as a fact—is more often on the lips of sales applicants today than it was thirty years ago.

It is also true that implicit in the use of the word is a seeming intention to evade personal responsibility. "Let Uncle Sam do it!" "That's the government's worry!" "Let the company see to that!"

Such attitudes irritate the self-reliant man whether he be of the so-called "old school" or born into the modern milieu. For the wise man of affairs knows that, finally, each individual must make his own security, by his own thought, labor, and thrift.

But if the sales manager is to motivate his younger men, the majority of whom, even now, are of the post-1933 school, he must understand *why* they feel the way they do, even if he doesn't wholly agree with their point of view. Management of salesmen must begin with what they *have*, what they *think*, what they *need*. It is futile, indeed, for the sales manager to hope to shift their standpoint *before* he begins to motivate them; for it is through the process of skillful motivation that they may eventually be changed, if they are to be changed at all.

This consideration of the emotional block set up in a typical sales manager by the word "security" seemed to us to be a needful prelude to a discussion of the average man's basic need for security, as a means of motivation and as an instrument for better management. For often, the mere mention of the word will trigger a tirade of scorn and abuse. Until a sales manager has sufficiently relieved his—we were about to say relieved his *mind*. But it is not his mind; it is his *emotions* that he relieves when he delivers a denunciatory preachment on "security."

Assuming now that the accumulated tensions on the subject have been dissipated, let us return to a discussion of the human being's basic need for security —a need which is literally as old as Adam, and which traces back to the days when man was closer to an animal than a human being. It is out of this greater soil, indeed, that the current economic and social thinking on the subject grows.

Out of that ancient evolutionary heritage arises the fact that all men, including the sales manager and the writer of these lines, are afraid, to a greater or lesser degree. Instinctively and unreasoningly afraid—afraid of their environment, afraid of each other, afraid of the unknown.

At times, there hovers over each of us a vague, undefinable, but nevertheless profound sense of isolation and "alone-ness", a feeling possibly of being an unwelcome alien in a strange land. Sometimes the sensation is acute and immediate; at other times, it is forgotten. And different people have the experience in differing intensity. Almost nobody talks about this experience; few admit it to themselves. But it exists in all of us; and no braggart need claim he knows it not. We *all* know it!

It drives men together into tribes, nations, unions, clubs, political parties, and all sorts of groups. Without it, churches would have no purpose; and even God would be unnecessary to man.

In this shoreless ocean of life, the individual gropes for whatever anchors, whatever fixed and enduring reassurances he can find, whether they be mental, emotional, or physical.

And because within man there exists this ancient and deep-seated need for security, *the sales manager is handed by Nature a powerful instrument of motivation and improved management!*

What aspects of security does this yearning encompass? Let's enumerate a few:

1. His salesman wants the security of GOOD CURRENT PAY.
2. His salesman wants the security which comes from "room to grow."
3. His salesman wants the security of knowing that good work, loyalty, and decency on his part will not go unrecognized or unrewarded by the boss.
4. He wants that feeling of security which comes from knowing that his boss is not generally prejudiced, capricious, fickle, changeable, or unpredictable.

There are many more "securities", to be sure. But experience shows that these are most often "on top of the salesman's mind."

The manager says: "Why don't you quit worrying, Charley, and put your whole mind on doing better work? You've got a good job at good pay; you've got a chance to grow and to go up the ladder; you know I never overlook good work; and you've got plenty of proof that every man here gets a fair shake. No teacher's pets, nobody on the black list!"

That's motivation by showing how Charley's need for many "securities" is being met in his present job—a subtle hint to transfer his "worry-energy" into "work-energy", a suggestion that he start growing up in the "room" provided for him, a seed-thought that perhaps he ought to match his manager's "open door" policy with a little more striving on his own part.

Here we see the practiced touch of the trained organist upon the delicately balanced keys of the Great Organ of Human Motivation!

Security, Yes! But Not Too Much!

To the less experienced manager, perhaps a word of caution is due: There can be, of course, *too much security!*

How much is *too much,* and how little is *too little,* only experience and good judgment can decide.

But, when security begins to be taken for granted, when the idea is everywhere prevalent in the sales force that security "comes with the job", that to secure it, no *quid pro quo* is required from the salesman—then security ceases to be a useful instrument of motivation for the sales manager.

The late Brigadier General Albert Browning, one-time Vice President of Purchasing at the Ford Motor Company, emphasized the truth of this "too-much-security" idea, when speaking of the eventual uselessness of the executive bonus plan previously in effect in that company. For many years, whether Ford made money or lost it, the bonus had been paid, *willy-nilly.* It had become not only a part of the job, but one of the employees' inalienable rights; in other words, a costly *vice.*

At the time of the General's comment, young Henry Ford was fighting to regain a long-lost market position; they were losing money so rapidly that we hesitate to quote Browning's figure, for fear that it would seem ridiculous. Top management decided to withdraw the bonus! Quite naturally, they were worried about the reaction; for it is difficult to tamper with a man's "spondulix nerve" without getting a loud and violent reaction.

"We were amazed," recounted Browning, "when we brought the bad news to our second-string executives, to hear them heave a sigh of relief and exclaim—

'Thank Heaven! As long as our subordinates were getting the bonus even though sales were down, we couldn't do anything with them.'"

"Security" is a valuable key on the motivation organ, only so long as it elicits a response when pressed. When the security story becomes "old stuff", in other words, when the salesmen feel that their need for security is fully met, then the sales manager may as well "tape over" that key and play only those still connected with active response-mechanisms.

4. Room to Grow

"People are funny!" The sales manager must accustom himself to that fact, using the word "funny" in the sense of *irrational, illogical,* and changing the word "people" to "salesmen." Pascal, it will be recalled, warned us of this general fact about human beings, a long time ago, when he said: "Men are organs, it is true, but odd and changeable and variable, WITH PIPES NOT ARRANGED IN PROPER ORDER."

Salesmen, generally, do not demand that they be advanced in status regularly, as is true in other types of jobs. But they insist on ROOM TO GROW!

And, they insist that the room to grow be *out in the open and clearly visible every step of the way!*

To say it in other words, salesmen insist upon having constantly before them "the vision splendid"; but they are not as insistent, as are many other types of workers, upon having the vision come true in periodic and clear-cut promotional steps involving job-title changes. This attitude is partly accounted for, of course, by the fact that a salesman's pay increases are almost automatic in many companies, being tightly geared to his sales volume—usually by a payment scheme which is little more than a thinly disguised commission plan.

But this situation does not wholly explain their attitude about room to grow. Salesmen are eternal optimists; they are likely to be self-confident; and despite their being called "loafers" and "security seekers", as a class, there is to be found among them a higher proportion of the self-reliant than is likely to be discovered in most other occupations. Notwithstanding what their tongues may *say* about "security", they have more than average faith in their ability to "manufacture their own future!"

The tendency to automatic pay-increases based upon performance, the natural and persistent tendency of the salesman to be optimistic, plus his general mood of self-confidence, combine to make a self-motivation pattern that explains the importance of this *visible room-to-grow* factor which the manager should continually keep in the spotlight.

The shrewd sales manager understands that, in the salesmen's dictionary, the phrase "room to grow" really means "room to earn more money"; or to say it more prosaically, a high *ceiling* on earning possibilities.

Experience shows that salesmen, generally, are not satisfied as much by the ego-inflating "increase-of-status" process as are men in other types of jobs. The salesmen for an ethical pharmaceutical company, for example, will not object to their title being changed from "salesman" to "medical service representative"; but the manager, who hopes that such an "improvement-in-status" gesture will be accepted as a substitute for an increase in pay, is due for an awakening. Unless the "status-elevation" is backed up by a pay increase, or offers a higher earning possibility, the men will scorn it. Privately, they may even accuse the company of trying hypocritically to substitute a shift of title for a raise in pay; such a policy very properly makes men angry.

But let none of these minor issues obscure the main point. Salesmen want jobs in which they can see room to grow, room to grow in money-earnings. Even if the growth in income fails to materialize as fast as they had hoped, they will be patient with their company, their sales manager, and themselves—so long as that room to grow is *visible and real!*

(Not a few companies have a common blind spot in their compensation plans with respect to the mature and highly productive, veteran salesmen on their field staffs. They have a fixed ceiling on top earnings for all salesmen; and no matter how much one of these veterans produces, and no matter how much below the average is his sales cost, *he cannot be allowed to earn more than the ceiling figure!* In these cases, is it not clear that top management has taken away from the sales manager one of his most valuable tools of motivation—one which he could employ with immense effect upon that small segment of his sales force which comprises his top-level producers?)

Don't Overplay the Room-to-Grow Angle!

The sales manager ought to keep in mind that this room-to-grow concept can have a dangerous recoil, if this motivation is used insincerely, with tongue in cheek.

The president of America's largest food manufacturing and distributing company was discussing with us the results of a highly interesting field survey which we had just finished in connection with their sales force of 900 men.

"With hardly an exception", we reported, "your salesmen asked one question wherever we went: *'Where do I go from here?'* "

"Why", the president answered confidently, "those who are competent will be promoted—first to district representative, then to district supervisor, then to district manager; and above those jobs, there is still lots of room—division sales manager, regional sales manager, zone sales manager."

"If all of these managerial men were wiped out tomorrow by an atom bomb, how many jobs would that catastrophe open up?"

"About one hundred twenty-five!"

"In other words, about 14 per cent of your sales force could be promoted if a company-wide debacle should occur. But, in the ordinary course of business, how many of those 125 managerial jobs were ever unfilled and available at one time?"

"At most, not over a dozen!"

"Twelve out of nine hundred—less than one and one-half per cent! What then, is the hard-boiled answer to their question: 'Where do I go from here?' "

"I never thought about the figures in this way before, but the truth is, there isn't any *good* answer. We're training men as salesmen, a large number of whom are bound to end up as sales managers and field managers for our smaller competitors!"

In a large sales organization, if there are current promotable possibilities for three to four per cent of the total field sales force, that figure is better by far than the typical room-to-grow-into-management-jobs opportunity in most large companies. Is it not fortunate for the sales manager that the average salesman's yearning is not oriented toward increase in status, but rather toward increase in pay?

And is it now easy to see how this room-to-grow appeal can be overplayed on the motivation organ, overplayed so much as to result in an explosive recoil?

Visible room-to-grow is one of the sales managers most powerful motivations; but it must be sincere and truthful. Otherwise, it's dynamite!

Personal Place, Personal Accomplishment, Personal Recognition

These three keys on the sales manager's motivational organ can be played singly, or as a great diapasonal chord.

Played one at a time, they set the salesman's feet marching to a more rapid tempo; they step up his mind to faster thinking, and focus his attention more fixedly upon his essential tasks and objectives. As a chord, their relentless rhythm is compulsive and difficult to resist.

For these motivations reach to the very core of a man's being, to his deep-seated, inner sense of "I-ness", his unduplicated and unduplicable individuality, that uniqueness which belongs to him and no one else!

Peter Drucker, in *Concept of the Corporation,* his book on human relations at General Motors, said that workers wanted two basic satisfactions from their jobs. He called these yearnings "status and function"—in other words, a place of their own to work in and important tasks to do.

We have previously dealt with the desire for an important task, under the heading of Responsibility and Work of Importance, Basic Need Number 2. The desire for a place of his own to work in, this hunger, is equally important—and useful—to the sales manager.

5. PERSONAL PLACE

"Place" is one of the most important words in the humanist's dictionary. It is the label for many differing facets of human yearning, none of which is quite quantitative or definable, and yet each of which is very important to understanding and motivating men.

A Need for Sanctuary

It is a subtle and fascinating study—this human need for *place.* In one sense, this is the outward manifestation of a need for *protection.* Protection *from what?* From the world, from all its threatening evils! We get a little taste of this need in the famous old hymn "Rock of Ages." Remember how the singer pleads for sanctuary in that inanimate symbol of security: "Rock of Ages, *cleft* for me." Observe that it is not enough to *cling* to the rock, it must be *"cleft in twain"*, so that a safe physical refuge may be provided. Let us call this first aspect of the word "place", *a need for sanctuary.*

A Living Place

A second meaning of "place" lies in the yearning for a place to live; that is, a *home*—with all the implications which time and association have built around that word. Something of the sense of sanctuary pervades the aura around this word "home", even in this usage; but it is more than that. Home, in this present meaning, is that place where the mechanics and process of living can be carried on in an organized way. It is the living place in the same sense that the work bench is the working place. The yearning for home threads itself through the life of Jesus, for example, starting with that incident prior to His birth when the hotel clerk, true to tradition, faced His parents with that depressing announcement: "There is no room in the inn!" Later Jesus Himself exclaimed about it, saying: "The foxes have holes, and the birds of the air have nests; but the Son of man hath not where to lay his head."

"Place" in the Opinions of Others

A third meaning of the word "place" has to do with a man's standing in the respect, esteem, and affection of his co-workers at the plant, of his neighbors in his community, of his fellow-members in his church, lodge, service organization, or union.

Family "Place"

A fourth aspect of this need for "place" has to do with a man's position in the intimate circle of his own family. In the not-too-long-gone days of counts and princes, it was said that "no man is a hero to his valet", because the servant repeatedly saw his master as he really was—bare as he was born, stripped of the pretentious braid and brocade that adorned him before the public. To remain a colossus at home is, for all of us, even more difficult than to maintain a hero's status before a valet. And this very difficulty heightens the poignancy of this need and enlarges its relative importance, especially in the case of a man of pride.

A Working Place

A fifth and very practical aspect of this phase of motivation is the need for a working place—a desk, or work bench, assigned to one man where he may work and where he may keep the tools of his trade safe and undisturbed by the curious and contaminating hand of an intruder. Anyone with shop experience knows how jealously the fine tools of his craft are regarded by the skilled tool and die-maker, or the deft fashioner of patterns for the foundry. There is no surer way to call down the curses of Satan and all his imps than to tamper with a skilled workman's tools. These are included in his concept of that private, exclusive, and individual work place which he calls his own.

In government offices in Washington, for example, we see the association of work status and work place carried to ridiculous extremes. Status is automatically indicated by type of work place and equipment—a single pedestal desk, proletariat; double pedestal, on the first rung of the ladder; big desk, going places; private office, arrived on the first plateau above the *hoi polloi*, may some day be a commissar; rug, telephone, and push buttons, symbols of supreme authority, only one step below the top man himself!

The work bench, desk, and office concept does not quite include the work place of the salesman, which is his sales territory, that piece of "geography" which is at once his responsibility and his opportunity. But, as we shall see in a moment, the desire to possess his territory exclusively, without intrusion or interference, is very important to the salesman.

Such, then, are the five facets of meaning which surround the word "place"—sanctuary, *living* place, "place" in the opinions of others, *family* "place", *work* place.

These aspects, of course, are not mutually exclusive; on the contrary, they are mutually interacting. They are not only synergetic; they are *synergistic!* Through these needs, the sales manager has the opportunity to influence, in varying degrees, the salesman's work place (his territory), his standing in the opinion of his co-workers, his status at home; and in a tangential way, may partly assuage the yearning for personal security which in its larger framework, we have called "sanctuary."

Remembering that the opportunity to influence is also the power to motivate, let us explore the motivational possibilities of this basic human need for *place*.

Manager's Opportunities for Motivation

The sales manager's first opportunity lies in the area of providing each salesman with a work place of his own; that is, his *territory*. If the manager is himself governed by integrity and insight, he can powerfully motivate his sales force by giving each salesman a sales territory with fixed boundaries, in which the sales potential is his, exclusively.

Upon first thought, the typical sales manager will respond: "Sure, but every company does that nowadays!"

But every company doesn't do it! As a matter of fact, comparatively few companies really stick to this simple, honest policy in allocating sales territories.

The methods by which managements "chisel" their own salesmen are so numerous as to defy listing. And often, those devices which they believe to be the most cunningly ingenious are really the most transparent and naive. Here are three commonplace examples!

The so-called "house accounts", often the largest volume accounts in the territory, "reserved" (!) for handling by the president, vice president, or sales manager, in order to save paying the commission or bonus properly due to the territory salesman—or allotted to the president's worthless brother, nephew, cousin, brother-in-law, etc., so that the relative's indigency shall not become outright mendicity.

A common variation of the house-accounts racket is that of the central buying office, which exists in the case of chain and syndicate stores which buy at one central point and ship the goods into warehouses, or individual stores, in many other territories.

Then, there are "personal accounts"—a selected list of customers buying substantial volume, located in a regular salesman's territory, and distinguished from the usual run-of-the-mill accounts by the fact that they were previously handled by a salesman who has now been promoted to sales manager, for example, or moved to another territory. The core of that peculiarity which justifies this special classification is this: *No one but the former salesman can hold the business!*

Only in a few rare cases are these exceptional situations warranted, either ethically, or by the facts of the case. Where they are, adequate remedies can be provided in behalf of the territory salesman so as to offset his potential reduction of opportunity. Further, if the regular territory salesman is deprived of all income from such reserved accounts, he should not be required to invest any time or spend any effort in selling or servicing this business! In other words, if he *sows,* he must be allowed to *reap!* And if he is not to *reap,* he must not be asked to *sow!*

But it may be asked: "Why introduce these negatives into a discussion of the art of positive motivation?"

ANSWER: Of what use to a sales manager is his finely whetted skill for motivating his men, if there is in-built, by company policy and long-term practice, insidious negative motivations which continually act to counterbalance and destroy important segments of his positive motivating attempts?

In other words, the sales manager cannot apply his plus-motivations in a vacuum of his own creation; he must introduce them into the framework of the total motivation picture, knowing that in practice, the negatives must be subtracted from the positives to determine the net motivational power at work.

Let us return to the more constructive aspects of the salesman's territory as an opportunity for motivation.

Ideally, this should be a territory in which the potential has been evaluated, and the task (in terms of call-load and travel-load) measured—*and the two factors matched!* In other words, there should be, in the territory, sufficient realizable potential to pay the man properly for the time and effort required efficiently to cover the area and to get the business therein. That task should not be greater than the reasonable capacity of a competent man.

This balanced territory should then be allocated to one salesman, as his exclusive responsibility and opportunity.

Under these conditions, the salesman has a fair sales opportunity, a reasonable and "do-able" task, an undisturbed chance to do his best. Pride, possessiveness, the prospect of good earnings, the sense of security that comes from having his own work place—all these powerful emotional drives *go to work for the sales manager*. This is a prime example of what we mean by motivation.

In another aspect of the word "place", the salesman's standing in the opinion of his fellow workers, the manager has a further opportunity to exercise his skill as a motivator. If he praises in public, but criticizes in private, he contributes to the good opinion of the salesman's associates.

A wiry Scotsman, down in Pennsylvania, division manager of a successful mutual funds sales operation says: "I always make a public event of a big sale!" His shrewd policy adds to the esteem in which the sales force at large holds the successful producers.

Every sales contest bulletin that praises the effort or results of any salesman, not only pleases that particular individual, but also elevates him in the esteem of his fellow workers. Even the story of a salesman who LOST A BIG SALE, but went down battling to the last, will raise that man in the eyes of his comrades who have fought similar battles, perhaps with different results.

And how can the sales manager help his salesman to improve his status within his own family? In many ways, by remembering that the same facts which raise a man in the esteem of his fellows, are useful for a similar purpose at home. The manager should also keep in mind that the best status-raiser within the family circle is a bigger pay check or, a sizeable bonus.

But, on the home front, physical evidence of achievement is valuable, too; it backs up the boasting which is often the unshrewd salesman's only weapon in holding his ground with the wife and kids. And since many of us have the un-happy habit of boasting the most when we are least secure, a contest winner's cup, a gold watch for being a top-closer, a check for twenty bucks as the runner-up—these are valuable implements both of defense and attack, useful physical evidence to help us subdue those who make up our severest critics, the folks at home.

The ribbon of the Legion of Honor, the Distinguished Service Medal, the decoration of the Purple Heart, the gold-plated lapel pin of the winning sales team—each, in its own way, is valuable to the individual in raising his opinion of himself. But every award has a greater value, that which comes from exhibiting it to others, not the least of whom are the "others" near and dear to us within our own family circle.

6. PERSONAL ACCOMPLISHMENT

Men hunger for the thrill of personal achievement. They want to be part of a successful team, too, itself a definite need which will be discussed later. But the hunger to be on the winning team is a group quality, an aspect of "belonging", an urge toward "togetherness", while the yearning for individual accomplishment is strictly a self-polarized, ego-centered reaching up. The need for strictly personal fruits of action is more intense in some men than in others, depending mainly upon the basic type of the individual, but deriving also from a prior sense of deprivation and insecurity; and like all other drives, the more urgent this yearning, the more powerful it becomes as a means of motivation.

Perhaps this craving to demonstrate individual personal ability can best be described by an example of the deterioration of morale and drive which often occurs in a sales force where the set-up, for one reason or another, makes the targeting of individual effort impossible. This repeatedly occurs, for example, in metropolitan city sales groups operating in "pool" territories, where group quotas are set up, group volume reports are made to the men, group contest results are posted on the bulletin board, and group bonuses are distributed on a per capita plan, rather than on the basis of each individual's contribution to the total result. On the evidence of wide experience, such set-ups have a stifling effect upon individual initiative. Lacking a personal target, in the form of a quota, deprived of regular reports showing individual progress, being unable to focus the powerful emotions of pride and possessiveness upon resulting volume, and unable even to pinpoint their private feeling of excellence upon the final consummation of their efforts, the bonus check—the motivating power of that personal sense of attainment is lost, lost to the salesmen, and more important to our present discussion, *lost to the sales manager!*

(This is a good place to point up a truth often overlooked. Many of those normal, natural, and intrinsic opportunities for managerial motivation, which are literally "built into" human beings, can be largely nullified by a type of sales organization structure that unwittingly seals off the emotions in an hermetically sealed container, such as the group territory set-up just described. The difficulties are intensified, from the standpoint of the sales manager's freedom to motivate, if, for example, the sales force makes its sales to jobbers and yet has, as a part of their duties, the need to resell to retailers and to help them to merchandise the goods out of the store into the hands of the eventual buyer-user. In such a case, the linkage between the salesmen's efforts and sales volume is loose and untraceable, for indeed, it is almost always hopeless to attempt to trace the retailer's purchases back to his jobber. That comment, however, by implication, does not deny that such a "two-way" selling situation involves many real problems both of organization structure and sales force operation. Our plea is this: When the sales organization is first set up, or when it is revamped, do not blindly and unthinkingly block the possibility of motivating the salesmen by devising a structure that hamstrings the future sales manager in his operations! Such defects usually result from a lack of knowing what constitutes good sales organization structure, or a failure to recognize that, when it comes to the operating stage, the greatest untapped source of sales horsepower lies in the emotional response-mechanisms of the human beings comprising the sales force!)

7. PERSONAL RECOGNITION

Elbert Hubbard, early twentieth century business writer and everyday philosopher, revealed his insight into the human heart when he wrote: "We can deal with our sorrows alone and in silence, *but it takes two to be glad!*" It takes two to be proud, too, and two to celebrate a victory, using the word "two" to mean those beside ourselves whose esteem, affection, and approbation are important to us, important for many reasons; but for one, because their joy in our accomplishments, our triumphs, reflected back upon the screen of our own pride, helps us to double the enjoyment of our victories.

This seemingly contradictory pattern of emotional response which arises from accomplishment needs to be understood, down to its very roots, by the sales manager. Why? Because, generally, we assume, without thinking very much about it, that the human being needs another when in trouble. In fact, the typical man or woman has a much greater need for the emotional response of others when he has a superior accomplishment, or a triumph to enjoy.

Hence, the need for personal recognition!

History reveals that the wise leader in any field—military, political, religious, sports, or business—gradually develops a comprehensive apparatus of recognition, providing various forms of acknowledgment for a wide variety of accomplishments, the whole being differentiated into functions and levels, in order to make available an appropriate award or gesture for almost every conceivable type of achievement. Napoleon, for example, had his famed Legion of Honor; the English Kings, their Order of the Garter; and the Pope, as head of the Roman Catholic Church, has his Order of St. Gregory the Great, the Order of the Holy Sepulchre.

Sales managers have an almost endless array of baubles, charged with legitimate auras of honor and given for various types of accomplishments—the President's Cup, the Founder's Cup, the Quota Buster's Prize; assortments of buttons, badges, ribbons, plaques; plus hats, overcoats, raincoats, one- and two-pants suits; and merchandise awards galore!

We can sit in the seat of the scorner and describe as "corny" these everyday symbols of selling success. But "corny" or not, they have been established in response to a deep-rooted need of the human being—the need to enjoy the fruits of his labors in terms other than monetary rewards.

Presented at an appropriate moment, with suitable staging and fanfare, these physical symbols of accomplishment and esteem give a file his "little day in the sun!" And long, long after the applause has died away and the brilliant arc lights of his "great moment" have grown cold, the memory of "the day" will still pull tight the cord of his courage and will still whisper, perhaps into an aging ear, the hopeful reminder: *"You can do it again!"*

In the previous pages dealing with the several aspects of personal "place", much has already been said about *recognition*. For it is not enough to *give* a man place. That place must be *conspicuously recognized* by management and its secure existence must be continually *reaffirmed*, both by the acts of the manager, and the physical symbols of recognition. For recognition is not confined to its braid and badges, its mere physical accoutrements. It may be a word of unexpected praise, privately or publicly spoken; a spontaneous pat on the back; a "you're-my-kind-of-a-boy" tone in the boss's voice when he says, "Hello, Tom"; a dime-store greeting card on his or his wife's birthday; an invitation to lunch with the boss on each anniversary of the date he was first employed—all these little acts are the instrumentalities of managerial recognition. For, in its simplest form, recognition is *first*, an awareness that the individual exists as part of the group; *second*, it is evidence of managerial esteem; and only in its most "physical" manifestation, are the formal symbols of recognition required.

8. Participation in Group Accomplishment

The sales manager will find, in almost every man, a desire to "belong to the group." Even the occasional individual who seems to be a hold-out or "lone wolf" often turns out to be merely an inept mixer, one who has not yet been able to lay his hands on the key that admits him into the hearts of his comrades.

There are many reasons for the individual salesman's wish to join the group. For example, being one of the team offers the man, especially the new man, a kind of undefined *security*, particularly *job* security. It requires no more than shrewd native instinct for a man to reason: "If I am a member of the group and act generally in accordance with the way the others act, I am less likely to be fired. They can't very well dismiss the whole force; therefore, my uniformity with the group is a kind of protective coloration which preserves my job tenure!"

Membership in "the gang" also removes the possible stigma of being called "exclusive", or "superior" by his associates, and eliminates the man from the possible suspicion of being "teacher's pet", or "a company man." It makes him an official member of "the grapevine", and cuts him in on the open wire of the salesmen's scuttlebutt, that *potpourri* of fact, rumor, gossip, personal "dirt", and just plain fiction, which more or less harmlessly murmurs its way as an undercurrent in almost every organization.

However, WHY the man wishes to participate in group accomplishment does not matter too much. It is his *desire,* particularly his negative desire not to be "included out"—to use Sam Goldwyn's classic phrase—which is important to the manager who seeks to motivate.

We recall, do we not, that the intrinsic opportunity in managerial motivation lies in deep-seated *human needs;* in this case, the need for being part of the group. That *need,* however, as it becomes stronger, turns into *desire* which, as it rises in intensity, can be called a *thirst,* a *craving,* an *eagerness,* a *passion,* even a *necessity.* To use the phraseology of the physicist, the *need* is the *potential,* the latency; while the *desire* is the *activity,* the *manifestation.* The *need* is the throbbing motor of the high-powered car, ready and waiting to be put in gear; the *desire* is the transmission which channels the waiting horsepower into the active motion of the wheels that speed the car around the oval at 150 miles per hour!

The pertinent question now becomes: How can the sales manager use as a motivating force this desire to participate in group accomplishment?

Believe it or not! He can use it in two directions—*positively* and *negatively!*

In the case of comparatively new men, for example, (for it is with new men that this desire is most powerfully contained), he can tacitly assume in his relations involving the man and the group, that the individual is already accepted by his comrades. He can allow him to take "pot luck" in a sales contest, for instance, although he may know that the salesman can't possibly make the winner's column. He can take pains to avoid referring to him separately, or in any manner or mood different from that in which he deals with the rest of the group.

On the negative side, the sales manager has ways of motivation so powerful that they may easily become *brutal.* He can isolate the newcomer in a special class, refer to him as a novice, a beginner, an outsider, a "youngster who hasn't gotten his feet wet", as one who has not yet "won his spurs"; and by an endless array of similar characterizations, make it clear that he has not yet been initiated into the mysteries of the brotherhood. These managerial tactics, if not carried to such an extreme as to arouse the sympathy of his fellows, could provide a most potent spur to a new man's effort. A tough-fibred, ambitious salesman would be challenged and compulsively driven to a peak of exertion. A weaker man, however, could just as readily be discouraged, crushed, and rendered useless under the same handling.

In other words, this particular motivation key must be touched only lightly, and then, only by the practiced hand of experience. Like every managerial technique, it must be applied with judgment, with that rare discernment which recognizes the subtle differences in men's emotional natures and reactions, a discrimination that traces back not only to a storehouse of rich experience, but some of whose roots are to be found in the compassionate recesses of the human heart.

A wise father, richly endowed with wisdom distilled from life's experiences, was counselling his son on techniques for dealing with the opposite sex. "I can sum it up in three words, Son—tough but tender!" Sales managers will please copy!

9. A Goal—and a Road Map

Salesmen, generally, have an intense desire to know WHERE they are going and HOW they are going to get there. This means that:

1. The manager must establish a clearly defined GOAL.

2. He must provide his group with a ROAD MAP.

These necessities automatically impose a beneficial discipline upon the sales manager who, if he is himself a promoted salesman as most managers are, may not be naturally as systematic and analytical as a leader ought to be.

In other words, his desire to motivate his men will compel him to think his way through his program and arrive at a goal sufficiently specific to meet the salesmen's desire for an official target, or destination. In the process of arriving at that goal, the sales executive will be compelled to work out at least a rudimentary method of operation, along with a time schedule; and this he can easily formalize into a map of the itinerary which will serve to meet the salesmen's inborn desire to see the route ahead.

There are many effectual sales managers whose technique, viewed from the standpoint of an outsider, seems to be that of "flying by the seat of my pants"; in short, managing in an opportunistic manner by the *"feel"* of the situation. This system of "management-by-hunch" might be good enough, if the manager's objective were to do the work himself, instead of getting it done by others.

But in an organization, the salesmen who carry the burden of getting the results which their manager envisions, do not possess his vision, nor his experience, and certainly not his confidence in his own intuitive powers; hence, their deep-rooted yearning for a goal and a road map still remains to be satisfied. And, of course, this unfulfilled need is not only the manager's obligation, but also his opportunity to motivate.

England's Field Marshall Montgomery rated these particular motivating opportunities very highly, so highly in fact, that he insisted not only that every man in his Eighth British Army, know WHERE the army was headed, and HOW it was proposed that they were to get there, but WHY the movement was undertaken, WHY it was *timed* as it was, and *why* the particular *battle strategy* had been chosen.

It can be imagined what a communications burden was placed upon his staff in carrying such information to each man in the ranks; and what a challenge this revolutionary philosophy must have been to the traditional concept of close-mouthed secrecy about future battle plans. But Montgomery's philosophy was carried out because he thought it worth in results whatever it cost in practice.

Like Montgomery's men, salesmen need to know their group destination far enough in advance to think about it, to weigh and measure the task, the time, the means, and to get accustomed to the whole pattern of the project. In fact, a man never really settles down to his task until his objective is clear.

The runner wants to know whether he is running a 30-yard dash or a five-mile grind. Why? Because he plans a sprint differently from a marathon, motivates himself differently, sets his whole mental and physical musculature into different patterns to meet the varying needs of the task ahead.

A salesman has no less need for similar knowledge and similar preparation. His plans, small and inconsequential as they may seem to his manager, must nevertheless be made. His boilers must be fired, his fuel tanks filled. And he must adjust his thinking to whatever is new and novel and different in the current project. All this requires time.

Psychologically, this setting up of an objective forces the salesmen to accept part of the responsibility for reaching it; hence, the mere establishment of goals becomes a helpful device for management use, and aids the salesmen better to understand their jobs.

You will recall the remark of Willy Loman's boy (in the play, *Death of a Salesman,* by Arthur Miller): "Dad is never so happy as when he is looking forward to something."

It is the manager's job to provide that goal and to picturize it in the salesmen's minds. Once that craving for an objective has been satisfied, the insatiable appetite of the human being demands, as we have previously pointed out, a second bit of reassurance in the form of a road map.

To feed these two hungers is to motivate salesmen in the right direction; to *fail* to satisfy these needs is automatically motivating them in a negative way, for the effects of a lack of objective can be devastating—vacillation, uncertainty, hesitation, reluctance to take that important first step which begins the journey, lack of confidence in the leader, unexpressed and haunting doubts of his competence, fear that even he may not be sure of his destination.

Sounds like a big price to pay for a single sin of omission, but to paraphrase and expand upon Michelangelo's remark on perfection: "*Morale* is made up of a long list of trifles; but when it comes to *results,* morale itself is no trifle!"

10. Excitement

Salesmen, to reach their peak of performance, need to be kept EXCITED! Therefore, the manager must generate a state of excitement which will satisfy this need.

How is it done? By keeping sales contests and competitions going regularly, by awarding "early starter" prizes for those who get into production quickly, by filling contest bulletins with exciting accounts of the neck-and-neck race in the current campaign. Further, the manager will pit one region, or one division, against another. He will encourage the salesmen in each district office to make a few side bets among themselves, as to the results in their local contest. He may even privately and tacitly encourage the local district manager to permit the two or three top men in the district office to engage in some rather heated personal interchanges as the contest warms up. All these carefully planned devices add to the air of dramatic conflict and tension which pervades the sales staff as the contagious aspect of the "excitement principle" begins to infect the whole group.

One life insurance general agent builds up and maintains excitement by long-distance telephone calls to each of his men, about midnight on Saturday, or around 8 o'clock on Sunday morning. A slight variation is to write each of the men a special delivery letter containing an explicit personal suggestion for getting some additional business, timing this to arrive—like the phone calls—late in the evening, or early on Sunday morning.

An adroit sales manager builds up excitement in an almost endless number of ways: by posting the "score" promptly after the sales are made; by arousing the competitive spirit between divisions, districts, teams, and even between individuals; by making an exciting "event" out of every out-of-the-ordinary accomplishment—a big order, a victory over tough competition, a sale of a seldom-sold line or item, the closing of a sale to a prospect who has resisted the salesman's efforts for many years, a big order sold on the first call, or an order secured only after a long series of attempts, the closing of an account that even the sales manager was unable to sell. He conveys to his whole group an almost nervous sense of urgency, of important matters pending, of great things just beyond the veil of tomorrow.

He takes the monotony out of the inevitably repetitive tasks of his men; he injects them with a sense of purpose, worthwhile, meaningful purpose. The first day of the week is no longer "Blue Monday"; it is the dawning of a period of pulse-raising sales battles and pocketbook-lining victories over the inertia and resistance of buyers. Under the manager's magic touch, every hour is newly glinted with the golden glow of the morning sun, for his is the magic wand that starts the once-plodding hands of the corner clock spinning at breath-taking speed, so that the day does not seem long enough to contain the efforts the men wish to make.

Sounds like hyperbole, doesn't it? But it isn't; it is the result of the application of one of the great gifts of leadership—the capacity to get excited about what to others seems a humdrum job and successfully to communicate that excitement to other men! Observing the dreary activities of the sales force that must work without this priceless fire of personal leadership, we are tempted to say that *it is the most important skill which the sales manager can possess!*

Of the many keys which open the organ-valves to human action, these ten are among the most useful and perhaps also, among *the most easily used.* But they do not constitute *all* the keys. Nor do the simpler melodies we have suggested and exampled comprise the sum-total of the "tunes" which the practiced hand of the professional will be able to play on this subtle and sensitive instrument— the human being.

This matter of the virtuosity of the instrument brings us logically to a very important consideration—*the manager's need for virtuosity in fingering the keyboard of the motivation console.* To express the thought in different words: It is important that the sales manager know how to change his pace, to alter his techniques of management from time to time without abandoning his basic tenets.

For "the law of diminishing returns" in economics has its almost exact counterpart in the processes of human thinking. The brain has the habit of rejecting a repetitive thought, an "old" thought, a previously accepted mental impulse, as being of no use, since it only duplicates what is already in the storehouse of impressions.

Just as a wife, for example, complains about her husband telling "the same old jokes", and ceases even to listen to them time after time, so also do salesmen tend to tire of the same techniques of motivation, if these be used too openly. Not that the men on the sales force, generally, are consciously aware of the manager's actions in terms of formal methods or techniques; but they have a sort of instinctive knowing, a faint subconscious awareness of the repetitiousness of that of which they have been the object. Eventually, if the sales manager's techniques are too obvious and too often repeated in the same framework, his men acquire a certain shrewdness in anticipating his "next move". In some instances, advance recognition of what is about to happen will evoke from his sales group no more than a knowing smile of tolerance; but there is always the danger that the brain will suddenly invoke the law of diminishing interest which, stated simply, means that the manager's old, familiar motivational manipulations are no longer getting across. They have lost their "bite!"

The foresighted sales manager avoids this unfortunate loss of control in several ways:

1. He applies his motivational tactics, not with a heavy hand, but with a light and delicate touch. He avoids the crude and the obvious.

2. He practices his motivation, as far as possible, in a natural setting, covering his efforts skillfully with the screen of the obvious, the logical, the expected. He focuses these efforts within the framework of the salesmen's interests because in such a milieu, they are seldom examined, much less questioned.

3. He changes his methods of presentation and application from time to time, always taking his wine from the same old cask, but pouring it, as it were, into new and more interesting bottles, from year to year.

Political and military leaders are compelled to learn early in life the art of concealing their methods of motivation and manipulation. The fate of a political party, sometimes of a nation, hangs upon the ability of the head of the state thus to conceal his techniques. For it is the common practice, in government, for the opposition to attack the *methods* to be used, when they dare not challenge the good ends which are sought. The moral is: *Keep the methods out of obvious view until the job is done!*

In the advertising agency business, we learned never to permit the client to view the artist in the process of making a rough layout. In every art, including that of practical management, there is a mid-point in the process of doing the job where only the practiced vision of the creator can foresee the order and beauty that soon will emerge from the disorder seemingly apparent. To watch the hand of the artist, laying on the litho-crayon in what will eventually be a dynamic, attention-attracting advertisement, only frightens and sometimes almost nauseates the uninitiated. Method is for the technician; only its *results* need be known to those whom the skilled technique benefits the most!

This sounds very Machiavellian, very "subliminal", almost subversive, does it not?

But it is nothing more than wise advice on how to practice expertly what the sales manager *must* practice if he is really to *be* skillful, or even merely to be *regarded* as skillful, by his superiors or his associates.

For the average man must be taught, guided, motivated, and directed into the right channels by other men who have acquired the ripe skills of leadership; *otherwise, only a few men will succeed either in their jobs or in their lives!*

And it is the unhappy truth that they must be thus guided by a hand so compassionate and so skilled *that they are not aware of the guidance!* Were it otherwise, even skilled leadership would often fail, for the false pride, the rebellious spirit of man, that "imp of the perverse", as Poe called it, which so often consciously activates and controls us, would refuse the leader's hand and direct us instead, into what wisdom so readily recognizes as the blind back alleys of failure and despair.

In other words, to succeed, men must have leaders—wise, capable, skillful leaders. And they must have executives who conceal their skills and lead without seeming to do so. Otherwise, the "bucking broncos" behind them will have none of it!

We have invested several precious pages touching upon the subtleties of skilled leadership. These subtleties are required solely because of the primitive, and only slightly-concealed "rawness" of the led. In short, waste no sighs upon those who are motivated. Without such inspiration and guidance, without the sublime patience and subtle skills of those who lead—men, generally, would be far behind that present point which with the help of leadership, they have attained; but which most of them believe they have achieved through intrinsic merit and brilliant application of their own talents.

CHAPTER X

Criticism That Does Not Crush

W hen Austin Igleheart was the operating executive at General Foods Sales Company, his employees repeatedly said that they preferred a "bawling out" from him to a word of praise from some other executive.

This was a unique tribute to the great skill with which he handled his human relations. And yet Austin Igleheart, as we know him, is not a professional "do-gooder", not a reformer, but a practical businessman of considerable wealth, employing his great talents to develop the sales volume of his Company. Nevertheless, of all the executives we have known, he has the keenest insight into the human heart; and he has a most practical way of using that insight to build men so as to get improved results for them and, in turn, for the company.

However, even at General Foods, where human relations had been a subject of careful planning and development over a long period of years, now and then —as in any organization—it was necessary for the executive in charge of manpower to criticize and correct some of the men on his staff. Igleheart did not make these criticisms in any halfway manner. Neither was his approach delicate or tentative. It was built, we believe, upon two foundations—his keen understanding of men and his deeply-rooted sense of fair play.

He had the gift of criticizing and correcting without leaving scars on the man's emotional nature. He could discuss what was wrong with an executive and his work without giving him an inferiority complex that persisted for months—or years! With his kind of criticism, Igleheart could lift a man up, while another manager might have been knocking him down; and he could send him away in a constructive state of mind, thankful to his stars for having had the privilege of the critical interview.

All of this is no small accomplishment; and a manager must possess rare gifts to secure such results.

THE EXPERT'S TECHNIQUES

What are the tactics, the techniques which are applied by men of great skill so that their criticism does not crush? What do they do that other men, less competent, fail to do? What mistakes do they carefully avoid which lesser managers often commit?

Let's discuss eight of the more important aspects of the fine art of criticism and correction.

1. CRITICIZE IN PRIVATE—NOT IN PUBLIC

Every experienced manager knows the first principle—if you must criticize, do so in private, *never in public*. The practical application of this humane precaution has two advantages, one benefiting the salesman, the other protecting the manager.

For the salesman, privacy "saves his face", avoids emotional trauma, and prevents loss of self-respect.

For the manager, privacy in administering criticism has a value seldom recognized—it prevents a possible loss of managerial stature and protects and maintains the esteem in which he is held by his staff.

For example, have you ever listened in when another man was being "bawled out"? Let us say you agree that the call-down was needed. In the beginning, you were in sympathy with the boss, but as he poured vitriol on the victim's head, did you not feel your sympathies were changing in favor of the man under fire? Strangely, the shift did not seem to originate within your own mind—it seemed as if it were being forced upon you by some unknown outside source, and, as the pressure increased, you experienced a seeming inability to restrain your steady change of "sides". You ended up saying: "Well, Joe sure deserved a 'hiding'; but when the boss got started, he poured it on too thick!"

As the manager's rebuke heightened in intensity, did you not begin emotionally to identify yourself more and more with the offender? Before long, the "weight" of your emotional reaction overbalanced your original logical opinion, and bingo!—the manager lost a protagonist.

A Safe Code of Conduct

> No man shall ever become less in his own eyes, in the eyes of his associates, or in the eyes of his family, because of anything I have ever said to him in private or in public.

If the sales manager sets up this objective as part of his creed, there is not much danger that the emotional nature of any of his salesmen will be seriously injured, nor is it likely that the manager's own stature will shrink. The consideration he has shown to others will earn similar consideration for himself.

2. Don't Question a Man's Motives or His Character

One of the broad concepts which favorably distinguish the English politician from many of those we are familiar with in the United States, lies in the fact that the more seasoned British statesmen seldom resort to public denunciation of an individual. Read the speeches of Winston Churchill, even in the days of his first service in the House of Commons, and you will find it difficult to discover a single situation in which he condemns a man as a *person*. He may condemn a man's *acts*, his *objectives*, his *actions;* but seldom, if ever, does he indulge in personal condemnation of the motives or the character of an individual. Borrowing liberally from George Bernard Shaw, the former Prime Minster once said: "I will go all out against what the man stands for, or the action he proposes, but I will not go all out against the man."

Winston Churchill has maintained his stature as a statesman over the years, notwithstanding the differences in party point of view and in spite of the fact that he himself has jumped the fence and changed parties at least once. Can this success be traced to the fact that he has taken wise and humane precautions not to bruise the inner psyche of any man, that he has taken care not to refer to anyone as a "crook", "thief", or "low-motived scoundrel?" And yet, none of us would say that he has failed to register his clear disapproval in pungent and unforgettable prose, whenever he thought the occasion appropriate.

What the Manager Can Learn from British Politicians

A sales manager can learn a great deal from this civilized trait of British politicians, typified by Mr. Churchill.

He can learn, for example, never to strike at the inner core of what a man essentially *is*, even though he may make harsh criticisms of what the man stands for, of his objectives, and of his methods of attaining them.

He can learn never to indulge in uncontrollable and angry name-calling which, as one of the oldest and most primitive forms of registering disapproval, is as much the mark of the cave man as is the stone axe.

Name-calling usually strikes at a man's personal attributes and qualities and the resulting psychic shocks often leave scars that time never succeeds in erasing. For example, there was a New York sales manager who called one of his men "coward". That salesman confessed to us *fourteen years later* that the name had fastened itself into his subconscious mind and re-haunted him every time he failed to make a sale. Eventually it crushed him; he never recovered from it!

Sales managers seldom see the long-term results of their management mistakes, but if this manager could have that privilege, he would stand aghast at the extent of his own power, power to build up or to destroy—MEN!

3. GET ALL THE FACTS BEFORE YOU "BLOW YOUR TOP"

Lives there a sales manager in all this world who has not gone home more than one night kicking himself for having popped off with an unconsidered criticism, the result of his failure first to get acquainted with *all* the pertinent facts? Until the manager has made a thorough investigation, it is not safe for him to assume that he knows all of the circumstances in a given case, no matter how strongly he may feel it ought to be corrected. The manager who "blows his top" without being adequately informed invites trouble. He himself lays the foundation upon which his employee can build a claim of unfairness.

"Bill, damn it all, the last thing you and I agreed on was that you would call on the James Metals Company if you didn't do anything else on this trip!"

"But boss, Mr. James was away from the office!"

"I know, Bill, but you are not supposed to handle these situations like a high school girl. You've been in this business eight years and you ought to know what to do in a case like that. Dig around, find out where he is. Get to him one way or another. This is important!"

A little later, Mr. Sales Manager learns that Mr. James was away at his mother's funeral. He is aware *now* that it would have been bad taste for his salesman to have tried to find the prospect, and that to have succeeded would have caused more harm than good.

As a result of the sales manager's failure to get the facts, who looks like the donkey?

In similar situations, every sales manager should take the time to get the facts. Usually, if he keeps calm and doesn't build up too many emotional barriers, he can get the truth directly from the salesman.

Thus equipped, he can act with fairness; otherwise, he may turn out to be more guilty of offense than the man he set out to rebuke.

4. Let the Salesman State His Side of the Case

It is the custom in this country to consider a man innocent until he is proven guilty. When the sales manager has need to indict one of his salesmen, let him prepare the bill of charges as completely as he wishes. When the case for the "prosecution" is in, the sales manager must not "tag" the man guilty until the latter has spoken in his own defense.

Take care not to frustrate the man under fire by refusing to hear his side of the case; for if you do, he will charge you, in his heart, if not openly, with being closed-minded, unjust, unfair. And the sales manager's office is no place for star-chamber proceedings.

Emotional Criticism Obscures the Facts

If the sales manager has raised the emotional level of the interview to a high pitch, he can count on the salesman to be even more agitated than he otherwise would have been. It is not to be expected that complete judicial impartiality will prevail. If there was fire in the indictment, there will be heat in the defense— for emotionality *breeds* emotionality. The salesman is bound to bring forth alibis, to rationalize his failure or his error by a process which, in the light of logic, may seem entirely ludicrous in its far-fetched conclusions. But this is insufficient cause to deprive a man of his innings, or of his right to state his case in his own way.

The sales manager must needs recognize that, in most garbled situations, only the salesman knows the whole story of what actually transpired—and even *he* may not know all the facts, or possess sufficient emotional objectivity or intellectual honesty to present them in a frank, uncolored fashion.

To sum up, for two reasons it is wise for the sales manager to make a thorough investigation in advance:

1. To anticipate with some accuracy what kind of case the salesman is likely to make for himself.
2. To avoid "blowing his top" and then suffer the consequences for having reached his conclusions on the basis of inadequate information.

5. Don't Overplay Your Hand

In all of us there is a bit of the stern disciplinarian typified by the old-time schoolmaster, knuckle-rapper in hand, on the alert to catch the first boy guilty of breaking the rules.

In other words, the opportunity to dress down an errant pupil is a temptation few men can resist. The act of criticizing often acts to enlarge the human ego and sometimes gives the criticizer a false feeling of superiority over the one being criticized. Coincident with these results is a tendency to overdo the faultfinding once it has gotten started, to hit harder than is necessary, and to enlarge the fault and make it greater and more important than it really it.

The mature sales manager will recall, somewhat ruefully, that upon certain occasions in his experience his critical energy seemed to feed upon its own fury, until the first gentle swirling of the critical waters became a fast-spinning eddy; and this, before he knew it, turned into a towering and destructive waterspout beyond his power to control.

Such an outburst may occur when the manager is not well, or when he is hard-pressed with work, or when his nervous energy has been overdrawn. Sometimes he loses his temper because he has previously withheld the fire of his criticism upon a succession of occasions when he strongly wished to uncoil the lash of his rebuke. Then comes a day when the salesman makes only a minor mistake; but minor or not, it "triggers" the pent-up emotions of his boss who unleashes a hailstorm of criticism, all out of proportion to the error.

Immediately, the executive loses his managerial stature; he himself becomes the proper subject for reproof; and certainly, under these circumstances, no manager can expect his criticism to be respected. Therefore, a wise manager takes percautions not to allow a salesman's faults to remain undiscussed, to pile up and be repeated, thus avoiding their building up a dangerous head of steam which may explode the safety valve. He carefully plans to make "the punishment fit the crime"; and he is especially careful to weigh up the good that may be accomplished by fair criticism against the emotional damage that might be inflicted by going too far. Between these two opposites is a point of balance which represents the maximum of good and the minimum of negative reaction. This is the target he aims for in his counselling interviews with his salesmen.

6. PRESENT THE PLUSSES AHEAD OF THE NEGATIVES

Seldom do we find a salesman who is such a paragon of perfection that he cannot be legitimately criticized and corrected on some points. But even the salesman who has much that needs correction, certainly has done many good things and exhibited many plus qualities which have contributed to his remaining on the payroll and doing the job he has so far accomplished.

At the beginning of a criticism session, it is very wise to review, in a pleasant way, some of the bigger accomplishments of the man; to recall difficulties he has overcome, the hard work he has done, and the cranky customers he has successfully dealt with. The manager need not review a long list, merely one or two favorable points before he unlimbers the big guns of his criticism.

This tactic of pouring oil on the soon-to-be-troubled waters has many advantages. It shows that the boss is aware of the good things the salesman has done. It gives the man a feeling of satisfaction and security which will help him live through the dark moments to come, when the criticism really gets rough.

This procedure helps the salesman to realize that he is not the recipient of a wholesale, "broad-spectrum" blast of undiscriminating criticism, but the subject of a selective examination and re-orientation of certain attitudes and aspects of his work.

I can recall an occasion early in my business life. I was on the "hot seat" when I felt my quick temper rising. But the kindly gentleman who was my boss settled me back in my chair to listen, simply by saying: "Remember, my boy, we don't spend any of our time cutting the specks out of *rotten* apples. If you weren't a good apple generally, I wouldn't be talking with you!"

In other words, as soon as he assured me that I was not being cast into the rotten apple barrel, I found the courage to go through the surgery of cutting out the bad specks!

The sales manager can help the man endure the surgery of excising his faults, by serving him first a platter of praise!

7. Don't Hand the Accused a Ready-Made Alibi

There are not many successful sales managers who really enjoy giving one of their men "hell". Many a manager—believe it or not!—reviews the problem repeatedly, and finally takes action only after he has screwed up his will to the point where he is intellectually and emotionally capable of giving his salesman the critical going-over he needs. In the overly-compassionate manager, there is often a tendency to soften the blow by the unwise act of tossing in some possible alibis.

"I don't know what happened, Bill—perhaps you were tired, or you didn't feel well, or you were worrying about the wife or kids. Whatever it was, this sure turned out to be a bad mess!"

If the salesman under fire is only partially a smart operator, he will immediately pick up one or more of these suggested alibis (which his manager has approved) and enlarge them to suit his purpose. In a jam, he may not even bother to pick one that is true. He merely chooses an excuse his manager has given him and which, instinctively, he believes will serve his present need.

The sales manager should compel the salesman to originate his own reasons for his failure or his ineptitude; let him dig into his own thinking for his answers and his alibis. Is there any point in making the chore easier for the salesman by giving him a ready-made check-list? State your complaint—let him defend himself! The sales manager cannot successfully be the spokesman for both prosecution and defense.

8. Complete Your Job Before You Quit

Almost every sales manager will recall a situation where contentious words were spoken, and the discussion degenerated rapidly into a cat and dog fight.

Yes, a plain, low-down wrangle! Neither side accomplished anything; neither admitted any errors. Nothing was changed, except that the mutual exhibition of bad blood made the future relationship potentially worse. This meant continued irritation and conflict, which is much more harmful than handling the issue promptly and cleanly and disposing of it at one sitting.

The sales manager should plan his criticism interview so that sufficient time is available to state the indictment, to hear the defense, and to work out a mutual plan of corrective action, thus disposing of the matter finally.

Get Agreement on Action-Objective and Face the Future

When the sales manager is about to conclude, he clinches the fact that the argument is finished and the course of action settled: "Now, Bill, do you understand the modifications I want you to make in your approach?"

When Bill agrees, the manager again: "Have I made clear the direction I want you to go and the things I want you to try to accomplish beginning tomorrow morning?"

After the manager secures acquiescence, he makes the final "cut-off". "You know I'll not nag you about this or bring it up in the future unless I am compelled to do so. You also know that I will expect you not to neglect the steps we agreed upon as the right course of action. I've stated my point of view plainly; I hope you have done the same. Some of your own ideas have been incorporated in the new plan. I'm sure it will succeed if we both head for the same destination. I'm not going to waste any time looking backward, because, like Lot's wife, I might turn to a pillar of salt. My eyes are on the future—that's the only direction we can go to make money."

EVALUATION OF "CRITICISM SESSION"

Held with __Elmer Meikeljohn__ _____ Date __April 14__

Outline briefly situation requiring correction __E.M. has been borrowing__
__money from customers for five months and failing__
__to pay it back. Several complaints have come in.__

Place a check mark opposite each question in the appropriate column to the right	A	B	C
1. Did I arrange the date, time and place of corrective interview so that others would not be aware of purpose of the meeting?	YES	NO ✓	
2. Did I conduct the interview in strict privacy, away from all others' eyes and ears?	YES ✓		NO
3. Did I lose my temper during the interview?	NO		YES ✓
4. Did I call the subject "bad names?"	NO ✓		YES
5. Did I question his personal motives, or indicate any intrinsic defects in his character?	NO ✓		YES
6. Did I have the major facts substantially correct in my formal statement of the fault or error?	YES ✓	NO	
7. Did I give the subject ample time and uninterrupted opportunity to state his side of the case?	YES ✓		NO
8. Was the "intensity" of my rebuke in proportion to the "immensity" of the error?	YES	NO ✓	
9. Did I mention some good points about the subject or his work before I presented the "indictment?"	YES	NO ✓	
10. Did I present the subject with my own ready-made excuses or alibis for his criticized conduct?	NO ✓	YES	
11. Did I get the subject to agree that the action being criticized was erroneous?	YES ✓	NO	
12 Did I outline a specific and constructive course of remedial action to be followed in the future?	YES ✓	NO	
13. Did I get subject's pledge to cooperate in following out the recommended corrective program?	YES ✓	NO	
14. Was the essential human dignity of both parties mutually respected throughout the interview?	YES	NO ✓	
15. Did I close the interview on a constructive note?	YES ✓	NO	

105 = Perfect Above 70 = Excellent 63 to 70 = Good 49 to 63 = Fair Below 49 = Poor		A	B	C
	TOTAL CHECK MARKS	10	4	1
	MULTIPLY BY	7	✕	10
	GROSS SCORES	70	✕	10
	DEDUCT COLUMN C	10	✕	
	NET SCORE	60	✕	

EIGHT TESTED SUGGESTIONS FOR SUCCESSFUL CRITICISM

1. Criticize in Private—Not in Public!

2. Don't Question a Man's Motives or His Character!

3. Get All the Facts Before You "Blow Your Top"!

4. Let the Salesman State His Side of the Case!

5. Don't Overplay Your Hand!

6. Present the Plusses Ahead of the Negatives!

7. Don't Hand the Accused a Ready-Made Alibi!

8. Complete Your Job Before You Quit!

CHAPTER XI

How to Sow the Seeds of Enthusiasm

One of the up-state Illinois salesmen of a Midwest feed manufacturer began, on Wednesday of a certain week, to sell an average of six deals per day to farmer-prospects, although in the previous six weeks during which the deal had been in effect, he had not attempted even one presentation.

What happened to him?

He "got religion"—and suddenly became enthusiastic about a deal that had previously left him unmoved and cold-as-ice. He began to make a big slice of extra money out of the very same deal that heretofore he had said he "wouldn't touch with a ten-foot pole!"

How did he "get religion"? His General Sales Manager phoned him on Monday morning. Here's about the way the conversation went:

SALES MANAGER: "Mr. Elston, how does it happen you're not doing anything with the new mineral feed deal?"

MR. ELSTON: "Got no use for it; it's no good—wouldn't touch it with a ten-foot pole."

SALES MANAGER: "O.K., tell me what's the matter with it. The boys in other districts are doing well with it."

MR. ELSTON: "We never used to have these crazy deals. My feeders just don't 'go' for them."

SALES MANAGER: "Well, I'd like to talk with you about it. What say we meet in the morning at the hotel in ——?"

MR. ELSTON: "O.K., I'll be there at 7 o'clock."

When the Sales Manager arrived, his first comment was: "Mr. Elston, if you're right about this deal, I'm the first fellow who ought to know it! So, I want you to take me around the country today to call on some feeders. I'll take them as they come. You don't believe in the deal, so I won't expect you to make the sales pitch. But, I *do* believe in it; so I'll make the 'tries'—and you can listen in. O.K.? By the end of the day, we should both be wiser."

By starting early and working until late supper-time (they call it *supper* out there), they made presentations to nine feeders. *They sold eight deals!* —an incredible and probably unduplicatable bit of good luck, since other salesmen were averaging only about half that score.

At the day's end, Mr. Elston's only comment was: "How dumb can a guy get?" Next morning, he went to work with a zing and really made a record for himself.

The new will-to-work the deal, the new enthusiasm made the difference. Nothing else had changed—the same company, same deal, same territory, same farmers that lived there yesterday.

Just enthusiasm; but that's a big "just".

Before we close this chapter, we are going to try to find out the method, the technique that produced the amazing metamorphosis in this salesman.

JUST WHAT IS ENTHUSIASM?

Ever since you were a cub salesman, you've been hearing about the importance of enthusiasm—how it is the indispensable quality for success in selling.

Looking back, you'll probably say that you either had it or you didn't. On some deals you did, on others, no! And, no doubt, you would be hard-put to explain why you were enthusiastic on some occasions, lukewarm on others.

It's difficult even to *define* enthusiasm in a practical business way.

The old Greeks called enthusiasm an "at-one-ment with the gods." The ancient sages of the East called it Raj-Agni, "King of fires". Yes, enthusiasm *is* a kind of *fire*. We can agree on that!

But how do we kindle this indispensable flame? Whence comes the tinder? Where do we get the first igniting match?

Let's go on a search, you and I, for the priceless answers to these questions. Let's try to find the ingredients of enthusiasm, the seeds and sources of its transforming fire.

But let's go further. Let's see if we can find the secret whereby the leader *communicates* the fire of enthusiasm to his men. For, it is not enough for a sales manager to know how to get enthusiastic in his own person; his big job is to engender this quality in *others*. And finally, he must *get back* a powerful *response* to his communicated enthusiasm. Without this last step, his effort is *unproved!*

John Wesley, the 18th century evangelist, understood this fiery quality of enthusiasm. It will be recalled that in Chapter III, "The Seven Basic Types of Men", we analyzed the life trend of this powerful preacher, discovered him to be a basic Type Six enthusiast and devotee, modified by a strong Type Three quality of adaptability and action, and further tinctured with more than a modicum of Type Two humanitarianism.

But the particular point about Wesley which is worth repeating here, is his answer to an inquirer who asked him to explain the secret of his power to draw and move great audiences from every walk of life.

Wesley's reply, as the reader will recall, was: "I just set myself on fire! People come to watch me burn!"

Wesley not only knew how to *generate* enthusiasm within himself, *he had mastered the magic of communicating it to others!* Yes, he went even further; he not only generated and communicated enthusiasm, but also successfully *evoked a fiery response from his followers.* And that response had sufficient "horsepower" to drive thousands of converts up the aisle to the improvised altar.

Those three steps are *essential* to the sales manager who wants to get the power-drive into his sales force:

1. To Generate Enthusiasm

2. To Communicate It to Others

3. To Evoke Response from the Others

Before we start digging for the "how-to-do-it", let's analyze our situation in terms of its basic variables, because these variables modify the technique.

First, we know that all salesmen are not alike, neither in respect to their own ability to generate enthusiasm, nor in their ability to absorb and respond to the enthusiasm of a leader.

Second, we know that all deals, companies, products, markets, pay plans and earning possibilities, are not the same in terms of the amount of enthusiasm with which they are accepted by salesmen.

Third, we know that not all sales managers are alike in *their* capacity to generate and communicate enthusiasm and to evoke a response from others; in fact, the variations we find among the human beings who are the salesmen, are likely also to be found in similar form and force in the human beings who are the sales managers.

This third group of variables may appear to be of no significance to the individual sales manager who is reading this book. But, when these variant individuals are grouped into classes indicative of their capacity to accept, absorb, and respond to enthusiasm; then, it is highly important for the sales manager to study these classes and to identify himself with that one whose characteristics seem to be most like his own. And further, he should discover what typical gifts, if any, the members of his group possess in handling enthusiasm, or what handicaps, if any, their common personality traits impose upon their effectiveness as leaders.)

It is interesting to note, for example, that the feed salesman, mentioned in the opening of this chapter, worked under a district manager who possessed an extraordinary capacity to communicate enthusiasm to his men; and if possible, an even greater capacity to evoke a response *from* them. But, he himself was a difficult field manager to enthuse. In other words, on the "intake" side, he was slow to absorb communicated enthusiasm and slow also to respond to it; however, on the "output" side, he justified the description *"terrific"*. In other words, he was much more of a problem to the General Sales Manager than his men were to him.

As proof of this, his whole district was relatively "cold" to the mineral feed deal we mentioned in the example; the General Sales Manager knew this because of the district-wide poor sales; but his decision at that late date was to "sell" one of the district manager's key men, which he felt would be more easily done than to try to "sell" the district manager himself. The results of this astute decision proved his judgment to be sound; for, once the result of Mr. Elston's experience was grapevined throughout the district (as it was very quickly!), the rest of the boys took the hint. In point of time, it is even fair to say that the salesmen of this district manager were "sold" on the deal, via Mr. Elston, before the district manager himself fully accepted the fact that it was a volume-producer. Here is a case where the General Sales Manager's shrewd appraisal of his field "opposition" resulted in the salesmen enthusing their manager, a reversal of the normal sequence.

Despite the favorable outcome, however, we must not leave this example without pointing out that the home office sales manager had failed to enthuse the district manager at the time of the "kickoff" of the deal; otherwise, these delayed remedial measures would not have been necessary. Even though the remedy succeeded admirably, a good deal of valuable time was lost in this district.

Where This Sales Manager Failed to Rouse Enthusiasm

We give this example here to emphasize several important points. The General Sales Manager had either:

1. Overestimated his own ability to enthuse this District Manager at the "kickoff" meeting—or,
2. Underestimated this District Manager's slow rate of intake of communicated enthusiasm—or,
3. Failed to test the effectiveness of his enthusiasm-communication by checking this District Manager's response.

Having known, for many years, all of the people mentioned in this example, our observation is that the General Sales Manager partially failed in all three aspects of manipulating enthusiasm. He was a powerful human being, had a great deal of confidence in his own ability. This led naturally to his failure to evaluate the unexposed resistance of his field managers, which in turn meant that it never occurred to him to check up on the response he evoked within them. He took for granted that his enthusiasm-communicating process was successful and that it developed sufficient "horsepower" for the job, which, in the case of this District Manager, was not true.

This situation highlights the conclusion reached in the discussion of the three groups of variables; namely, that all salesmen are not the same in their basic "enthusability" and further, that not all sales managers have equal ability to do the enthusing job.

THE FOUR CLASSIFICATIONS OF SALESMEN'S "ENTHUSABILITY"

Let us now proceed with a further analysis of these variables, an understanding of which, as we shall see as we proceed, is one of the keys to smoothing out the peaks and valleys of individual "enthusability". The sales manager's necessity, first, is to recognize that variations exist, and then to class men into a few typical groups, a task we are now about to attempt.

From the standpoint of "enthusability", experience with many groups of salesmen indicates that they can be classified roughly into four groups or types:

1. *The Self-Starters,* who grab the ball and run with it; in other words, who *sell themselves* and thus enthuse easily, with scarcely any burden on their manager.

This group includes those who are intensely loyal and devoted to a leader; he has their complete confidence: If *he* is sold, they are sold.

2. *The Easy Starters,* who willingly *take* the ball if it is handed to them, and who run with it if the play is carefully charted *for* them. In other words, they enthuse easily, with a minimum of "hypodermic pep injections" from their manager.

3. *The Dead-Center Boys,* who neither accept nor reject, but merely vegetate on the payroll, without the fires either of assent or dissent. These are the "half-way" men, the lukewarm, who are "neither hot nor cold!"

4. *The Reverse-Gear Boys,* who are difficult to enthuse, slow to accept a new product or program. These include the doubters, the skeptics, the non-believers, those who are thinking in the opposite direction, unless you overwhelm them with evidence. But once "sold," they *stay sold!*

A Two-Thousand-Year-Old Example of Generating and Communicating Enthusiasm

In order to make the usefulness of this classification a little clearer, let us examine the example of a classic group of twelve men plus a leader, a group with whom we are all somewhat familiar, since the brief story of their operations is found in the most widely circulated book in the world.

Jesus, and His twelve apostles.

He selected these men—four fishermen, two tax collectors, two carpenters, two teachers, and two men of the law—without the aid of aptitude tests, a selection aid which in His case was not needed; because, as the Good Book tells us, the Master possessed an extraordinary power of in-seeing which enabled Him to know "what is in man".

Out of this assorted dozen of ordinary men who were given the extraordinary task of selling a new product, and an intangible one at that, to an unwilling and unready market, let us pick only two for the purpose of our present illustration—Simon Peter, the fisherman, and Thomas Didymus, the lawyer.

The Dynamic Self-Starter Type

If we can believe Michaelangelo's illustrations, Peter, who, in Greek, was called Petros, the Rock, was a large, powerful, impetuous man, familiar alike with the rough Sea of Galilee and the rugged life on its shores.

While he did not really understand, intellectually, the seemingly new philosophy his Master was teaching, he was nevertheless, emotionally devoted to the Man who led the group. It was Peter, you remember, who in the heat of devotion and anger, drew his sword and cut off the ear of the soldier about to lay hands on Jesus after the latter's betrayal by Judas. And it was Peter, too, who first refused to let Jesus wash his feet, thinking that the Master was thereby demeaned. Upon being told however that, unwashed, he had no part with Him, Peter then changed his tune and cried: "Not my feet only, but also my hands and my head".

Peter was clearly among those few intensely loyal men who are included in our first type—the Self-Starters. It is not likely that Peter "sold" himself. He was perpetually "sold"—*pre*-sold, in fact. If the Master believed it, *he* believed it; if the Master wanted it done, he wanted to do it. He enthused easily, and if he was ever a burden on his Leader, the problem arose from Peter's excess of zeal, not his lack of it. Jesus, like a good sales manager, appreciated Peter's perpetual readiness to do His bidding. He valued his unquenchable enthusiasm, even though at times it led him too far into indiscretions. It is no wonder then, that at the last days, the Master said to Peter, the Enthusiast: "Unto thee I give the Keys to the Kingdom of Heaven" . . . and "upon this rock (Peter) will I build my church." And He awarded this great responsibility to Peter, even though He knew that in a later moment of crisis and tension, Peter would prove weak and deny Him thrice. The sales manager can learn something from that incident. Jesus did not seek for perfect men—there were none then; there are none now. He used the manpower at hand. Under His guidance, they somehow succeeded in a strange new task for which none of them had had any previous experience.

The Reverse-Gear Man

A completely different man was Thomas Didymus, the lawyer, one of the two men of the law in the group. He had the skeptical, the legalistic mind; he was acquainted with the predominance of false testimony. Nothing short of incontrovertible physical evidence, viewed by him at first hand, would convince Thomas.

After the resurrection, when his brother apostles told him that in his absence, their Master had visibly appeared and talked with them, Thomas, cautious, suspicious, doubting the validity of this heretofore unheard-of phenomenon, said, perhaps almost scornfully: "Except I shall see in His hands the print of the nails, and *put my finger into* the print of the nails, and *thrust my hand into* His side, I will not believe."

Observe here, disbelief at its very acme. Thomas admitted that he did not trust even his own eyes. That's carrying skepticism pretty far, isn't it? Not only must he SEE the print of the nails, he must FEEL them. It was not only that he did not trust the eyes of his colleagues—he did not trust *his own!*

Thomas was definitely one of the Reverse-Gear Boys. A sales manager is likely to have one or two of them even in a sales force of twenty-five men.

But Thomas did not get his "walking papers" from his Leader. Instead, Jesus appeared again, this time when Thomas was present. He accosted the skeptic of the band, and to him He said: "Reach hither thy finger and behold My hands; reach hither thy hand and thrust it into My side and be not faithless but believing." And thereupon, Thomas did as he was bid, and he believed, and called Him by name, and accepted from Him a rebuke: (how much more) "blessed are they who have seen Me *not* and have believed."

Under equivalent conditions, no doubt many of us who think like sales managers would have been tempted to fire Thomas. But no! The Master remembered what Thomas had said when the news of the death of Jesus' beloved friend, Lazarus, had come to them: "Let us go also that we may die with him!" Amazing courage, incredible devotion and loyalty, this man Thomas had shown—the same man who was born an iron-minded skeptic, an unbeliever, so much an unbeliever that even today we use his name as a symbol of his type—"a doubting Thomas."

Perhaps, just to finish the story, we should add a memory-refreshing postscript. Jesus' judgment was not wrong. After the ascension, Thomas continued loyally in the Cause, founding the Christian Church in Syria, preaching in Persia and India, and ending his days as a martyr, so legend says, slain in public in behalf of that Cause which once he could not believe in, much less be enthusiastic about!

This almost 2000-year old example emphasizes that the problems of generating and communicating enthusiasm are not new. Nor are the types of men and their varied degrees of enthusability new. If a Leader of transcendent powers met these same problems and these same types of men so long ago, whereof shall we complain now?

SECOND AND THIRD TYPES ANALYZED

Besides types one and four, the Self-Starters and the Reverse-Gear Boys, we have the second group, the Easy Starters. Their kindling is laid, but they wait for the manager to fire it. And this no manager can reasonably refuse to do.

Believe it or not!—the third type, the Dead-Center Boys, those lukewarm half-way men who are "neither cold nor hot"—these are the most likely candidates for a termination notice. Almost any experienced sales manager will tell you that he would much rather motivate the Reverse-Gear Boys than try to pep up these paralyzed parasites who have taken up permanent and upholstered residence upon his mid-line fence. This idea of eliminating those who cannot decide is not a new thought, for long ago it was written: "Because thou art neither cold nor hot, I will spue thee out of my mouth!"

What the Four Classifications of "Enthusability" Mean to the Sales Manager

Regardless of the areas and degrees of difference in the resistance of the four types of salesmen, the important point to remember is that not all salesmen enthuse equally well; they offer neither the same *kind* of response mechanism nor the same *extent* of enthusability. While the sales manager will not be able to segregate them by type and offer each group a different formulation of information-conviction-persuasion, he will take care to include in the total indoctrination process, the essential ingredients of knowledge, proof, and emotion which will successfully fire all four types to the limit of their enthusability.

Four Classes of "Black Sheep" the Manager Must Deal With

Outside of these four fairly well standardized and easily definable groups, there are some other individuals who are poseurs, or to be bluntly American, phonies who put up a fake front and, either consciously or subconsciously, play a completely false role. These individuals can be defined and described quite readily. Call them aberrant types or, as they would be designated in the horticultural field —"sports" who have deviated from the customary family characteristics and have become black sheep, as it were, for one reason or another.

These deviates we call by names of our own choosing:

1. Pseudo Believers

2. Pseudo Unbelievers

3. Pseudo-Independent Thinkers

4. Advance-Alibi Artists

These pseudo types are discussed here because the inner "phoniness" of their outwardly assumed role is concealed. A sales manager may harbor one or more of these pretenders for a long time before he discovers them. Yet, the need to recognize and uncover them is great, for they are hidden resistances to enthusiastic indoctrination. They may be the destructive rotten apples in the barrel of otherwise good fruit.

1. The Pseudo Believer

He is the familiar "yes" man, the fellow who is not going to jeopardize his position by letting the boss know that he lacks enthusiasm for his job, his company, or a current promotion program. Basically, he may be one of the Dead-Center group, or the Reverse-Gear group; but this fact he shrewdly conceals from his boss, perhaps even from himself. He speaks glibly at sales meetings; laughs at the boss' jokes; applauds loudly and long when pep-instilling speeches are finished. And, rather obvious flattery is one of his favorite tools. Once in a while, one of these Pseudo Believers will wear the mask expertly enough to fool his fellow-salesmen, but not often. Usually, his colleagues quickly get his number and for his kind, they have a rough name. But seldom will they "snitch" to the boss about him. And even if they did, the boss many times wouldn't believe them because he mistakes the pseudo enthusiasm for the real thing.

2. *The Pseudo Unbeliever*

This chap is another poseur. He makes an obvious show of *not being sold*. This pose may arise from one or more of many sources. For example, some cases come to mind where this attitude was assumed in group gatherings intentionally to give the sales manager trouble, as a sort of revenge for some real or fancied hurt or injustice worked upon the salesman at some previous time. Perhaps the man failed to get his expected raise, or lost out on a bonus, or was turned down on some request for a special deal for himself or one of his customers. In emotionally immature salesmen, this "getting-even" tendency is very evident and this is only one of the several directions it may take. One particularized offshoot of this pseudo unbeliever is—

3. *The Pseudo-Independent Thinker*

This is the chap who believes his pose indicates a kind of superiority over his fellow-salesmen who, by joining in the group's enthusiasms, become to him "poor, dumb, driven cattle."

Some men, for example, resist any demonstration of personal enthusiasm just to be different; or, for the same reasons that a listener holds out against the exhortations of a Billy Graham, or in earlier days, of Billy Sunday. Some deep-seated feeling of inferiority or insecurity prompts such men to take attitudes opposed to those of the boss or of the group, because they feel that such action sets them apart as intellectuals, stoics, or men of great personal will-power, uninfluenced by the persuasive efforts of others. It is an ego-satisfying role, a compensatory rationalization, but a difficult and dangerous one if the sales manager lets it run wild. Once again, this fellow seldom fools his colleagues. They don't bother to classify him in terms of his mistaken and misdirected inner drives. They simply dub him a "wise guy" or a "smart aleck"—and let it go at that. Another of the singular offshoots of the Pseudo Unbeliever type is—

4. The Advance-Alibi Artist

Here is a man plagued by inner mental misery. He has a powerful "expectation-of-failure" complex. He has lost all confidence in himself. Secretly, he expects to fail in whatever he undertakes. But he has drive and guts, and he fools one sales manager after another, getting away with his act, perhaps for a whole lifetime. Such men prepare, in advance, the most elaborate and carefully-planned excuses for failure.

This fellow is perhaps the most difficult to uncover of all the "pseudos".

One of our clients hired such a man as Field Supervisor. He was well-educated, dressed well, spoke with great fluency, was highly personable as a human being and as far as could be discerned, he had all of the basic traits needed to succeed in this supervisor's job. His work history contained a concealed hint of something wrong; it revealed that he had held several good jobs, each for a year or two; then, a change without any appreciable advance in pay. But this occurred after the war when most careers showed interruptions and abnormal patterns; thus, no one bothered to check into this situation, nor thought to regard it as a warning signal.

This fellow could not be enthused about any aspect of his work. He criticized the company, its products, its marketing and distribution policies, and its promotion programs.

The General Sales Manager replied: "Sure! We've got lots of things to correct; your job is to correct them!"

But no! This chap turned every assignment calling for constructive corrective action into a personal diagnostic survey of what was wrong with this and that aspect of the company's activities.

"We already know that; do something about it!" repeated the General Sales Manager, impatiently.

But he could not change. Because he was so sure, subconsciously, that he was bound to fail in the end, he didn't even make the effort to operate on the constructive side of his job.

For him to become enthusiastic was potentially dangerous. Enthusiasm implied an admission of rightness, constituted a presumption of potential effectiveness—in the company's policy, project, or campaign. This in turn foreshadowed the probability of success. To show enthusiasm, then, was literally to commit himself to success in advance of trial. To him, such a course seemed fatal. If he gave up his well-prepared indictments, how could he explain his inevitable failure when it happened? Such was his fearful and confused thinking.

After three costly years, he was discharged, not because he was recognized as an Advance-Alibi Artist, but on the grounds of his constant criticism and bickering, which led to suspicions of outright disloyalty. Neither he nor his manager ever suspected the nature of his real trouble. It was never accurately evaluated.

This situation has been exposed here in considerable detail because sales managers seldom penetrate behind the veil of the deep psychological mystery involved in such cases. And, they are more numerous than is generally suspected. But, an astute leader, with extraordinary powers of insight into the hearts of human beings, might have cured this chap by leading him by the hand, by assigning "easily do-able" tasks to him and helping him to carry them out under such close surveillance that he could not fail. Gradually, the fear-of-failure complex might have been supplanted by a habit-of-success belief. Admittedly, that is a slender hope and an unlikely triumph of personal leadership, because it would have called for an insight beyond the powers of an ordinary man and a patience that would have made Job seem a first-grader in this ever-needed school.

What the Sales Manager Must Do to Cope With the Deviationist Classes

It is hazardous, however, for a sales manager to class a man into one of these "deviationist" groups without considerable observation, experience, and consideration. There must always be in mind the possibility that the state of belief or unbelief is sincere and not pseudo. One test is the extent to which the suspected "pseudo" parades or flaunts his attitude before his fellows. If he does it flagrantly, almost challengingly, suspect a deviate. Even then, the suspicion should be patiently verified. Armed even with prima facie evidence, it is easy to be wrong in such matters. And there is always the temptation, in moments of managerial anger or despair, to slap the "deviationist" tag on a man, as if the act of naming him solved some of his peculiar personality problems. Of course, tacking the tag on is only the first step. (In fact, if it is done publicly, it may worsen the problem!) The real test comes in the application of corrective measures that some day will permit him to remove the label. And certainly, in his indoctrination and push programs, the sales manager will avoid slanting them to the peculiarities of the deviates.

Having finished, for the time being, with the four pseudo types, we return now to our four standard classes. In these groups—Self-Starters, Easy Starters, Dead-Center, and Reverse-Gear Boys—the question of what and how much the sales manager is *required* to do, will depend to some extent upon the personality pattern of the manager himself.

This brings us to a brief analysis of the second conditioning aspect of the total situation.

How the Sales Manager Himself Is Classified

It was pointed out, a few pages back, that the sales manager, having once been a salesman, was likely to find himself considerably like one of the four standard types of salesmen we have previously analyzed. His experience in management may have modified his natural personality leanings to some slight extent. The necessities of a manager's responsibility may have taught him the compelling need for being a good actor; that is to say, the need for seeming to be enthusiastic in front of his men, even though he may just have come from a wall-shattering argument with the production department about their failure to meet the current market needs in terms of price, finish, design, etc. Being able to PRETEND enthusiasm where none is felt, may be an asset for the sales manager. Admittedly, there are times when this ability may be the sales manager's only "out." But it is no substitute for the real thing.

Therefore, let us not obscure the basic problem involved in the sales manager's type of temperament, by *assuming* that he possesses histrionic or forensic talents which may cover up or counterbalance his basic temperament-problem. In other words, let us analyze him as relentlessly as we dissected the salesman.

Is he a Self-Starter, an Easy Starter, a Dead-Center Man, or a Reverse-Gear Type?

If you are a sales manager, and if you have realistically and objectively classed yourself into one of these four groups, you are about to make an unexpected discovery: Your being in a given class does not affect your problem of enthusing men in the same way as it affects the "enthusability" of salesmen in the same group.

For example, let's say you've identified yourself as a Self-Starter. For a salesman, that's good news. For the sales manager, it is good news too, but not to the same extent. For if you enthuse *too* easily, you may have a tendency not to prepare yourself with enough ammunition to convince the Reverse-Gear type of salesmen. You may build yourself a beautiful but flimsy house-of-enthusiasm, resting on tall stilts, high above the rockbed of reality on which your skeptical salesmen live and move and have their being. In that event, you are likely to come up with plenty of pep, but no proof.

As a manager, your need, if you are a Self-Starter, is not to be carried away by your first enthusiasms. Keep on digging for objections, weak spots, negative angles. Patiently offset these negatives with positive plus-point proof. As the old man said to his son who was about to build himself a stone barn: "Son, you get twice as much stone as you think you'll need; then, you'll have half-enough!" Get twice as much evidence as *you* need to convince yourself; then double it; and you'll probably have sufficient proof material to handle your "class four" skeptics, those "doubting Thomases" we must always deal with.

If you place yourself as a manager in the Easy Starter Group, your problem lies in the same direction as that of the Self-Starter. It may be a little less acute in degree; but in essence you face the same dangers; you have a tendency toward making the same omissions; namely, you go into the duck blind with your shells only half-loaded. Read again the suggestions to the Self-Starter and apply them to yourself.

Should you courageously associate yourself with the Dead-Center Boys, ponder upon the fate of that famed, but extinct bird, the *Eoornis Terrevelox Gobiensis,* the "swift-winged" bird of the Gobi desert. Its fossil remains were found buried beneath the sands of time between two vessels each filled with corn. The bird died there with plenty of food in sight because he couldn't make up his mind as to which container of corn to eat first.

John H. Patterson of National Cash Register fame spread a sign before each manager-training group, a sign which read: "A MANAGER IS ONE WHO DE-CIDES." If you can't reach a prompt decision, better give up trying to be a manager; the seeds of managerial success are not in you!

Should you find, however, after honest self-appraisal, that you associate yourself with the fourth group, the Reverse-Gear Boys, do not despair. Perhaps, like the Thomas of Biblical fame, your skepticism will turn out to be a blessing. In a manager, tough-fibered resistance to being easily enthused is also a protection against building the illusionary house on stilts, provided always that with his resistance, there is coupled a dynamic drive to get the evidential material needed to convince his skeptical salesmen. The evidence that the doubting sales manager accumulates to enthuse himself, he converts into the proof material that sells his men. But if the manager, in addition to being a Reverse-Gear Boy, is negatively closed-minded and not given to driving action in evidence-gathering, he is in a dilemma indeed. He will be a wet blanket, not a fiery, enthusiasm-communicating, enthusiasm-evoking sales evangelist. Such a sales manager must delegate the salesmen-enthusing job to an associate or subordinate; and furthermore, take pains to keep his personal lack-of-enthusiasm under cover. Better still, let him seek a new job, where he can *become* enthusiastic; if he can't do that, then let him get out of sales management and into a position where enthusiasm is not important. However, we know of no such job which is worthwhile, for we agree with Emerson that "nothing great is ever done without enthusiasm."

At this point, let's sum up and see how far we have come:

1. We have decided that the sales manager's problem, with respect to enthusing his men, has four aspects:
   a. Generating enthusiasm within himself.
   b. Communicating it to others.
   c. Evoking a response from "the others."
   d. Determining whether the "horsepower" of the response is sufficient for the task to be done.

2. We have seen that not all salesmen respond equally to the sales manager's efforts to enthuse them.

3. We have classed salesmen into four basic groups, according to their tendency and capacity to accept communicated enthusiasm and to respond to it—
   a. Self-Starter
   b. Easy Starter
   c. Dead-Center
   d. Reverse-Gear
   —plus four "black sheep," or "deviationists," who depart from standard types: the Pseudo Believers, the Pseudo Unbelievers, the Pseudo-Independent Thinkers, and the Advance-Alibi Artists.

4. We have discovered that the "enthusability" of salesmen is conditioned and modified by the temperament-pattern of the sales manager.

5. We have found that not all sales managers have equal capacity to generate and communicate enthusiasm to salesmen and to evoke a response from them.

6. We have classed sales managers into the same four basic groups as salesmen.

7. We have found that temperament-patterns of the sales manager, as represented by these four groups, do not affect his basic capacity to enthuse men in the same manner, or to the same extent, as the temperament-patterns of salesmen affect their "enthusability."

In other words, of the three variables previously mentioned—salesmen, companies, and sales managers—we have discussed the first and third, leaving only the second to be dealt with now.

Influence of Company Factors on Enthusability

Because matters in our second class of variables are largely the result of top-management decisions and, therefore, are not subject to substantial modification by sales management, suggestions about these situations would be made largely without hope of getting action. Furthermore, these areas are not as directly related to the *human* side of sales management as are those of the salesmen and sales managers.

There is set out, in the left-hand column of the chart, immediately following the next page, ten typical situations about which salesmen generally get enthused. In the second column are ten opposite situations which generally leave salesmen "cold." Admittedly, these are highly-generalized types of situations, all of which may not apply in every business, but they *do* give the sales manager a clue to those conditions which arouse *natural* enthusiasms. Normally, the more of these basic enthusiasms he can start with, the less "pepping up" from the outside will be necessary.

SALESMEN GENERALLY ARE:

ENTHUSIASTIC ABOUT—	UNENTHUSIASTIC ABOUT—
1. NEW PRODUCTS, which offer fresh, new approaches for sales talks.	1. OLD PRODUCTS, where they must continue to flog the same donkey over the same old flank.
2. Products where the ELAPSED TIME between first call and final sale IS SHORT.	2. Products where the ELAPSED TIME between the first call and final sale IS LONG-DRAWN OUT.
3. EASY-SELLING items.	3. Items that require MUCH SALES EFFORT.
4. ONE OR TWO PET ITEMS.	4. THE REST OF THE LINE.
5. LOW PRICED ITEMS.	5. HIGH PRICED ITEMS.
6. CALLING ON OLD CUSTOMERS.	6. COLD CANVASSING NEW PROSPECTS.
7. REAL LIFE SALES DEMONSTRATIONS, made by supervisors to actual customers—to show "*how* it is done."	7. PRINTED-ON-PAPER INSTRUCTIONS, telling *what* to do.
8. Pay plans that PAY BONUS SOON AFTER SALE.	8. LONG-DELAYED BONUS PAYMENTS.
9. Deals with LIMITED-TIME, ACTION-GETTING CLOSE.	9. Deals that are AS PROFITABLE to customer TOMORROW AS TODAY.
10. GIVING OUT Demonstration SAMPLES.	10. INQUIRING ABOUT what use the prospect has made of demonstration SAMPLES.

ENTHUSIASM DEFINED AND EXPLAINED

Now that we have examined the two groups of human beings involved in the generation and transmission of enthusiasm and have explored the variabilities which distinguish their actions, we have before us a fairly comprehensive blue-print of the framework within which must take place the sales manager's process of enthusing his men.

This, of course, brings us to the very core of what we first sought when we set out upon our search; namely, a definition of this force which we call enthusiasm.

WHAT is it? WHERE does it come from? HOW is it generated, communicated, and evoked in others?

No author, so far as we can find, has ever attempted these answers, not even within the less-confining boundaries of philosophical or metaphysical concepts; nevertheless, let us rush in bravely where angels fear to tread.

Enthusiasm is a quickening of the mind and emotions, usually as an *inward* response to an *external* stimulation, although it can be initiated by impulses originating from within. It is directed toward some person, object, idea, or course of action. It partakes of the qualities of fervor, ardor, zeal, inspiration, passion; and in its higher aspects, it reaches ecstacy or exhaltation until, at the zenith, it becomes a sort of frenzy, even fanaticism.

Observing a human being controlled by enthusiasm, we can see that this energy is not something wholly new; both observation and experience show that its intrinsic potency as well as its capacity to persist and endure, are conditioned by past events and tinctured by the individual's prior experiences. These "storings-up" of the past are mingled, in what seems to be a random manner, with those new thoughts and suggestions which have sprouted and grown from seeds currently planted in the mind by the sales manager, for example, or from some other outside source.

In other words, enthusiasm is a complex of many forces, some springing from the reasonings of the intellect; others from the wells of deep-sourced belief and conviction. Some of its components, it brings from the past; others are as fresh and current as this morning's pep-talk from the sales manager.

In its maturing journey, enthusiasm goes through the plodding, sequential processes of the concrete mind; yet often, without warning, it may soar into the levels of the reproductive imagination, seizing handfuls of old familiar parts and pieces and recombining them into dazzling, splendid new forms and patterns.

But enthusiasm is not something of the intellect alone; nor is it derived wholly from faith or belief; nor can it be referred to as the single-parented child of the imagination. Until that which is intellect or reasoning, and that which is belief or conviction, and that which we call imagination, are all fired and fused in the furnace of the emotions, *enthusiasm is not born!*

We have repeatedly compared enthusiasm to *fire;* and intellect and reason are certainly not fiery; in fact, do we not refer to logic, that child of reason, as *"cold"* logic? Intellect, reason, logic, conviction, belief—these, considered as ingredients of enthusiasm, must be thought of only as fuel for the flames of *emotion;* otherwise, enthusiasm is a cold and lifeless thing. *And a cold and lifeless thing is not enthusiasm!*

WHAT THE SALES MANAGER MUST DO

Therefore, he who would enthuse others, must first identify the type of temperament with which he deals and aim his blows at this single target. To clear the way for an enthusiastic response, he must *inform* the *intellectual; reason* with the *logical; convince* the *skeptical; excite* the *fancy* of the *imaginative; motivate* and *persuade* the *immobile.* He must *reroute* the *thinking* of the *prejudiced* and *capitalize* upon the *favorable convictions* of those already fervent in his cause. Finally, he must toss all of this as kindling wood into the furnace of emotions, since only the emotional power leads to action.

He who would influence others must not lose sight of the wise admonition of Pascal, that "people are generally better persuaded by reasons which they have themselves discovered than by those which have come (from within) the minds of others."

In other words, toss in the SEEDS, the *seeds,* mind you, not the complete concept—and let the thinker discover, plant, and cultivate them himself. To change the metaphor, give the other fellow the *materials,* but don't build the *house*—let *him* do that!

In the last three paragraphs is to be found the WHAT TO DO in order to build enthusiasm. To sum it up, the sales manager employs upon his salesmen the same techniques of informing, convincing, and persuading that he used upon prospects when he was a salesman. The only new thought is this: Salesmen are people (as we intimated in the first chapter) and as such, they *ought to be sold as people,* when management wants enthusiastic action from them. And that process must not cease until it has unleashed the fires of emotion.

SALESMEN ARE TOUGH CUSTOMERS

But, as we have indicated, few salesmen are Self-Starters. And, even those who are, need to be informed and convinced, if not persuaded; while those in the other three groups require all three steps, just as does the prospective buyer. In fact, it has always been our observation that salesmen are the hardest to sell of all factors in the distributive process. Dealers can be sold more easily than salesmen; and prospects and customers are pushovers as compared to the sales group. Salesmen offer a sort of professional skepticism; an "educated" resistance to all new ideas, new products and promotions. The total sales power that sells a prospect is not sufficient to sell a salesman. It is as if salesmen retain, from their experience, a recollection of all the resistances, all the objections they have ever encountered; and these rise up, like ghosts, to restrain their enthusiasm.

How to INFORM Salesmen

Each sales manager knows best what information to give his men. He knows, for example, that salesmen need to know not only what a product *is*, but what it *does* for the prospective buyer. Again, salesmen like to have management define the primary markets and to instruct them on the specific needs of each of those markets, telling them how the product meets those needs. They like to know specifically what *claims* to make in each industry or business and what evidence is available to back up the claims. They like to know the major motivations that move buyers. In industrial selling, for example, certain high-priced machinery is sold in one industry to improve quality; in another, to cut costs; while in still another field, the sale of such a machine is tough going because there is no well-developed desire for high quality, nor are the buyers basically interested in cutting costs.

How to CONVINCE Salesmen

It is in the conviction stage, where skepticism, doubt, and disbelief are the barriers to engendering enthusiasm, that salesmen are really tough. They can spot hyperbole (bull, bunk, hot air) a long way off. Mere assertions unsupported by evidence do not interest them, any more than similar empty claims interest a prospect. Like prospective buyers, they want evidence, proof, demonstration. Specific case histories, backed by testimonials, comparative cost reports, "before-and-after" studies—nothing less than this hardpan-proof material will convince trained and experienced salesmen, particularly men in the Reverse-Gear group.

The sales manager would do well to include in his knowing something of what the successful trial lawyer is compelled to know about evidence—evidence being that which the lawyer defines as "the raw material of proof."

From the sales viewpoint, there are three major factors which affect the value of evidence as proof material:

1. BELIEVABILITY of the witness
2. DIRECTNESS of the evidence
3. METHOD OF PRESENTATION of the evidential material

Believability of the Witness

Witnesses, generally, are believable in this order:

(a) The HOSTILE witness, one whose interests are opposed to yours. If *he* says "it's good", that testimony weighs heavily as evidence.

(b) The AUTHORITY, the specialist, who testifies from out of intensive training and authoritative experience in a given field. (The "expert witness" of the courtroom.)

(c) The NEUTRAL witness, the fellow who doesn't "give a damn" either way. When he testifies in your behalf, it indicates that he has departed from his neutrality and this rates relatively quite high on the total scale of the believability of the witness.

(d) The SATISFIED CUSTOMER, who approves your product after using it.

(e) The FRIENDLY witness, who gets a much lower believability rating because he is presumed to be already disposed in your favor.

(f) The evidence offered by YOURSELF or YOUR COMPANY has, of all, the lowest believability rating, because you are expected to speak well of your own products. This is only a modern acceptance of an ancient rule: "If I bear witness of myself, my witness is not true."

Going back to Thomas Didymus, in our example, he didn't accept the witness of his own associates (whom we would class as "f" on the believability scale), because he distrusted not their integrity, but their objectivity. A simple claim, made by the manufacturer or his representative, is always thought of as a self-serving declaration with very little evidential value, unless it is corroborated by other witnesses. The old law declared no man could be convicted on the evidence of a single witness; there must be two or three. That requirement of corroboration still exists in modern law.

Directness of Your Evidence

The second factor affecting the evidential value of your proof material is the directness of your evidence.

(a) FIRSTHAND evidence, the "I was there; I saw it; heard it—in person."

(b) SECONDHAND evidence, the story as told by a second party, sometimes called "hearsay" evidence.

(c) PARALLEL evidence, where the present situation is set out as being parallel to, or almost exactly like, some other situation. (The close-fitting analogy belongs here.)

(d) "JUST-SUPPOSE" evidence, often called "hypothetical", where the reasonableness of a claim depends upon the similarity and "logicalness" of a carefully constructed hypothesis.

In both parallel and "just-suppose" types of evidence, a good deal of imagination is required, first to reconstruct the exact parallel situation and second to construct a tight and reasonable hypothesis. Since imagination enters into the formula of construction, it must also enter in some degree into the hearer's acceptance of the analogy or hypothesis; in other words, these two types of evidence will be readily acceptable to the more imaginative, whose powers of projection and visualization are sufficient to enable them to follow, picture, and accept the imaginative presentation as true. It is wiser not to rely too heavily upon these types of evidence in appealing to strongly materialistic thinkers—a classification which includes most salesmen.

Referring again to Thomas Didymus, our convenient stereotype of skepticism and doubt, he refused to accept the secondhand evidence even of his trusted associates; he had to have the firsthand evidence of his own eyes, and even that, you will recall, was not enough. He had to put his hands in the nail holes, and touch the wound in his Master's side. He not only distrusted the objectivity of his fellows; he distrusted one of his senses—his eyes—unless, what his eyes saw was corroborated by his sense of touch.

Methods of Proof-Presentation

The third factor determining the value of your evidence is the METHOD OF PRESENTATION.

(a) ACTUAL PHYSICAL proof is the most effective form in which to present evidence. (Actual trial runs, demonstrations, testing of samples—these are everyday forms of physical proof.)

(b) VERIFIED DOCUMENTARY evidence is the second most effective form of presentation. (A movie showing a physical demonstration of a machine in actual operation, case histories accompanied by testimony of results written on the company letterhead and signed by an executive—these are examples of verified documentary evidence.)

(c) UNVERIFIED DOCUMENTARY evidence is effective, but generally less believable than the verified proof. A case history *without* a testimonial letter is a good example of simple documentary evidence.

(d) VERBAL case histories are the most frequently used method of presentation in selling; but intrinsically, they carry the lowest of the several believability ratings. They are undocumented and unverified, and their effectiveness depends largely upon repeated corroboration.

There are some salesmen who, like Thomas, will believe only if they themselves *see* and *hear* or *taste* and *feel* the physical evidence at firsthand. Unless their previous knowledge or prior experience provides them with a confirmatory background for belief, they will not accept anything short of firsthand, physical evidence.

Analyzing the Feed Salesman's Resistance

If we examine further the case of Mr. Elston, the feed salesman whose experiences opened this chapter, we discover that his skepticism, his disbelief, sprang from several causes:

1. He had no PREVIOUS KNOWLEDGE or PRIOR EXPERIENCE with "these crazy deals", as he called them, so that within his thinking was only the age-old resistance to change; there was nothing on the plus side to urge him to action.

2. His imagination was not vivid enough to enable him to project and visualize himself in a hypothetically successful situation, using the deal as it was intended to be used.

3. His district manager was himself skeptical, uncooperative, even combative about the deal; and, consequently, he had not communicated any enthusiasm to his men. In fact, he had done just the opposite; and like Shylock, the men had "only bettered (his) instruction."

But when the General Sales Manager set out to inaugurate corrective measures, Mr. Elston's basic confidence in the Manager—plus his loyalty—were sufficient to gain his acceptance for the belated proof-experiment. And, when the General Sales Manager had demonstrated for a whole day in the field, not only *WHAT* could be done, but *HOW*—Mr. Elston capitulated quickly. His skepticism was cured and his enthusiasm had been aroused. He went to work with zest the next morning.

What kind of proof moved Mr. Elston to enthusiasm?

First: As to the BELIEVABILITY OF THE WITNESSES, the feeders, to whom the General Sales Manager sold the deal, were the very same feeders whom Mr. Elston had foretold would be HOSTILE. Since a hostile witness carries the highest believability rating, this was the best kind of proof to be had from the believability-standpoint.

Second: As to DIRECTNESS OF EVIDENCE, you will recall that firsthand evidence, seen with your own eyes, heard by your own ears, is the most direct evidence you can get. So, we can credit the General Sales Manager with shrewd wisdom in bringing the salesman along, thus presenting him with the best type of proof material—the evidence of his own eyes and ears; yes, and order book!

THIRD: As to the FORM OF PRESENTATION, in this case, the evidence was presented in repeated *actual physical demonstrations* of the saleability of the deal. The General Sales Manager proved the saleability *by selling the deal,* which is PHYSICAL PRESENTATION, the highest form of proof available in this area.

In other words, the General Sales Manager brought evidence from *hostile witnesses,* the *most believable* of all witnesses; he presented it at *firsthand,* which is the *most direct* kind of evidence; and he demonstrated in *physical form—* in his own person before both prospect and salesman—which is the *most convincing* form of presentation. In this case, the three-way proof formula quickly demonstrated its validity and effectiveness in practical field application.

Let us digress here to make a collateral observation.

No claim is made that this General Sales Manager had the three-point formula consciously in his mind when he initiated his feed demonstration. He was only "doing what came naturally." But, it was out of hundreds of such practical field situations—situations involving not only sales managers enthusing salesmen, but salesmen enthusing prospects—that the outlines of this practice gradually emerged. From the outlines, the formula was devised and tested again and again, until it had proved itself reliable enough to be classed as a definite technique. Wherever, in this work, you find procedures "definitized" into a formula or a check-list, you may assure yourself that they are not the result alone of mental cognition, but represent the organization and crystallization of many mens' field experiences. These have been patiently observed, analyzed, and organized into a definite technique or method which is teachable and learnable.

This basic approach to the technique-evolving procedure is inserted here because many able, practical sales managers have a suspicion that any material which is *well organized* is, willy-nilly, *theoretical.* As a matter of fact, the only reliable source of technique is field practice; when you find similar practices used by many men in many lines, you can be sure you have discovered something basically sound and usable. Observe numerous examples of a practice used in field work, analyze them, isolate the similarities and differences, reconstruct the process in its sequential steps, and lo!—there emerges a sound, organized, teachable technique.

In the present case, the practical steps taken by the General Sales Manager exercising the natural skills derived from his experience, were exactly the same as they would have been had he been following the formula. The formula doesn't *change* the practice; it only recognizes the usefulness of that practice; then it simplifies, organizes, and crystallizes it into a brief and understandable "package."

How to MOTIVATE and PERSUADE Salesmen

Up to this point, we have discussed some basic considerations in INFORMING salesmen, and have introduced a simple formula for preparing and presenting EVIDENCE with which to eradicate doubt, skepticism, disbelief.

There remains only the task of MOTIVATING and PERSUADING salesmen to accept the material which we will presume the sales manager has presented up to this point, and to act upon it.

It is at this stage when the coldly intellectual, the calmly logical, and the evidential must be raised to the fiery and exciting emotional level.

Salesmen are true hedonists, in the literal sense of that word, as Epicurus would have used it. They pursue pleasure and the prospect of gain; and they tend to flee from pain and loss, using those two words in their broader implications.

Their underlying response-patterns, however, manifest in specialized forms, conforming to their peculiar occupational interests and activities. In Chapter IX, it will be remembered, we listed Ten Basic Needs of Salesmen, needs which are so universally present that we might almost call them *built-in* opportunities for managerial motivation. These needs are the specialized outcroppings of the pleasure-gain, pain-loss concept which comprises the larger framework of that ancient philosophy which we might call, in its modern form, *economic* hedonism. For the convenience of the reader, we repeat that list of basic needs:

10 Basic Needs of Salesmen

1. Money
2. Responsibility and Work of Importance
3. Security
4. Room to Grow
5. Personal Place
6. Personal Accomplishment
7. Personal Recognition
8. Participation in Group Accomplishment
9. A Goal and a Road Map
10. Excitement

It will be observed that these ten needs, as basic keys to motivational opportunity, have a longe-range, almost *permanent* usefulness. In other words, in the larger aspect of motivating his men to success, the sales manager will play upon these keys more or less continuously. A further glance at the list will also show that these basic needs provide almost equally numerous opportunities for arousing the less permanent, more temporary fires of enthusiasm for a single campaign, contest, drive, or special project.

For whether you are John Wesley, moving people to religious conversion, or Huey Long, the demagogue, marching the masses to the ballot boxes with emotional slogans like "Every man a king!", or John Q. Salesmanager persuading a sluggish sales force to go out and sell, these needs are the age-old keys to action. Without applying them, it is doubtful whether anyone can secure worthwhile action in any important cause.

Go Easy on "Pep-Talks"

Emotional appeals are important in arousing salesmen to enthusiastic response, but the young high school coach's "get-out-there-and-fight" appeals which are mostly sound and fury without the solid content of specific information and convincing evidence, serve very little purpose. They neither fool salesmen nor enthuse them.

Test the Group Response

At some point shortly after the persuading or motivating process is concluded, the cautious sales manager checks the intensity of the response which his enthusiasm-instilling tactics have evoked from his listeners. Is its horsepower sufficient for the task ahead? Let him not make the mistake of being over-confident or of assuming that the enthusing job is well done. Before it is too late, let him test his accomplishment by direct inquiry, by observation of the general mood, by the old "washroom survey" method, or by enlisting the cooperation of certain trusted key lieutenants as observers and opinion-testers. These indirect approaches are almost always needed, for men generally avoid giving negative opinions to the boss; and if he relies solely on direct inquiry, he may get a false report.

He can eliminate some of the negative opinions by a frank open-forum question and answer session before the close of the meeting. Often, men will expose their attitudes in such an impersonal session more readily than if directly queried later on. These cautious steps in evaluating the after-attitudes take some time, but the investment pays off in freedom from later surprises and failures.

Summing Up

We have come a long way since this chapter began. Let's take a backward look and see where we have been.

We have seen that in the matter of manipulating enthusiasm, actually, the sales manager has a four-fold task:

1. To *generate* enthusiasm.
2. To *communicate* it to others.
3. To *evoke a response* from the others.
4. To *test the "horsepower rating" of the response* before concluding his presentation.

We have discovered that among those whose task it is to enthuse, or among those who are to be enthused, there are wide variations—first, among managers, for example, in the capacity to enthuse others; second, among salesmen, in their capacity to generate their own enthusiasm, or to accept the communicated enthusiasm of another and to respond to it.

We have classed all the human beings involved into four classes; but, we have found that the effect of being in one or another of these classes does not have the same significance in the case of the "enthuser" as it does in the case of the "enthusee."

We have defined and explained enthusiasm.

We have set out WHAT the sales manager must do to engender enthusiasm in his men, and have agreed that the necessary three steps—to inform, to convince, to persuade—are the same steps we have used so long in selling prospects and customers.

We have made a specialized application of the process of informing-convincing-persuading fitted to the sales manager's problem of building up enthusiasm, developing at some length the "how-to-do-it" of proving his case to his salesmen; finally, presenting the techniques of motivating and persuading them to favorable and enthusiastic action.

There remains but one step to be taken—and only the sales manager can take it. Try out these procedures, test them on your own men, against the background of your own problems. Only then will you know certainly whether the time spent on this chapter was well invested!

THE SEEDS OF ENTHUSIASM

Its Sources and the Process of Its Cultivation and Development

I **WHAT** **IT IS —** Definition and Description	ENTHUSIASM is a quickening of the mind and feelings, resulting in a kind of fervor, ardor, zeal or inspiration, which may reach exhaltation or ecstacy, and in its highest expression, manifest even as frenzy or fanaticism. Its force is directed toward some person, idea, object, or course of action.
II **ITS** **SOURCES or** **SEEDS** (Where It Comes From)	Usually, enthusiasm is an internal response arising from suggestions projected into the mind and feelings from the outside; but in some people, and upon some occasions, it can be excited and raised to an emotional level by impulses originating from within the memory and the imagination.

III
BASICALLY
CONDITIONED
BY —
(Background)
	The intensity of the enthusiasm engendered in a given individual is conditioned basically by his temperament-pattern, which includes his type of mind and his typical emotional response characteristics. From the standpoint of *enthusability,* these individuals fall roughly into four groups:
	
	    1. The Self-Starters
	    2. The Easy Starters
	    3. The "Dead-Centers"
	    4. The "Reverse-Gears"
	
	plus four pseudo types, the Pseudo Believer, the Pseudo Unbeliever, the Pseudo-Independent Thinker, and the Advance-Alibi Artist.

IV **CURRENTLY** **CONDITIONED** **BY**	The result thus far secured is further conditioned by the salesman's feelings of loyalty towards his leader and his company; and, by the kind and amount of current information given, the effectiveness of the evidence submitted, the pointedness of the sales manager's appeals to the salesman's action and loyalty motives, and his desire for money and other promised gains.

CHAPTER XII

Compounding the Successful "Personality-Mix"

"*S*ay, *who do you suppose I met at the Union Club this noon? Bill Waldron—remember him—that salesman you let go last year because he couldn't seem to make the grade? On his way out, he stopped at our table to talk a minute; likes his new job; has already gotten himself into the Top Ten Club!*"

Has something like that ever happened to you? Sure it has, and to almost every other manager as well. More than once, the average sales executive has been puzzled and frustrated; yes—and Heaven forgive him!—even a little *irritated* by the quick success of one of his ex-salesmen under a different manager. And he has often asked himself: "What's this other fellow got that I don't have?"

One sales manager we know made it a point to get acquainted with the other manager for the sole purpose of studying his successor under his personal microscope. He went so far as to make an appointment with the executive who had succeeded where he had failed. On that occasion, he laid bare his own frustration in an effort to get hold of the other fellow's secret. But the latter was as much at a loss to explain his success as the former was to account for his failure—and so nothing worthwhile came out of the meeting.

Only one manager's answer seemed to fringe upon the truth, as we discovered it later. His reply was: "It's a good deal like a marriage; take two nice people who don't 'hit it off'—finally they split up. Nobody can figure it out. I believe it is a matter of—what shall we say?—*polarity?*"

And "polarity" comes mighty close to the heart of the problem. But polarity implies duality, the pairs of opposites, such as positive-negative, white-black, good-bad—any pair of words connoting opposite extremes.

THE "PERSONALITY-MIX" DEFINED

After observing, analyzing, hypothesizing, and playing around with the question for some twenty years, we find that it involves not a duality, but a triplicity.

It is not a problem touching sales management alone—it presents itself *whenever two human beings come into contact.*

Sometimes, we call it *the magic triangle of relationship;* or let us coin a phrase and call this transitory relationship between two people a "personality-mix".

THE "PERSONALITY-MIX" EXPLAINED

For example, when Sales Manager "A" comes in contact with Salesman "Y", between those two human beings there is automatically set up a relationship—a mutual interchange of power, of mental and emotional energies. Out of that intercourse a child is born. Let's call it "X". Manager "A" is one of its parents; Salesman "Y" is the other.

In any contact of two human beings, the birth of this third person cannot be avoided; it is automatic and inevitable. Once two sides of the triangle come into relationship, the third side demands to be put into its place. The picture looks like this:

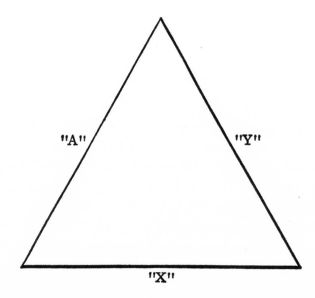

To say it another way, the unseen guest at every contact or conference is the combined product of your "output", commingled with the "output" of your salesman.

When created between you and Brown, the product is not the same as it is when created between you and Jones. From the salesman's point of view, the same truth applies—the "mix" between himself and *you* is different from the "mix" brought about between himself and another manager.

When Mr. Salesman "Y" leaves your employ and goes to work for the ABC company, the "mix" of which he was a part when he worked with you, is left behind. A new and different triangle of relationship is set up, resulting in a new "personality-mix", where "B" is the new sales manager, "Y" is the same salesman, and "Z" stands for the new "personality-mix". The new picture looks like this:

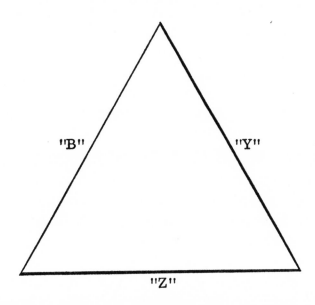

The new company's products, its training methods, its "environment" may be practically the same as those of your company; but the "Z" factor—the new "personality-mix"—is certain to be different. And, if it is more suitable to Salesman "Y" than was the "mix" created between *yourself* and him, his chances for success in his new job are proportionately greater.

It is not a matter of determining which boss is the superior sales manager. It is a matter of "personality-mix". This explains why Salesman "Y", leaving the employ of Sales Manager "A" will succeed better under Sales Manager "B", even though there is no discernible difference in the quality or amount of training, the amount or method of compensation, or the amount or quality of general supervision.

In fact, as consultants, it is part of our never-ending task to study the "measurables" which contribute to the success or failure of one salesman or an entire sales force. Yet, we cannot recall a single instance where such a study shed any light on this problem of personal relationship, which is at least circumstantial evidence indicating that the "mix" is abstract, intangible—in other words—*unmeasurable!*

But this "mix" does exist as an important fact—just as, for example, kindness and patience, and other abstract, intangible and unmeasurable attributes exist.

Different Types of "Mix-Components"

The "mixes" are bound to be varied because the people who make them up, are varied.

There are men who are "putter-outers" and others who are "taker-inners". There are men who are shrewd enough to be "putter-outers" when putting-out is needed and "taker-inners" when a situation calls for "taking-in". Usually, if a man is a leader, he will lean towards being a "putter-outer". But there are times, if he is a *wise* leader, when he will understand the necessity of making himself receptive, listening interestedly while the other fellow pours out what is in his mind and on his heart. In other words, the shrewd manager will know WHEN and HOW to change the specific gravity of the "personality-mix".

As soon as the sales manager begins to consider these matters in his sum-total pattern of salesmen relations, he will begin to find that there are methods of improving the "personality-mix", methods which he has never heretofore known about or practiced.

"That's what I want to hear about!" says the practical-minded sales manager, interestedly, "how can I use this 'personality-mix' idea in my daily work?"

How the Manager Uses the "Personality-Mix"

Well, once the manager really understands not only the WHAT but the WHY of this concept, he will use it in many ways.

First: He will cease being perplexed, frustrated, or self-condemnatory when one of his separated salesmen makes good under another sales manager.

Second: He will begin to think more deeply about his human relations. If he has been unwittingly a bit stand-offish or authoritarian, he will soften that appearance of isolation, and begin to give more of himself to others.

Third: He will cease trying to manage any man in a vacuum, be it his own or the vacuum of the salesman. Isolation of an individual—either of the sales manager or the salesman—does not usually result in successful human relations.

FOURTH: He will begin to manage men in terms of the total "personality-mix" which he and each of his salesmen comprise. He will patiently observe which "mix" is most successful with each individual, and that "mix" he will use to manipulate each man to greater selling success.

Some Hidden Hungers of Salesmen

We know that isolating salesmen from their sales managers tends to worsen human relations, as we pointed out in Item 3 above. And experience indicates that salesmen generally don't like "vacuum" management.

In fact, one of the great hungers we have repeatedly and continuously encountered in our work with thousands of salesmen and dozens of sales managers, is the hunger of the salesman for frequent contact with his leaders. It does not matter whether that leader is the district manager, the divisional manager, the sales manager, or the president of the company. Mr. Salesman yearns for visits with people who are more in the "headquarters-know" than he himself. He wants this contact because:

a. He seeks the RECOGNITION, the status or place that comes from meeting and associating with his superiors.

b. He wishes to unburden himself of a lot of QUESTIONS which have been piling up inside him—and he hopes to get authoritative, reliable, and official *answers* to those queries. Sometimes, his desire may be partly to assuage his own natural curiosity, but more often, he is endeavoring to equip himself to give authoritative answers to the questions which his prospects and customers *ask of him!*

Let's recall a highly-pertinent example of this need for authentic information. A large pharmaceutical house was in the first stages of some freshly-filed patent suits that were to determine which one of several companies was to have the right to patent a valuable new drug.

Of claims and claimants there were many, two or three of them giants in the field. Already there existed among the "big boys" a complicated network of cross-licensing agreements, not all of which were publicly known, but merely bandied about in the rumor stage.

The sales force was tense. The questions that physicians, hospital personnel, and druggists shot at them in the field, they could not answer. Yet to their customers, these sales representatives *were* the company.

We ran across the consequent turmoil in the course of a national field survey of sales operations for which the company had engaged us.

We asked the president if the company's policy of secrecy might not be abandoned in this case.

"Secrecy!"—he almost shouted with surprise and irritation—"We have no policy of secrecy. We can give the men every fact that we know ourselves!" True to his word, the whole story was clearly and fully explained at the next field manager's meeting.

The managers heaved a sigh of relief. "There is no skeleton in the closet after all! Now, our representatives can give intelligent, factual answers to the questions we have been getting from physicians, hospitals, druggists, and wholesalers!"

The pressure was off. The morale bounced back like a released rubber band.

But the story must not end until I recount the president's reason for not having released the facts earlier.

"I didn't think the field needed that kind of information," he alibied.

Verily, verily, there is a huge psychological chasm between top-management, ensconced serenely on the sixty-second floor of an air-conditioned New York skyscraper, and the sales representative pounding the hot pavements in Minonk, Illinois. Sometimes, that distance is as great as the space between our little earth and the fixed star Arcturus. Only the perpetual watchfulness of an alert sales manager can bridge—and keep bridged—that chasm of incredible unknowingness!

The Basic Yearning for Human Interchange

There is still another reason for the salesman's yearning for executive contact:

He wishes to be *reassured* by the generally *friendly,* frequently *optimistic,* conversation of those members of the executive staff who are "in the know".

Perhaps, what he wants most of all, though he seldom expresses it clearly, is *friendly interchange* with someone above himself. He wants to bask in the warmth of another man's personality. Let us say kindly, he wants "official companionship"! He finds warmth and satisfaction in the right "personality-mix". It gives him a chance to express *his* personality to that other fellow, whether he be a top executive, his home office sales manager, or his immediate field superior.

In short, he yearns for that interchange of mental and emotional energies that two human beings put out when they meet together. He derives something of value from it. A deeper sense of "belonging"; perhaps, in some cases, a chance to "show off" and boast a little to a man "up-the-line". In other cases, an opportunity to "get next" to the boss.

But whatever the motive, even if it is a bit immature, these contacts help to build morale. Even those self-seekers who seldom take their eyes off the "main chance", do not, as a rule, abuse these contacts with superiors. They value them and do not wish to risk losing them.

It might help the sales manager better to understand this yearning for human contact, if we turned to another field, the U.S. Armed Services, and quoted some paragraphs from General S.L.A. Marshall's *Armed Forces Officer*, on this matter of isolation, of "aloneness", as it affects morale on the battlefield.

> The battlefield is *cold;* it is the lonesomest place which men may share together. *The harshest thing about the field is that it is empty.* It is this emptiness which chills a man's blood and makes the apple harden in his throat. (That sense of isolation again!)
>
> The (soldier) must have at least some feeling of spiritual union with (his comrades) if he is to do an efficient job of moving and fighting. It is the touch of human nature which gives men courage and enables them to make proper use of their weapons. One file, patting another on the back, may turn a mouse into a lion . . . The thing which enables an infantry soldier to keep going with his weapons is the near presence, or the presumed presence of a comrade. The other man may be almost beyond hailing or seeing distance, but he must be there somewhere within a man's consciousness, or the onset of demoralization is almost complete. He becomes a castaway in the middle of the battle.

Of course, the tensions of the sales firing line do not equal the life-and-death intensity and finality of those on the field of battle. On the selling field, those in the battle lose orders, but not lives; their pride is wounded, but no blood is lost; nerves may be frayed, but no arms or legs are blown off.

There is a difference between soldiering and selling—a tremendous difference, both in the quality and the quantity of what its participants must endure.

But—

Is it not likely that the need for human interchange which we find in salesmen arises from the same deeply-buried lack of self-sufficiency, the same basic insecurities, the same fears which beset the soldier? (In fact, to be truthful, which beset us all!)

Frequent contacts between a salesman and his manager eradicate the "management in a vacuum" error; they do away with the salesman's fearful feeling of isolation or aloneness.

In brief, the sales manager needs not only to understand the "third-person-at-every-conference" concept, but he will do well to learn how to use this triplicity of powers to satisfy many of the salesman's basic hungers, and thus to arm him with more courage, drive, determination, confidence, and loyalty to his leader.

THE BELL "TOLLS FOR THEE"

Perhaps the sales executive would profit much if he were to take to heart the message which John Donne, English poet and preacher, gave out four centuries ago:

> No man is an island
>   Alone in the Sea.
> He's part of the mainland—
>   of *you* and of *me!*

In other words, in a sales force, there is no such thing as a separate and personal triumph—all other men are lifted up by any one man's accomplishment.

And neither are there any separate and isolated defeats—for when one man loses, all share, in many ways, in his lack of triumph. And in an even larger measure, and more directly, is this true of the sales manager, for his success is indeed built on the accomplishments of his men.

To paraphrase Donne a little further, let the sales manager "not send to ask for whom the bell tolls"—for whether it be the glad paean of victory or the solemn tolling of defeat, the answer is the same—the bell "tolls for thee!"

CHAPTER XIII

The Kind of Manager
Salesmen Like

For a sales manager to succeed, it is not absolutely essential for him to be *liked* by his salesmen.

But it *helps!*

The goodwill of the salesmen toward their manager—which, under right conditions, deepens into a genuine affection on both sides—is an intangible but powerful force that sustains the morale and enthusiasm of the whole field sales group in times of poor business, through periods of widespread customer complaints, or during other stretches of temporary discouragement. In short, a favorable disposition towards the sales manager is a valuable asset to him at precisely the time he stands most in need of it!

What does a sales manager need to *know*, what is he required to *be*, what must he *do* in order to personify the kind of manager whom salesmen *like*, and whom they *follow* through thick and thin?

It would be arrogant for any author to claim to know all that lies within the minds and hearts of other men; but here are *an even dozen dependabilities* which, if found by any sales group in their own sales manager, will instill in them a sense of worthwhileness in their work, and a feeling of security in their jobs.

12 ATTRIBUTES SALESMEN WANT IN THEIR MANAGER

1. They want a manager WHO KNOWS HIS JOB.

2. They want a manager WHO PLANS THE GROUP OPERATION IN ADVANCE.

3. They want a manager WHO EXHIBITS SELF-CONFIDENCE WITHOUT ARROGANCE.

4. They want a manager WHO DOESN'T BLAME *OTHERS* FOR *HIS* MISTAKES.

5. They want a manager WHO DOESN'T "HOG" THE CREDIT FOR ACCOMPLISHMENT.

6. They want a manager WHO HAS A HIGH "BOILING POINT."

7. They want a manager WHO WILL FIGHT FOR HIS MEN'S RIGHTS.

8. They want a manager WHO UNDERSTANDS HIS MEN AS HUMAN BEINGS.

9. They want a manager WHO CAN REACH A DECISION.

10. They want a manager WHO IS PREDICTABLE.

11. They want a manager WHO BELIEVES IN HIS MEN.

12. They want a manager WHO PROTECTS HIS MEN FROM THEIR OWN WEAKNESSES.

Let us examine these attributes one by one, determining if we can, why they make such a strong appeal to the men who must do the bare-handed, front-line selling.

Before we begin this study, let us agree that no one manager will possess all of these traits. If he did, he would no longer be human. But it isn't needful that the manager encompass all these virtues in order to have his men like him; in fact, if he but demonstrates half of them, he will be much admired, respected, and followed by the salesmen who have put themselves under his leadership.

1. A Manager Who *KNOWS HIS JOB*

Salesmen fear a leader whom they do not believe to be competent. To himself, each salesman readily admits that he doesn't know it all! And when he hits his own blank spot, who is going to fill in if his manager is not knowledgeable and thoroughly competent?

We personally know many field sales managers in the pharmaceutical field, for example, who are inwardly frightened at the thought of making an effective detail call on a physician. There are managers in the merchandising field who would avoid, at all hazards, any attempt to sell a franchise to a new dealer outlet; and, in the chemical field, some managers fear to call on a prospect's technical man to discuss one of the more modern applications of one of their company's technical products. Experienced salesmen have many opportunities to discover how "rusted-over" are the once top skills of the men who manage them; and out of earshot of the manager, they will tell you a little sadly that, in fact, they would prefer to make the call WITHOUT the leader.

But their demand for managerial competence extends much beyond skill in salesmanship. Men want a manager who knows their markets, who is skilled in pricing, who knows the right people to see on reciprocity deals, who knows from experience the realities of their day's work, who doesn't expect the impossible, and, on the other hand, won't accept a half-way job. They want a leader who stands well with top management, who is respected by competitors, who can figure out a smarter deal than the other fellow when a sale hangs in the balance.

In other words, they want a manager whom they believe to be equal to whatever situation may arise.

A Manager Who PLANS THE GROUP OPERATION IN ADVANCE

Salesmen, as a rule, are not good planners. Generally, they do not believe in planning and consequently, they do *not like* to plan.

But they reach for, and readily pay tribute to, the manager who is himself able to plan ahead for their whole group. That sounds inconsistent on first hearing—and when examined closely, IT IS! But people are full of such inconsistencies, and the experienced manager accepts them with a wise smile and goes blithely on his way unfrustrated. To him, this paradox means that the very salesmen who tell him that planning (for them!) is a waste of time, believe it to be essential to the man who does the managing. He knows that this means that they are more susceptible to being taught the technique of personal planning than their conversation would indicate. Most salesmen avoid planning because actually they don't know how to plan; not knowing how, they have never tried it; and not having tried it, they admit to themselves, at least, they don't really know whether planning is or is not worthwhile.

Under the leadership of a manager who plans ahead for the whole group, salesmen feel more secure. Even if the boss changes his plans now and then, they do not lose that sense of security if they observe that the changes were carefully thought out before being made and that they were made for a good reason. In other words, a *better* plan supplanted the original *good* one.

3. A Manager Who EXHIBITS SELF-CONFIDENCE WITHOUT ARROGANCE

The late Albert Payson Terhune, famed writer of dog stories, once explained why some persons are repeatedly bitten by canines, while others seldom have that experience. Said he: "Some people fear dogs; when approached by a dog, that fear seizes them, and they secrete adrenalin. This taints the blood with a slight odor which almost instantly finds its way into the blood stream. This odor signals that the human is fearful, and this, in turn, tells the animal it is safe to attack." So the dog-fearing man, or woman, is bitten, bitten because of a signal given off by his own metabolism.

Salesmen, in a not dissimilar way, are instinctively on the watch for fear-signals in their manager. If they observe him to be uncertain about the group objective, if they see him change courses repeatedly without any apparent reason, if his assignments turn out to be "wild goose chases," if flagrant violations of instructions go unreprimanded, if the laggards remain unprodded—the group as a whole quickly comes to the conclusion that the manager is unsure of himself, doesn't know his job. (Every *new* manager, particularly, is under fierce and continuous observation by his men. If the group sniffs the scent of fear, they may give the manager a bad time. This hardly seems sportsmanlike, but on the salesmen's part, it is a natural "testing" procedure, and as Napoleon said: "He who wears the crown must bear the weight of it!" In many groups the new manager may as well make up his mind that the rule is almost that of the jungle—"Rule, or be ruled!")

Yes, salesmen demand a manager who is self-confident; not in an external, bluffing way, but deeply, genuinely so. On the other hand, men have little to offer to the unfortunate leader whose confidence reaches the point of arrogance; for, above all other managerial weaknesses, they detest arrogance, bluff, and pretense.

They want confidence backed up by experience, by "guts"—the confidence that isn't afraid to confess that "this is going to be a tough battle!" Men aren't afraid of a tough battle; but they *are* afraid of a faltering leader!

4. A Manager Who DOESN'T BLAME OTHERS FOR HIS MISTAKES

When you uncover a man who repeatedly shifts the responsibility, and blames *others* for *his* mistakes, you can label him as "emotionally immature"—for that habit is one of the first and clearest symptoms of childlikeness.

Historically, blame-shifting would appear to be the oldest of the symptoms of emotional immaturity. You will recall the event, as recorded in the Good Book:

The Old Serpent, in a little tête à tête with Eve in the Garden, urged her to eat of the fruit of the tree in the midst of the Garden, despite it having been specifically forbidden to do so, promising: "thereafter, you will be like gods, knowing both good and evil."

The Serpent had an interesting gleam in his eye, and a brilliantined hair-do—so Eve yielded.

And like a good partner, she passed the good thing along to Adam.

And *he* did eat!

And at once, they both became reluctant nudists, ashamed of their nakedness. They fabricated some fig leaves into modesty patches, and hid from the Lord in the reeds and tall papyrus plants.

But, as Adam should have known, there was no hiding from God, who sternly inquired of Adam: "Hast thou eaten of the fruit of the Forbidden Tree in the midst of the Garden?"

And Adam cringed a bit, and reached for an alibi instead of the truth, replying: "The woman Thou gavest to be with me, *she* gave me of the tree and I did eat!"

As far as we can discover, that's the first recorded incident of "passing the buck!"

In analyzing this incident, we find that the technique really hasn't been improved upon to this day. In fact, Adam tried to pass the buck in two directions, in one sentence. Observe he not only blamed Eve for inducing him to sin, but he made a sly pass at the Lord Himself, when he reminded God that the cause of it all was "the woman THOU gavest to be with me . . .!"—intimating, of course, that if the Lord had checked her references a little more carefully, He wouldn't have risked such a careless type of female in these brand new and unprecedented situations!

And Eve didn't bear up any better. She turned out to be not only the temptress, but when the Voice turned to her and asked: "What is this that thou hast done?"—She replied: "The serpent beguiled me and I did eat!" (But Adam is still one up on her—she got only one alibi in her response!)

Returning now to the main thread of the chapter, salesmen do not like buck-passing managers. In that respect, Adam would not have made a popular sales manager. He was a weakling, couldn't stand the gaff!

5. *A Manager Who DOESN'T "HOG" THE CREDIT FOR ACCOMPLISHMENT*

If we turn the last coin over and observe the reverse side, we find another trait men dislike, exemplified by the manager who is always grabbing as his own the credit for an accomplishment which was wholly or partly engineered by one of his salesmen.

Were you ever a jobbing house salesman travelling tandem with a big-shot sales manager from some manufacturer's home office? You knew the trade; you knew their needs; you knew whom to see; you knew what application they were most likely to be interested in; and, you did the preliminary selling. Mr. Big Shot came in at the end; took the order; and wrote it up on the company order blank, not even bothering to give you a carbon copy.

Did you or did you not detest his intestinal equipment with unparalleled fervor?

That's the type of manager we're talking about. The credit-grabber!

The astute sales manager is exceedingly cautious to make certain that his "boys" get credit for everything they do; and when it can be done delicately, and without obvious faking, he sometimes gives one of his men open credit for something which he himself may have previously set up behind the scenes. This type of sales manager never takes an order—that honor is always reserved for the salesman.

The fact repeatedly has been hinted at in this book that the traits which make a great leader in any field of human effort are the traits which make a great sales manager. We would like to prove it now, with Prochnow's account of a story straight out of the problem-freighted life of one of America's greatest leaders of men—Abraham Lincoln*.

> The battle of Gettysburg had been fought. Lincoln sensed an opportunity to end the war by driving hard against Lee's rear in retreat. A swift, daring attack might do it. As commander-in-chief of the army, he ordered General Meade to pursue. A friendly note in the President's handwriting accompanied the instructions:
>
> "The order I enclose is not of record. If you succeed, you need not publish the order. If you fail, publish it. Then, if you succeed, you will have all the credit of the movement. If not, I'll take all the responsibility."

Rereading that story, brings to mind a very personal question for our sales manager friends:

> Are you, in your own little sales management world,
> big enough to do an equivalent thing? Are you selfless
> and objective-minded enough to give one of your men
> a difficult assignment, telling him if it fails, you will
> take the rap, but if it succeeds, he can have all the
> credit, even the credit for thinking up the project?

* Herbert Prochnow: *The Public Speaker's Treasure Chest*. New York; Harper and Bros., 1942.

Yes, and never let anyone know differently?

Lincoln's note was the visual evidence of a sublime act of self-effacement, but we'll wager that Lincoln never thought of it as self-effacement at all. He had the gift of being able to stand in the other fellow's shoes. When he thought of asking Meade to make this daring movement, he asked himself: "What will Meade's position be? How will Meade feel? How can I protect Meade if my judgment is wrong?"

Lincoln never thought of *himself*. He did think it imperative to seize a soon-to-be-lost opportunity. His judgment, his wisdom, his intuition did tell him to strike immediately. In the simple processes of a great mind, he decided to put *his* name, not *Meade's*, at risk in case of failure. If success came, then let the glory be Meade's, as if in the everyday course of events. Here is complete and undiluted self-forgetfulness, so often the seed of grandeur and greatness in human actions!

Salesmen do not expect such heights of divine forgetfulness of self in the sales manager who directs their day-to-day affairs. But self-forgetfulness on a lower level and a lesser scale is the key to that quality they do look for—a manager who does not hog the credit for another's accomplishment!

6. *A Manager Who HAS A HIGH BOILING POINT*

A manager whose personal "pop-off" valve lets go at a very low head of steam is not likely to be one of the best-loved sales managers in the country. For salesmen like a manager who has a high boiling point. That means a manager who can build up quite a head of steam over some untoward event and nevertheless, can control himself so that his "pop-off" valve never even spews or sputters!

A hot temper is not an asset in any kind of work. But, in managing men, it can make more trouble than the kindly rebound of remorse can heal in a long time.

Salesmen fear a manager with a hot temper. They have learned that nothing constructive comes out of a temperish discussion. They have observed that *one hot temper in a group ignites many others,* and they know that the resulting conflagration destroys, never constructs.

Lacking that high boiling point, the manager flares up before he gets all the facts. Perhaps he feels that he is too busy and too short of time to talk to one of his men about what, to him, seems a trivial matter. Or, he may feel that the particular salesman is ALWAYS complaining; or that the man who is waiting outside for a gab-session about the new promotion, hasn't even given the deal a half-fair tryout.

And ALL OF HIS INDICTMENTS MAY BE TRUE! But a temperish outburst is not the solution to any of these daily annoyances; in fact, a show of temper will only make any one of the several situations worse! If you want men to *like* you, *bridle your temper*. If you want men to *respect* you, *bridle your temper*. If you want men to *follow* you, *bridle your temper*. It's an inexpensive way to buy a great deal from the men you are trying to lead.

7. A Manager Who WILL FIGHT FOR HIS MEN'S RIGHTS

The salesmen report primarily to the sales manager, but in important *secondary* ways, they must live within the rules of *several* departments, particularly the credit, traffic, service, and adjustment departments—to name a few which commonly touch the salesman's activities. Furthermore, the financial and accounting departments often impose and enforce what seem to the salesmen like strict and unyielding regulations regarding expenses, entertainment, parking fees, etc. These functionaries often give the whole sales force "a bad time" when one of the men in the field gets outside the corral of official policy. And the dilemma is worsened when the home office functionary bypasses the sales manager and inflicts his criticism directly on the offending salesman. To do so is manifestly bad practice, of course, from the standpoint of sound organization, for such communications should inevitably "go through channels." Nevertheless, such short-cutting is widely practiced and becomes the cause of much "bad blood" between the departments.

In such situations—and many others in which the salesmen are under fire from outside the sales department itself—the salesmen very much hope for a manager who will stand up for his men's rights, a man who refuses to "knuckle down" to top brass when he is certain that his men are not in the wrong.

A good example of this type of circumstance recently arose in one of our client companies selling to drug stores. Theirs is a product perishable over perhaps a year's time, and their general policy has been to pick up and replace the "stales", the old-dated packages, and items with soiled or damaged labels. But there was a limitation as to the AMOUNT which could be replaced on any one call—$10 worth at retail value.

In a store in central Illinois, one of the company's experienced salesmen came across a very unusual situation. The store had recently changed hands, and the new owner had been cleaning out the basement. There he unearthed sizable quantities of the company's products, which the former owner, instead of displaying and selling, had apparently been saving for the weevils and the termites.

Some of the items were so ancient that they were no longer being manufactured by the company. Other items carried old labels, superseded as much as two years previously. Obviously, company policy had not been formulated to cover such an unusual situation. The salesman, taking a common-sense view of the problem, decided the company would certainly not want those worm-eaten labels and antiquated products on sale in this store. So he took it upon himself to replace $50 worth of company goods.

His report had hardly hit the home office, when bang!—back came a sizzling letter of criticism, copy, of course, to the division sales manager. Early the next morning, the guilty salesman phoned his manager. "Come in tomorrow morning and we'll get it straightened up," commented the division sales boss, calmly.

At next morning's conference, he asked his salesman a few questions, picked up the phone, and called the general sales manager at headquarters.

"I got your letter about John's handling of the old merchandise last week at Ames Drug Company. George, I think he did exactly right in all ways but one; he should have written you a brief note setting forth the circumstances. The store has recently changed hands; the new owner dug up a lot of our stuff that looked like it might have been "stashed" away in King Tut's tomb. John figured we didn't want any of that stuff on the shelves or in the hands of consumers. So, he used his common sense and did what I think either you or I would have done under the same circumstances. I'd prefer to compliment him rather than to bawl him out, if he hadn't pulled that stupid boner and left you folks up there in the dark. Wouldn't you say so? . . . It's O.K. then? Fine! He'll pick up the balance next trip . . . says there is about half that much more still to come. Much obliged. John will be relieved . . . he began to believe he had committed a cardinal sin."

Turning to his salesman: "Everything's all right, John, but I know I'll never again have to remind you that a stupid little boner can sometimes get us all into as much trouble as a big one!"

No need to overstress the point. John thinks his boss is "a prince of a guy"; he stood up for him under fire; and he didn't bawl him out when he deserved it for pulling a stupid boner in another direction.

And that sales manager follows the same policy when one of his men is under fire from a jobber, a dealer, or a direct customer. He doesn't condone an error, nor does he shield the man who has made it, but he quietly searches for honest means to fight for his salesmen's rights. In trouble, or out, he treats his men as adult male human beings.

It isn't enough to say that salesmen LIKE that kind of manager. They *love* him!

Literally! When a leader stands up to *his* boss and defends one of his salesmen who is under fire from the head office, and then plusses his action by omitting the rebuke—assuming that the man is an adult and has given himself all the "going over" he requires—the effect on the whole sales force is *electric!* The news flashes around the field in a day, by means of that invisible telegraph which is always operating, but never located. Such loyal and comprehending management evokes real *devotion.* This leader may be lacking in several of the other desirable management attributes which salesmen look for, but they will overlook not a few of these missing traits, if they can get this kind of treatment in exchange.

8. A Manager Who UNDERSTANDS HIS MEN AS HUMAN BEINGS

This book began by insisting that "salesmen are PEOPLE." And they want to be treated like people—that is, as *human beings!*

A sales manager will complain to us about, let us say, the failure of his salesmen to make the proper proportion of prospect calls. We reply, hoping to supply him with some information which experience does not seem to have given him, that salesmen in every line of business are reluctant to make "cold canvass" calls on prospects. It is one of the salesman's less comforting tasks. Less comforting because the prospect is a stranger; he is likely to be less friendly; he hasn't been "warmed up"; his NEEDS haven't been exposed, and recognized, and admitted. Everything about a cold canvass call makes it potentially less productive, less friendly, less of a pleasant experience for the salesman, and so, it is only *natural* for him to shrink from the negatives of the prospecting task.

Therefore, we reply to the sales manager's complaint with an answer distilled from thousands of experiences: "But he hasn't any special INCENTIVE to make cold canvass calls."

Then comes the sales manager's emphatic rebuttal: "Incentive, hell! He's PAID to do cold canvassing; it's part of his job!"

That incident occurs frequently in our conversations with sales managers; and when it does, we know we are talking to a manager who does not understand his men as *human beings!* Whether he realizes it or not, he is subconsciously thinking of them as company-manipulated robots, automatically controlled by their pay-checks instead of being motivated by those emotional impulses which move the other members of the human race.

Salesmen need special incentives to induce them to tackle distasteful parts of their jobs. In short, management must make it especially worthwhile to push down on the accelerator when the men naturally want to put on the brakes.

Until the manager understands these facts, he doesn't understand his men as human beings!

Managers must understand, for example, that when the top salesman's baby is ill, he is no longer that specialized robot who sells like a machine; he is just another human being whose child is ill. Or, when a man has a nagging toothache, for instance, he is but a pain-racked member of the human race, even as you and I.

Salesmen like a manager who knows this without being told—and whose actions show that he knows it. (And just for emphasis, they very much *don't like* the manager who *doesn't* know it!)

9. A Manager Who CAN REACH A DECISION

The old Navy injunction—"In a situation demanding action, do *something*, even if it's *wrong!*"—is a dictum highly thought of among salesmen. They like a leader who can make up his mind. The procrastinating manager, the pussy-footer, the fellow who just can't reach a decision doesn't stand very high in the esteem of the gentlemen of the sales fraternity.

Without actually putting their opinions into words, the men think of this man as fearful, *afraid to act;* or as *ignorant*, lacking the facts upon which to base a course of action; or as "wishy-washy", lacking the WILL to act. They are likely to regard him as the prototype of that famous legendary jackass which starved to death between two bales of hay, having been unable to make up his mind as to which one to tackle first.

The manager who wants his salesmen to LIKE him, must have the know-how, the courage, and the will-power to take sound action—promptly!

10. A Manager Who IS PREDICTABLE

In the general opinion of the selling profession, we would say that the *manager's predictability* ranks very high in their list of desirable managerial traits.

They prefer a leader whose trend of mind and thought is sufficiently crystallized as to be predictable. In fact, experience indicates that they would rather be led by a mentally-crystallized and dogmatic leader than by an unpredictable one. Salesmen are nervous, uneasy, fearful, unconfident about the manager whose thoughts and actions they cannot predict with considerable accuracy.

The manager who constantly changes his plans, who reverses his decisions, who in comparable situations chooses widely differing courses of action—gives his sales force a permanent case of the "jitters."

Would you know the WHY of this yearning for the manager who is predictable?

It is but the echo of an ancient and universal fear—*the fear of change!* Back of the desire for predictability, is the conviction (not necessarily true) that the manager who is predictable will be likewise slow to introduce innovations. Out of this comforting belief arises the feeling of job security and personal adequacy which the men yearn to, and *do*, enjoy.

The new sales manager, coming into an organization he did not build, will be wise to present to his salesmen at least a facade of personal predictability, though he is at heart a confirmed innovator. As he destroys the old myth little by little, he can replace it, likewise little by little, with the higher pay which is the natural fruit of more aggressive sales management. Such a switch, shrewdly made, is not likely to cause him to lose any of the regard of his field selling organization. Money talks!

11. A Manager Who BELIEVES IN HIS MEN

The great Italian historian, Guglielmo Ferrero, in a great work on the politics of power, warned the people to place no trust in the leader who placed no trust in them. In other words, faith begets faith, and confidence brings forth its counterpart.

A somewhat similar axiom, namely, "Salesmen seldom believe in the manager who does not believe in them," is equally true. This belief is the eleventh of the attributes which salesmen seek in their manager—a man who believes in them. This means believing in their objectives and intentions; it means believing in their integrity, their loyalty, their actions. The manager who wants his men to *like* him will not ignore their need for his belief in them. By quiet and subtle deeds, he will demonstrate and project to them his belief, his confidence. Time after time, in small ways, he will make this faith known. And especially when he finds it needful to criticize them, as a body, or individually, he will do it shrewdly, tactfully, in a manner that avoids suggesting that his basic confidence has in any way lessened.

And he must sow the first seeds, make the first move; for it is from these seeds that sprout not only the spreading branches of *his* faith, but also the long out-reaching tendrils of *their* returning confidence in him.

12. A Manager Who PROTECTS HIS MEN FROM THEIR OWN WEAKNESSES

Let's look in on a confab between a sales manager and one of his salesmen who has just returned from a trip.

SALES MANAGER: Joe, you know better than to make these special deals. The Policy Manual says plain as day: "No extra discounts for district warehouse shipments to chain stores."

SALESMAN: Yeah, I know boss, but Finnegan says the Crown people are doing it, and he isn't going to pay a premium to do business with us.

SALES MANAGER: But, Joe, you don't have to be a continual sucker for that line of talk. It's Finnegan's job to try for a better deal every time you call—and for that matter, every time *any* supplier's salesman calls. He gets PAID for making HIS sales pitch, just like you get paid for making *your* sales approach. Either he is a better salesman than you, or you are an easy-mark. You didn't sell our policy to him; but he sold his idea to you.

SALESMAN: Look, boss, if I didn't have this account, I wouldn't make quota once in a lifetime. And besides his argument makes sense. We must save money on shipping big consignments to district warehouses over shipping smaller lots to individual stores.

SALES MANAGER: We've been all over that a hundred times. The Book says "No", doesn't it? And, I sat with you for an hour before you left and *I* said "No!" And besides, *the law* says "No!"—unless you can prove a cost saving. Not a half-dozen houses have ever been able to sustain a cost-saving case on the facts, and some of them have spent $50,000 to $100,000 on lawyer's fees and expenses just trying. If we do this and it turns out that we're guilty, then Finnegan is guilty, too. That's what the law says! Now, because *you* haven't the guts to handle him, *I've* got to take two days off and do it. And, I won't tell him a single thing you couldn't have told him when you were there.

SALESMAN: Well, you shouldn't have sent me there. You know I'm scared of these big guys. You know I always crack up when they start putting the pressure on me.

The last outburst of the salesman should be printed in red ink. It contains the point we want to emphasize. Under the pressure of his own manager's criticism, this salesman does what workers in many situations constantly do—*he blames his boss for sending him on a job which he later bungled.*

Instead of accepting responsibility for his error, he tries to push the burden of his failure right back on his manager.

Immature? Yes, even CHILDISH! Yet the situation is commonplace. In varying degrees, and among a small proportion of salesmen, this attitude recurs time after time, in situation after situation. Perhaps this explains why salesmen like a manager who takes care to protect them from the errors which grow out of their own weaknesses.

This is one demand that confuses and mystifies many managers.

"These fellows expect me practically to DO the job for them!" So exclaimed one sales manager when confronted with a much less severe case than the one just exampled. He threw up his hands in a gesture of complete futility, a gesture which said without words—"*I give up!*"

But the sales manager *can't* give up. And if he truly understands the problem from its roots to its top-most branches, he won't *want* to give up.

FIRST: Many men are unaware of their own weaknesses, or what may be even worse, they shut their eyes and are unwilling to admit them.

SECOND: They are not aware of the errors of judgment and practice which their weaknesses lead them into.

THIRD: They are unwilling to take responsibility for their own errors, as we just saw in the aforementioned example.

The comforting fact is that only a few men in any sales group are victims of the worst of these weaknesses; the rest of the sales force are only tainted slightly from contact with the weakness-rationalizing point of view now so prevalent. In most cases, these men can be educated out of their weaknesses by means of a little managerial understanding and patience.

It may help sales managers generally to understand the problem, if we point out that the corrective measures applied by the manager are seldom needed except in those cases where the man's parents failed to do a good job of "bringing up" the child.

Would you like to test the validity of that hypothesis? Go back to the file of the two or three worst offenders in your own force. Pick out the personal history record, and the interviewer's report. Watch for evidences of maternal over-protectiveness, "Momism." Was he an only child? Examine his educational periods, not his standings, but his participation in school life. Look into the qualitative factors, particularly any information reflecting upon his attitudes. If your records are even reasonably complete, the roots of today's weaknesses will be found in yesterday's soil. Perhaps the indications of over-shielding during childhood and adolescence and the consequent personal irresponsibility will be so clear-cut and so numerous that you will say: "We *shouldn't* have hired this fellow; and we *would* not have, had we known what these symptoms really meant!"

But we are not too much concerned about the exceptionally severe cases. They may need to be separated. The sales manager's chief problem lies with the majority of his men who are only slightly infected with the "irresponsibility virus." These are the men who are grateful for the manager with the insight to understand their weaknesses, for the man who views them, if not *compassionately,* at least *realistically,* and who takes the time and trouble to warn them of the probable pitfalls ahead. Best of all is the manager who helps them by specific personal direction to escape the errors resulting from their personal deficiencies.

In concluding this chapter on "The Kind of Manager Salesmen Like", let us repeat the obvious truth that no one human being can bring to his manager's job all of these desirable traits. However, just as the boy in Hawthorne's story grew up to become the benign image of the Great Stone Face in whose shadow he had lived, so also the sales manager—who keeps this list before him as he goes about his job, who attempts to practice through a conscious act of will the kind of management salesmen respond to—may find, after a while, that he has acquired almost unwittingly, the subtle skills that once seemed so remote from his thinking.

Salesmen know that a good manager makes a terrific difference in their satisfaction, their income, and their future. And, in a primitive emotional sort of way, they know what makes a *good* manager. They may not have crystallized their feelings into words, nor organized them into a rational pattern, but when they sense that their manager possesses even a reasonable proportion of the attributes they seek—eyes light up, hopes rise a little higher, and to their lips comes a wordless and unspoken pledge to do a little better than an average job for the man whom they recognize as a better-than-average manager.

As for the sales manager who has attained to that stature which men yearn to find in their leader, this is no little thing that he has achieved.

For sales management, successful sales management, is more than all else, a *human* task.

To have moved the directing finger which has pointed out to sometimes carping men, the constructive path; to have spoken at the right moment the shepherding word that has prevented men from straying from their proper flock; to have quelled with calm voice the feckless fears of men and sowed courage in hearts where courage before was not; to have sounded the ringing call to action which stirred men from their deadening lethargies; to have wielded the patient hand which turned them from their stubborn intransigencies into the paths of cooperation and success—in short, to have been the incarnate vehicle of that strong, firm will which guided men out of the dead-end byways into the straight, auspicious channels of success, and by the force of character, and faith, and skill bent their very destinies to better ends—this, indeed, is no small service in the world of men.

And yet, effective sales management really means all that.

That manager of salesmen who, to others, has seemed fortunate because he was a good deal skilled with men, will not be found before memory's mirror, viewing himself and his works with pride. No, you will find him still facing the East, looking outward towards the men he molded. The bright aura of leadership that glows about his head, he will never see, nor know. But about those he guided, his humanity, his grateful heart will build a greater light, and with that humility which marks the true grandeur of great leadership, he will exclaim with Brutus:

> My heart doth joy that yet in all my life,
> I found no man but he was true to me.

INDEX